TRAVELS
WITH
STANLEY

TRAVELS WITH STANLEY

DON'T STEP ON THE GARLIC

ROZ LABOW

TRAVELS WITH STANLEY
DON'T STEP ON THE GARLIC

iUniverse books may be ordered through booksellers or by contacting:

iUniverse
1663 Liberty Drive
Bloomington, IN 47403
www.iuniverse.com
1-800-Authors (1-800-288-4677)

ISBN: 978-1-5320-2876-2 (sc)
ISBN: 978-1-5320-2877-9 (e)

Print information available on the last page.

iUniverse rev. date: 08/14/2017

To my husband and travel partner of fifty-six years. I don't know anyone who will travel with us, and I don't blame them. Sometimes I don't want to travel with us either.

Contents

Contents

PREFACE

It was an article in the *New York Times* that initially started me thinking about writing this book of travel stories. It goes back to January 18, 1992, when Margot Slade wrote an article entitled *Travels with Mom and Dad*, which was published in the travel section. The article prompted me to reply, and it was published as a letter to the editor (see chapter 1). It did take me a while to get started, but once I had reduced my career responsibilities, it seemed like the right time. Writing this book turned out to be a great nostalgic journey reviewing the many trips we took, some with our sons and some just us. I started by reading the diaries that I had written for every trip we took from 1965 on. This provided the most important motivation for writing. Although certainly not an easy prospect, it was greatly facilitated by having my diaries. I could refer to the many pages of detailed descriptions of what we did over the more than fifty years of traveling together. However, another important motivation was to put on paper the travel stories that Stanley told over and over again every time he had a new audience. These stories were always well received.

It seemed important to have a permanent record of them. So, for this purpose, the book became a series of stories related to our travel. To this day, we are asked by friends, family, and colleagues, "Where is your next trip?" and "Where have you been recently?" And another comment that I frequently get is "You should write a travel book. I would love to read it."

Introduction

Travels with Stanley is not an ordinary travel book. Rather than guide the reader with things to see and do in a variety of countries as in a typical travel book, interesting and amusing stories about selected topics are conveyed together. During the course of our travels, we have been to all seven continents, including 129 countries. At first, we traveled ourselves (1965), but from 1981 to 1991, there were ten trips with our sons. We traveled at the Christmas–New Year's break, when everyone had time off. During those years, our sons were in high school and then university and then medical school. However, as time went on, it became clear that their professions and girlfriends would take precedent and we would have to travel ourselves. Though not our favorite way of traveling, we did go on tours in order to go to places that couldn't be reached on our own (safaris and cruises). On the rare occasion, we traveled with friends. For the most part, though, we traveled on our own. Our favorite way to travel is to get into our rental car and just wander.

When considering how I would format the book in order to recount our travel stories, the content of the book would not be "travel" in a guidebook format. The stories from the many places where we had been would be described together in a chapter of a similar theme. For example, in chapter 9, "Encounters with Wildlife," the visit to the mountain gorillas of Rwanda is recounted in the same chapter as rescuing a young girl from the jaws of a crocodile in Namibia. The chapter headings are, for the most part, those that would be found in a conventional guidebook, such as getting there, getting around, where to stay, food, wildlife, security, golf, fishing, and so on. In some cases, I tried to provide some constructive information on how to travel or at least for the most part how we like to travel and how it has worked for us.

In addition to the stories depicting our travels without a real purpose, there is a description of the trips to our grandfathers' birthplaces (chapter 15, "Finding Our Roots"). Another great part of our travels involved our surgical missions to Nicaragua (chapter 16).

There is no perfect way to travel, and that is, in part, what the book is intended to narrate. Although the primary goal of the book is to amuse, nonetheless, some worthwhile travel lessons can also be found. Our many experiences have taught us and may perhaps help readers.

List of Illustrations

Chapter 1

WHERE TO GO?

So how do you choose where to go? We are often asked, "Why are you going there?" and "How did you decide to go there?" And most of the time, I actually find it really hard to answer those questions.

Travels with Stanley began when we were married in June 1961. Before you read about all our travels, it might be interesting to know first of all how Stanley came into the world and then how we met. Stanley was a bit of a miracle. He was supposed to have been born in August but instead was born in May. We aren't really sure, but my mother-in-law was maybe twenty-eight weeks pregnant. It was May 20, 1936, and it was snowing in Montreal. She barely made it to Jeanne D'Arc Hospital, and basically, they did nothing and sent them home. She describes keeping him warm by placing him in a drawer in the warming oven, and she would shake him in order to see if he was still alive. He never cried. She said that she fed him with a dropper and with breast milk. The breast milk came from a variety of wet nurses, for which my father in law advertised in his pharmacy. One woman promoted herself by saying, "By me, it's cream." Many years later, Stanley got a call from the Supreme Court of Canada. It was Justice Morris Fish. He said, "Stanley, you owe me your life. My mother was your wet nurse who answered your father's ad in his pharmacy."

Another lucky quirk of fate was the fact that my mother-in-law never made it to the Jewish General Hospital, where they had 100 percent oxygen incubators. The high concentration of oxygen caused blindness.

My father-in-law was also involved in how Stanley and I met. It goes back to the polio epidemic in the 1950s in Montreal. Salk vaccine had just been developed, but it was in short supply. My father-in-law as a pharmacist and owner of a drugstore was able to get the vaccine. Since my parents were good customers, he gave them vaccine for me. My parents invited my future in-laws over for dinner to thank them and, during the evening, asked me to play a piece on the piano for them. I played *Fur Elise* and then went back to my room. After some time, my mother and mother-in-law met at the hairdresser and felt that it was a good idea to get their children together. At this point, I was sixteen and had just graduated from high school. Stanley had just finished his first year of medical school and was twenty-two. The story goes that one day his mother asked him to take out Rosi Fisher. He answered, "Mother, are you crazy? Me a medical student taking out someone who has just graduated from high school!"

She replied, "Do it for your mother. What's one night out of your life?"

After a couple of years of dating, I decided to take matters into my own hands and presented Stanley with some possible dates in June 1961 when the synagogue was available but added that if he'd like to wait a year that was okay also. He chose not to wait, and when I asked about a ring, he said he had $400, which he gave me so that I could go choose a ring with my mother.

Lou Goldberg produced a very nice ring. When we mentioned the amount of money we had, he answered with a question—"How did you know my cost price? On this ring, I'm losing money."

I don't know why we both loved traveling. Both of our parents traveled, but although the love of travel can be partially instilled, it has to be an integral part of one's personality. Perhaps a good way to explain how and why we travel is by answering questions that are in a gift that I received several years ago from one of my graduate students who also loves to travel. The gift is a series of cards entitled "Travel Topics to Go." Each card is a travel question.

The first question, which describes our first trip together perfectly, is "If you had six weeks to drive around the US, which region would you most like to visit?" We did have six weeks when Stanley started his residency program in Ann Arbor, Michigan, in August 1962. We left Montreal, the city where we were born, to launch our life together. We drove from Montreal, Canada, to Ann Arbor (where we would study for four years) to Los Angeles on Route 66 and then up the coast to Vancouver and across the Rockies down into Montana and across the United States back to Ann Arbor. This was our first real trip together after being married. I was always the navigator, and Stanley was the driver. It was rare that we took my car, which was automatic. Stanley's, to this day, is a shift, and although once briefly I tried to learn, I never did.

My navigating occasionally was off by 180 degrees, especially if I was holding the map upside down. One morning, I had the sun rising in the west. I didn't keep a diary on this trip, though I have kept one for almost every trip since. However, I remember one story that Stanley tells over and over. We were in Helena, Montana, having our car filled up. The gasoline station attendant didn't know where to start. The car was the British Sunbeam Alpine. We pointed him in the right direction, and his comment on the make of the car was "I have a Sunbeam also, but mine pops up toast."

Stanley and the Sunbeam Alpine in the Mohave Desert, California, July 1962

Five weeks and approximately ten thousand miles later, we knew that where we were entirely compatible was travel and perhaps food, which will be evident as our travel stories unfold.

Next question: "Would you rather travel by train, car, plane, or ship?" (chapter 2, "Getting There"). I could easily answer—car. Of course, this isn't always possible. But, in a country with reasonable roads, getting in the car and just wandering is my favorite travel method.

Another travel question—"Do you like for your time on vacation to be planned or spontaneous?" Certainly, some planning is necessary, but overplanning can eliminate the best part of travel—serendipity. This brings me to the first Labow rule of travel. We only have reservations for the first night of our arrival in a place. Recently (February 2017), we were in Puerto Rico. When talking to some young surfers at a table next to us at a restaurant, it turned out that one of them had parents who owned a B and B in the mountains. We made arrangements then and there to go to TJ Ranch near Lagos dos Bocas. It was the highlight of our trip. If we had booked our entire stay, this would never have been possible.

Our next trip was in 1965, also a crazy road trip. It was a bit of a classic *If It's Tuesday, This Must Be Belgium*, although we were on our own—no tours. We flew from Detroit to London and then Copenhagen and Amsterdam, where we rented a VW Beetle. We drove from Amsterdam to Brussels and then to Germany, down the Rhine to Basle and around Switzerland to Geneva, ending in Paris, with Frommer's *Europe on 5 Dollars a Day* as our tour guide.

And so, the next question: "On your fantasy road trip, who would be the perfect travel companions?" Although we had ten years of traveling with our sons, right now no one wants to travel with us, and we don't want to travel with anyone else. Fantasy or reality road trip, it's just Stanley and me.

So, the next question: "What's your best packing secret?" We try not to keep this Labow rule of travel a secret. And most of the time we are told from people we speak to that they just can't do without their favorite shampoo or face cream and a change of clothes for every day and, of course, lots of shoes. However, when traveling by anything other than a car from home, carry-on luggage only. We believe that there are only two kinds of luggage—carry-on or lost. Also, when problems arise with flights, the first question is always "Have you checked bags?" Less is more when it comes to packing. Of course, this rule limits shopping. But for us, shopping is not an essential part of travel. Throughout the book, I point out when checked baggage would have added to the problem.

The *New York Times* travel section has often given us ideas; it was an article in the *Times* that initially started me thinking about writing this book of travel stories. On January 18, 1992, Margot Slade wrote an article entitled "Travels with Mom and Dad," which was published in the travel section. The opening line: "Just picturing several days and nights spent in close proximity to the folks who raised us is enough to make most of us quickly realize that going on vacation with our parents is an idea whose time, if it ever came, has gone."

I responded with a letter to the editor on March 15, 1992:

> To the Editor:
>
> I thought I was going to save writing the book *Travels with My Adult Children* for my retirement (which it turns out I did), but Margot Slade's article entitled "Travels with Mom and Dad" (Travel, Jan. 19) required an immediate reply. We returned recently from a 20-day trip to Paris and Morocco with our 23- and 25-year-old sons, who are in their first and third year of medical school. Our Christmas break travels continue to be the highlights of our lives. Relationships between parents and children and between brothers are revitalized. Choosing countries that are not English speaking and don't have ready access to English language television encourages communication.

When I told my older son that I was writing a book about our travels, some thirty-five years later, he recounted minute by minute his favorite stories (chapter 9, "Encounters with Wildlife").

So, in the case of travels with our kids, we chose countries and locations in those countries where English wasn't spoken and there was no television. Of course, it would be a real challenge now to find places where there would be no Wi-Fi. The answer would probably be to leave the cell phones and the iPads at home. Good luck!

Tours—not our favorite way to travel. But if you choose locations where it is impossible or next to impossible to go on one's own, you have no choice. Examples would be

Antarctica (chapter 3, "Getting Around") or a camping safari in Africa (chapter 9, "Encounters with Wildlife"). The best trip we have ever taken (another travel question in that little box of travel topics) was with our kids to the mountain gorillas of Rwanda on a camping safari. There are several stories from that trip. The most beautiful place we've ever seen (another question asked) is Torres del Paine National Park in Chile, where we took several guided hikes (chapter 4, "Where to Stay"). Sometimes the price advertised is so good that it makes sense to take the tour and do as much of it as you want to. Our trip to China with SmarTours in February 2000 was only $799, airfare included. My Chinese graduate student arranged for us to meet with her friends both in Beijing and Shanghai, so we left the tour for a day here or there.

Another kind of travel is a volunteer vacation. Question: "If you went on a volunteer vacation, whom would you most like to help?" We went on twelve surgical missions to Nicaragua, where Stanley performed plastic surgery (chapter 16, "Surgical Missions"). And although we speak several languages, because of these trips, I would most like to be fluent in Spanish, the language most spoken in the world after English and Mandarin. (Question: "In what language would you like to be fluent?") Also, if we had to pick our favorite continent, it is South America, the Spanish-speaking countries. Often people ask, "How can you travel there? Do you speak the language?" I answer that Stanley speaks every language in the world. I actually found people who believed that. However, he can always make himself understood. Although often it's taken some time, he never gives up. Once, in order to get a cup of tea in Dien Bien

Phu, Vietnam, he ended up drawing a picture of a teapot and a cup. These days, it is rare to find somebody around who does not speak English, but language should never be a barrier for travel. It never has been for us.

Recently, we have visited the homeland of our ancestors. (Question: "Would you like to visit the homeland of your ancestors?) We went to Romania and found the town Stanley's paternal grandparents left around 1900 and went to Latvia, where my paternal grandparents left around the same time. In these Eastern European countries, persecution of the Jewish population was routine, which is why they left. (Question: How and why did your family come to America?) (See chapter 15, "Finding Your Roots.")

It is harder to choose places to travel with friends, especially if not on an organized tour. This requires lots of compromise, and certainly choosing people to travel with who have the same philosophy of travel is difficult. We have done it a few times over the many years, but now our time in travel is becoming more and more precious. Besides that, nobody wants to travel with the "crazy Labows."

I do have to include Stanley's intuition of a place coming into its own. So many times, out of thin air, Stanley says for example, "Our next trip is to Albania." Then, the following Sunday, the travel section of the *New York Times* features an article on Tirana, the capitol. This has happened many times. Who knows why?

On where not to go, I do always consult the travel advisories from the governments of Canada and the United States. Although adventurous travelers, when the website says, "Travel only if necessary," or, "Avoid all travel," we stay away. We aren't that crazy!

A word of explanation about the title: Although I have traveled alone from time to time and with my students to scientific meetings, all the trips I'm writing about in this book are about traveling with Stanley. At times, he may not be the most tactful and sometimes a little oblivious. Stories about his apparent or inadvertent lack of sensitivity are described throughout the book, but one that seemed the most appropriate to describe his behavior took place in Indonesia (chapter 9: Encounters with Wildlife). We were walking through rice paddies and garlic fields. There were ridges surrounding the plants, and we were asked to please walk on the ridges and, "Please, don't step on the garlic." I think Stanley didn't hear because he marched right through the garlic fields, avoiding the ridges. This was characteristic of Stan on many trips, as will become evident as the stories are told. I should add that some of the most interesting moments were when Stanley spoke to people at random and found out the most amazing things. This has been true no matter where we are, either at home in Ottawa or in some place very far away.

My diary from 1965 described in the preface the "art of travel." There is no right way or wrong way to travel. Sometimes the location dictates the kind of travel; whether you're on a tour or on your own or traveling with friends or with your children will determine how you travel. Our favorite saying when things aren't going exactly as we planned is "Are you having fun yet? Or this is part of the adventure?" The chapters in this book will tell our stories about the many different ways we have traveled over the years. With more than ninety trips to over 129 countries, there are many stories.

First of all: How to get there?

Chapter 2

GETTING THERE: MISSED FLIGHTS AND OTHER UNAVOIDABLE COMPLICATIONS

One of the most difficult parts of travel is the lack of control over flights. There are so many things that can go wrong and do. It can be weather, especially in the winter in Ottawa. It can be mechanical trouble with the aircraft. It can be a problem with another flight coming from another place with the crew that is supposed to fly the plane you're about to get on … or all of the above. But sometimes it is none of the above. It is simply a mistake that you have made. We now have two "trip meetings" as we call them—one way in advance to make sure we have the correct days and then another closer to the departure to make sure again that we have everything we need, such as money, passports, boarding passes, medications, and so on and so on. I prepare a travel checklist for every trip, and that is the meeting agenda. Often, a mistake is found. For example, I forgot to take into account that an overnight flight from Santiago to Toronto involves arriving the next day, and so scheduled events for that morning needed to be changed. We missed this on the first trip meeting weeks ago. So, no matter how hard you try to be organized, what you think is the impossible happens or, as Stanley quotes his mother saying, "The impossible takes a little bit longer."

New York to Quito, Ecuador (1990)

One of our favorite trips, which didn't start off too well and ended even worse, was our trip to the Galapagos in 1990 with our sons. We met up in New York, Brian coming from Boston, and spent a few days shopping and seeing plays. We saw the musical about *Buddy Holly* and *Phantom of the Opera*. And we ate at some great restaurants. Interestingly, when we were in New York City in April 2016, we were walking from Ground Zero through Chinatown and found that the Excellent Dumpling House on Lafayette Street was still exactly the same as it was in December 1990. We highly recommend this restaurant!

We woke up on December 28 to a seven-inch snowfall. Somehow, we negotiated ourselves around New York in the slushy mess and checked with Equatoriana Airlines that our flight to Quito was on time, leaving at 11:45 p.m. When we entered the departure lounge, we saw a huge line there, which made us suspicious. Sure enough, it was the Thursday night flight, the flight from the night before our flight. The plane had taxied to the end of the runway, but the pilot had changed his mind and decided not to take off in the snowstorm. Therefore, the entire flight was taking off Friday night instead. Stanley went wild, but there was no way we could get out Friday night. Somehow, we found a very capable and sympathetic American Airlines agent, who rearranged our entire flight, which turned out to be excellent. We flew on Pan American Airlines to Miami at noon the next day and then from Miami to Quito. In Miami, we waited for our crew. The pilots at American Airlines were calling in sick, but one hour later they showed up. We landed in Quito at night and were met by our Overseas Adventure Travel guide who was there waiting for bags that hadn't shown up the day before.

We had a couple of days in Quito. We felt the altitude right away and were so tired that when our bus broke down on the way back from the market and the volcano in the pouring rain, we hailed taxis to get back to the hotel. Although the beginning of the trip was not auspicious, cruising around the Galapagos Islands was one of our most memorable trips. The wildlife there is unique. Every day we saw huge varieties of birds and plants that only exist there. We swam with sea lions and manta rays. Our guide went on and on about conservation and bad tourists, but then he smoked nonstop and put out his cigarette on the ground. Not too impressive—unlike some wonderful guides we have had (chapter 14, "Guides"). We were with an eclectic group of tourists, a big range in age and backgrounds. An interesting subplot to the trip was Mary, a single mother of two. We always travel at Christmastime, and we are usually with Jews or divorced couples whose kids were with the other parent. Mary was propositioned by the guide the first night but then by the third night was sleeping with the captain. At first, she complained about all the advances, but then by the third night she was bragging about them. She said that the crew looked up to her because she was the captain's woman. Crazy! He was old, had terrible gold-capped teeth, and was very short and generally homely. The youngest on the trip, Matt, saw them in the same sleeping bag on the deck and was very confused.

Another single woman we met on the trip was Sarah. She turned out to be an invaluable connection. She was a lawyer who lived in Washington, but her brother was also a lawyer. In his law firm was an immigration lawyer who helped get Daniel a visa to stay and do his residency. He knew the chairman of surgery and convinced him that Daniel could switch to an H1 visa from his student visa. There were many tense moments at the time, but all turned out the way we wanted it to.

So, you'd think with all trouble getting to the Galapagos that we would have paid our dues to the airline gods and that our trip on the way back would be perfectly smooth. No such luck! The trip from hell began on January 9, 1991. Although the Quito airport was crowded, check-in with American Airlines was efficient, and we only left fifteen minutes late. But when we arrived in Miami, the immigration lines were something I had never seen before. It is great now that we have Global Entry as Canadians, which bypasses all the non-US-citizen lines. But at that time, we were in the same line as the passengers from flights from the Caribbean and Central and South America. We were cleared well in time for the flight to Newark, which had been delayed two hours.

We were about to take off when the pilot came on the loudspeaker and said, "Well, folks. This appears to be one of those days. A valve has just blown, and we have given up our position at the gate. So in order to save time we will go to a quiet part of the airport and let maintenance assess the problem."

After another hour, the maintenance crew said that the valve had to be replaced, and we were to head back to our gate. We waited and waited, and we didn't move. Well, the pilot came on the loudspeaker again, and it definitely was one of those days. One of the maintenance crew had fallen down the ramp, and the medics were fixing his leg and evacuating him.

We finally returned to our gate. By now, many people were in a panic as they had connections in New York City. We were not in such a bad situation, since we were overnighting in New York at the hotel where we'd left our extra luggage and shopping packages from the beginning of the trip (computers, cameras, and so on). We met another member of our tour wandering around the airport in Miami. He had to buy another ticket home because in Quito they had pulled all the coupons. At least those don't exist anymore. We were told that our plane would be ready at 7:30 p.m.

It was ready, but then the crew walked off the plane. Another crew would be coming at 9:15, and so we would take off at 9:40. In the meantime, I saw that there was another American Airlines flight leaving for La Guardia at 8:00. We would worry later about our luggage, which will be at Kennedy Airport. Why did we ever check luggage? We were delayed another fifty minutes, took off at 9:00, and arrived in NY at 11:15. At 1:30 a.m., Daniel went out to Kennedy to get our luggage and came back at 3:00 a.m. We got up at 5:30, said good-bye to the boys, and caught our flight to Syracuse and then Ottawa. Aside from all this craziness, this trip ranked in our top five best trips.

The most important advice from this experience: Never check luggage!

Paris to Morocco (1991)

We were on our way to Morocco, our last trip with our adult children in December 1991. We had spent a few days in Paris and were supposed to fly to Casablanca via Amsterdam. Brian and Daniel had been out the night before with friends, and we woke them in time for the flight, we thought. After we woke them, Stanley checked the tickets. We had missed our flight to Amsterdam. As mentioned above, tickets were coupons, not electronic. They were those coupons written on funny paper, line by line, each line being another flight. And so the impossible happened. On the way in from the airport (under the influence of Halcion) Stanley read 1:05, but it was 10:35—1:05 was on the next line (in other words, the next flight from Amsterdam to Casablanca). We were mildly hysterical! We called KLM, and all flights were booked to Casablanca for a couple of days. Then we called Royal Air Maroc. There were three flights that day. All flights were booked, but we decided to take a chance and went to Orly Sud. What a terrible airport!

We found a very sympathetic agent, who placed us as numbers one through four on a priority wait list, and we paid for four tickets to Casablanca. As we were waiting, needless to say very agitated, we saw mobs of people moving around very quickly. An area was being cordoned off. Police announced, "Bomb alert." Stanley and Daniel were guarding the luggage and were right in front.

We watched them blow the parcel up. Brian and I had gone upstairs to try to call Morocco and tell them our probable flight. Then as we came down, they cordoned off another area in the parking lot and blew up another package. We didn't get through to our driver but left a message. Sure enough, we made the flight, direct to Casablanca instead of via Amsterdam, and our driver was waiting for us even though we were on a different flight.

So we thought our problems were solved. We had been extremely lucky, considering that this was peak travel time. Aside from costing us the price of four one -way tickets to Morocco, we were able to meet our driver and get to our hotel that same night. Being cautious, Stanley had the hotel call KLM to check on our return flights. Sure enough, all our tickets were canceled. Since we didn't show up in Amsterdam, the return tickets were automatically canceled. Once more hysteria, but at least we had time to sort out the problem. We called Sandy, our friend and travel agent. In those days, we always booked trips through her travel agency. KLM put four business-class seats aside for us, and all was in order for our return trip. Certainly, things are different now. No more missing coupons!

Advice from this experience is what I do now, as mistakes can still be made: Print your boarding passes twenty-four hours in advance. That way you know you are on the flight.

Pokhara, Nepal (1994)

Our trip to Pokhara, Nepal, was part of a three-country trip in December 1994. We started out in New Delhi, flew to Bhutan and then to Katmandhu and Pokhara return, and then headed back to New Delhi, with a side trip to Agra and finally back to New Delhi. I get tired just writing about these trips. I guess we were a lot younger. Although this was all in all a wonderful trip, in this chapter, I want to describe what it was like to fly in Nepal in 1994.

We arrived in Katmandhu without reservations on December 26 and took a taxi to look at a variety of hotels. Although now it seems extremely nervy, we were able to book what was one of the best hotels called the Yak and Yeti. Not only that—we got a real deal at $75 with our InteleTravel travel agent card, when the regular price was supposedly $150. Our first mission was to make our flight reservations to Pokhara for December 28 through January 1. Katmandhu at that time was still full of hippies from the sixties who just hung out there. It was loaded with shops, restaurants, and ancient temples, which were in terrible condition. After the terrible earthquake in 2015, these structures were severely damaged and many were totally destroyed.

In spite of its interesting combination of Hindu and Buddhist traditions and history, the city didn't appeal to me. The air was terribly polluted. The area around the central square, Durbar, was filled with garbage, dog excrement and filth, lepers begging, and many others selling less than beautiful crafts. In addition, the most annoying thing was being constantly bombarded by little kids begging or wanting to guide us around. The boys, age eight to twelve, even after rejection, continued to follow us and harass, almost swarming us. One time I was reading my guidebook while walking and tripped on the uneven bricks. I went flying, scraping my knee and elbow. Fortunately, they were covered, but I still was worried about infection. I had a real "hairy." However, if you were tired after walking around, there was always an auto rickshaw that would drive you back for next to nothing. We found one great guy who took us on a tour of Katmandhu. He pulled, pushed, and peddled for over an hour, and all we gave him was three dollars.

We got a call from the front desk at the Yak and Yeti the night before our flight. Our flight to Pokhara was changed to much later. But we set out way in advance anyway to the domestic airport. I remember the international airport as being very nice when we flew in from Bhutan, but the domestic airport was horrible. The state of the washrooms still lingers in my mind; they were impossible to use, overflowing with human excrement. The rest of the terminal wasn't exactly marvelous either. We arrived in Pokhara, and I really cannot remember why we chose to go there. We weren't going trekking on the Annapurna range, but I guess we wanted to get close to it. The quality of the hotels was not great. We found one that wasn't heated that had vacancy, but none had vacancy for December 31. Our goal was now to return to Katmandhu and the Yak and Yeti for New Year's Eve.

We set out on a walk, which *The Lonely Planet* described as "a nice walk before breakfast." We tried to take a taxi to the base of Sarangkot Hill but got stuck behind a truck whose drive shaft broke. We had no choice at this point but to start walking up. We both had colds and were tired from our walk yesterday. The annoying kids appeared out of nowhere as in Katmandhu and continued to follow us up the hill. We hitched a ride with a truck for part of the way and then proceeded on our own. It got steeper and steeper, and I was about to drop. We finally made it to the restaurant on top, half-dead, and, after a short rest, set out down, walking for two hours down steep steps. Part of the way down, a thunderstorm started, and we were bombarded by hail and arrived at the road soaking wet. We were way out of town, but by some miracle, a taxi appeared and took us back to our hotel. The next day was December 31. I woke up very sick, probably a combination of a cold, stomach upset, and altitude. Or it may have been the very polluted air. It was impossible to see the tops of the Himalayan range. (It turned out that the best view we had, even of Mt. Everest was from the plane that took us to Katmandhu from Bhutan.)

Stanley spoke to his friend at Baba House where we had been eating all our meals. He told him that I was quite sick and that we had to get back to Katmandhu that day. We knew at this point that the Yak and Yeti had a room for us. He said that he had a friend at the airport, and Stan gave him twenty-five dollars. He called his friend, and we were on a 9:30 a.m. flight; we'd only left the hotel at 8:30 a.m. At that time, there were two airlines flying between Pokhara and Katmandhu. We were amazed that we got onto a flight so close to flight time. But then we waited. It was quite foggy and the planes were waiting to take off. Finally, one plane did depart. We were told that our flight couldn't take off yet. We didn't get the reason until we had been waiting for hours, and it didn't come from the airline. Somebody who flew this route regularly knew the reason. Only the pilot had an instrument rating. The copilot was rated VFR (visual flight rules) only. Fortunately, we made it, checked into our hotel room at the Yak and Yeti, and actually had room service for our New Year's Eve meal.

Air travel has only become more difficult. Perhaps it is due to the increase in the volume of travelers, but mostly it's due to the ever-increasing security that happened after 9/11. I try very hard to zone out and keep relaxed. After all, most of the time when you are going through security, it's because you are going on vacation. However, with all the rules and all the items that are necessary to be removed before going through the detectors—clothes, wallets, iPhones, boarding pass, photo ID, glasses, coins, liquids, computers, watches (I could go on and on) and, in our case, our two pieces of carry-on luggage—it's difficult to do. Putting yourself together afterward, with the other passengers milling around you, has become sometimes an overwhelming challenge. The increase in security seems to be following the same growth curve as our aging—not a great correlation. However, one benefit of aging is being exempt from removing shoes and outer jacket after age seventy-five. The rationale escapes me.

Advice here is to get all the clearance you can. Canadians have NEXUS, which also gives you Global Entry. So any time you land in either Canada or the United States you are known.

Ottawa to Montevideo (2000)

Yet another almost missed flight occurred on our trip to Uruguay in December 2000. At this time, there were still paper tickets. We had weather issues on the first leg of the trip to Newark, and our travel agent got us a flight the day before a storm was forecast. We had to stay overnight at the airport. Once again, Harold and Joanne picked us up for lunch. It was a beautiful day. But when we tried to check in for all our flights in Newark, Continental said that they couldn't do the next leg, since it was Lan Chile, and at that time, the different systems didn't communicate. So, when we arrived in Lima from Newark, we were not on the list for Santiago. It seemed totally strange since we were on the list from Santiago to Montevideo. How were we going to get to Santiago to take the flight to Montevideo if we weren't on a flight to Santiago? Our travel agent said that she had reserved seats for us that day on all the flights. The impossible takes a little bit longer.

Stanley started his routine about being a surgeon who was operating on a deformed face in Montevideo at the request of the government. I'm not sure this ever worked, but somehow there were five no-shows on that flight, and we got on. So four flights later we arrived in Montevideo. We stayed in Montevideo for one night and then rented a car to drive around Uruguay. The country is extremely small and has more cattle than humans per square mile. And at that time, Uruguay was empty everywhere we went.

After our usual first day, where we're stopped by the police, this time for not having our lights on, we didn't have much trouble finding our way. I emphasize much trouble; there's always some trouble. We stayed one night in Colonia, across the water from Buenos Aires in Argentina. We set out for the estancia that I had found on the Internet, without reservations and without really knowing where it was. I thought it was in the town of Florida, but it turned out to be eighty kilometers past that. Somehow we arrived there, and it was a fantastic find. It was originally owned by the Jesuits, who sold it to the Spanish when they conquered the area. It was privately owned for a while but had now been renovated into an incredible resort.

Stanley started his travel agent spiel (song and dance) showing our InteleTravel card. Stanley was just about to say that he had been sent by the Minister of Tourism to check out the resort when the owner said, "You are in luck. The Minister of Tourism is here now with his family."

We went right to lunch with the most incredible food. It seems that Uruguayans eat more meat than any other South American country. We went on a tour of the estancia with Belen, the manager. During the night tour, we were able to see a huge variety of nocturnal animals. We got an incredibly good rate and were very sorry to leave that outstanding place.

Although Uruguay is an extremely safe country, I did have a few life-threatening events while we were visiting. We were walking in the estancia, and Stanley brushed aside a bee that was circling around his head. It ended up stinging my arm, and I got a terrible reaction. We were on our way to Minas, the city where all the bottled water comes from. We went for a walk along a well-marked trail, past the mineral springs, when out of the grass bordering the trail came a brown, hairy spider, five inches in diameter, directly in front of my feet. Actually, all day I'd thought I was dying, as the bee sting had turned really ugly with the area of redness growing by the minute. It was swollen and itchy, and a red streak was moving up my arm. A waiter in the restaurant we went to in Minas, gave me some ice and said that it was probably one of those killer bees that supposedly were invading North America. Antihistamines seemed to control the reaction from the bee sting, and the spider did not attack.

We proceeded to La Pedrera, where it was possible to view the ecosystems on the Atlantic coast. The wildlife there was unique and prolific. We stayed in a partially finished group of apartments and were attacked all night by mosquitoes. However, we found a beautiful restaurant called La Baleonada. The food was definitely well prepared, but we were sitting in the restaurant alone. Once more, we heard that times were very bad in Uruguay from the owner. This was a recurrent theme on that trip. It was good for us, in that everywhere we went, Stan could negotiate a great rate for our accommodation.

Who should walk in but Belen, the manager of the estancia we had been at several days before and her boyfriend, who lived here. We arranged to meet for dinner the next night. It was another great meal, and before Stanley could do anything, her boyfriend had paid.

We continued on to Punta del Este, the city where all the Argentinians had their resort homes. So many houses were for sale that had been abandoned. They were beautiful, very large estates around five acres with ocean views. The bad conditions in Argentina affected those in Uruguay. We heard one story about a house that decreased in price in six months from $1.5 million to $750,000, and in another month, it was bought for $300,000, with all the dishes and furniture included.

Punta del Este is a peninsula, and there is a walking path that circles it. I said that this was the third time on this trip that Stanley tried to kill me. We were walking along the path. It was sunny and hot. Stanley said for me to look at this house and then put out his foot, saying that it was to shade me. I went flying on the stones, receiving a major wound. But I kept walking. It was close to five miles before we stopped for lunch. I wonder about these trips we took years ago. Somehow what we tried to do seems rather crazy. I guess that is why we say that no one would travel with us.

Our final stop on this motor trip in Uruguay was Montevideo. We returned our car and spent a couple of days there. There are still many Jews in Montevideo, and the history of Jews in South America is one of both persecution and sanctuary (see chapter 15, "Finding Our Roots"). On our one full day in Montevideo we met a family traveling with three generations, one grandma with her two sons, one daughter-in-law, and three grandchildren. The grandma had come to Uruguay having been imprisoned in the concentration camp, Buchenwald. Her husband had immigrated first, and she had lived in Montevideo for seventeen years. They hadn't returned for thirty-eight years and were going to find her house and the synagogue. We had also met an older Jewish couple on our first day in Uruguay driving from Montevideo to Colonia. The Rosens had escaped from Berlin in 1936 and 1939 (also husband first and then wife) and lived in Brazil for five years, after which they'd immigrated to Uruguay. They were at a beautiful resort for a vacation that their daughter had planned for them. As usual, as we were walking around this resort, Stanley started talking to them, suspecting they were Jewish. Chabad had made it here also of course, and since it was Chanukah, an enormous menorah was erected on the beach in Montevideo where we had been walking.

From Montevideo, we took the ferry to Buenos Aires. As we arrived on the dock, taxis attacked us and refused to put on the meter, Stanley's usual fight with taxis. So instead, we decided to walk the ten blocks to our hotel, pulling our luggage across eight-lane avenues in Buenos Aires.

The taxi fight continued a day later with the fare to the airport. We decided to walk away from our hotel and hail a taxi. We had been told that prices were fixed—thirty-five dollars by taxi, forty-seven dollars by private car, and fourteen each for the bus. Stanley started in with his twenty-dollar proposition. The driver called into his office for someone who spoke English, and we negotiated twenty dollars plus tolls. I had written in this diary that the chapter on taxi stories was turning into a novella, and it's true that almost every trip had some kind of taxi story.

We flew to Santiago, Chile, and were again assaulted by taxi drivers. We heard the whole range of prices and ended up settling for eight thousand pesos, which would be about fifteen dollars today. When we were in Chile last March 2016, our fifth trip to Chile, taxis were much more expensive, and we took the bus to our downtown hotel and then again walked many blocks. On our most recent trip in January 2017, we used Uber. What a difference that made—cheaper and at our doorstep in minutes.

Our second trip to Chile was in 2000. We had made contact with Adriana on our first trip to Chile in 1987 through common friends. She invited us to a Chanukah party at her home; all her family would be there. We hadn't walked much that day and so decided to walk. We set out, oblivious to directions, and after about an hour, we realized we were 180 degrees off.

We were at a gas station, and we met a man filling up. He said he would take us. He turned out to be the financial editor of *El Mercurio* (the biggest newspaper in Santiago) and he gave us his book about finances written in Spanish. We said to let us off near El Bosque, and again we started walking. Everything looked very different. The road had been widened, and the telephone poles and electrical wires had been buried. We eventually found our way to what had been the old Sonesta Hotel, which was now the Intercontinental. It was possible to recognize what was the old Sonesta on one side of the building. However, the building was now completely different front and back. The new construction of what was now called the Intercontinental had been added only on one side of the old Sonesta and so looked different depending which street you were standing on as the hotel stretched an entire block. This completely disoriented us. We knew we were close, but when we asked people where Glamis was, nobody seemed to know. Stanley said that we should call Adriana, but I had left her phone number at our hotel. Not too bright!

Finally, we met a couple who said Gladys, not Glamis, was one block over. Maybe we just didn't hear properly. However, I recognized the top of an apartment building one block over, which was Glamis. I said, "Let's walk over just in case." Sure enough, it was Adriana's place.

We were being anxiously awaited for by this point, as we were over an hour late. We were asked, "Have you converted to Latino time?"

One would think that the trip up to now would have been enough, but after all that traveling, we flew to northern Chile for a week. We stayed at Explora in the Atacama

Desert, the driest place on earth. We stayed in another Explora in Patagonia in 1996 (see chapter 4, "Where to Stay"). I described it as the most outstanding place we have stayed. There is pure luxury while minimizing the impact on the environment, fitting right into the geographical location.

On our return to Santiago on January 5, we didn't see the taxi driver that Stanley had arranged to pick us up when we drove with him on December 28. Sure enough, he came running to us after he had made a second circuit around. We figured we had saved fifty thousand pesos on the four rides to and from the airport. We stayed over one night, and then we left for the airport for our flight to Miami. After all our trouble on our way down, we had reconfirmed many times. However, when we went to check in, again we weren't on the manifest for the flight. Somehow, with lots of ranting, we got boarding passes to Miami (but only to Miami, not to Ottawa). We had to clear customs in Miami, check in for our flight to Newark, and then check in again to head to Ottawa. We also of course had to go through security again after checking in with Continental, which happened to be the furthest concourse away. When we finally got our bags, we realized never again. We made our flight to Newark and could check our bags through to Ottawa, but no matter how long we went away for, we never again checked bags.

So once more—never check bags! This will be a recurrent theme and piece of travel advice.

Ottawa to South Africa (2004)

The many stories from this trip are parts of other chapters (chapter 9, "Encounters with Wildlife"; chapter 15, "Finding

Our Roots"; and chapter 14, "Guides"). But again on this trip in 2004, a coupon of mine was missing in my airline ticket. It was the last leg of a multileg trip (Ottawa to Montreal by bus, Montreal to Amsterdam, Amsterdam to Cape Town, Port Elizabeth to Johannesburg, and Johannesburg to Cape Town, Amsterdam, and Montreal. What was missing was the Johannesburg to Cape Town leg. We e-mailed the travel agent who had made the reservation and figured we would follow up when we got to Victoria Falls, where the agency was based. When we checked in for the flight from Johannesburg to Victoria Falls, the agent again remarked that we were missing a leg. She said to purchase an e-ticket for that leg. It was South African Airways, but they didn't have a real solution. No one would take responsibility.

When we arrived in Victoria Falls, we went straight to the travel agency and gave them our tickets to sort out. We were sure they tried very hard, but from December 24 until January 3 when we checked in for our flight to Cape Town, we were no further ahead. Again, the only solution offered when we tried to explain our missing coupon story was to buy another ticket. For some reason, the process took forever, and boarding was called by the time the ticket was purchased. Our flight from Cape Town to Amsterdam was fine, but again upon checking in for our flight to Montreal, we had no seats. It got sorted out, and we returned home. All in all, it was quite an amazing trip.

Newark to Panama (2007)

We often have to fly through Newark, although we try to always avoid the New York City airports—unless of course we're stopping to see the kids. One of our sons and his family live there. Our trip to Panama and Nicaragua in March 2007 was one of those times. We flew to Newark; stayed over in New York City; and met Joanne and Harold, who lived in New Jersey. We often did this before setting off on our trips. Harold and Joanne would pick us up at Newark Airport, and we would go out for lunch, as often we had long layover times. This time, Harold happened to be in New York for one of his many medical appointments, and we set out from Manhattan well in advance of our flight time to Panama and Nicaragua. We had a great lunch very close by and set out for the airport, which should have been a fifteen-minute drive. The sun was out, although there had been heavy rain earlier. All was well until the exit ramp from the New Jersey turnpike, and we inched along for an hour and a half until we could see the tollbooth. There, it was total gridlock. Absolutely nothing was moving.

We decided to leave the car, and with our carry-on luggage (here's another testimonial to carry-on only) and knapsacks we started to run. We went through the tollbooth. Someone in a black van stuck his head out his window and asked, "Do you want a ride?"

We jumped in and he started going on side roads back and forth and somehow got on the road to the airport, which was empty. He was Flavia from the Liberty Trucking Company. We checked in forty minutes before flight time. The agent tried to tell us the flight was closed, but Stanley went into his "I'm a surgeon and have to operate tomorrow" routine, and sure enough, we checked in and the flight was notified. It was interesting that the line about operating tomorrow turned out to be true; seven years of operating in

Nicaragua, twice a year, followed because of someone we met at the hotel on our last night in Nicaragua on that very trip (see chapter 16, "Surgical Missions").

The trip back was equally historic. We had to return via Panama and so had to take a flight from Nicaragua to Panama. We had to overnight in Panama before taking off for Newark. Although the news about weather in Newark was bad, our flight took off on time. Luckily or maybe not, we were the last flight to land, just as Newark Airport closed. We sat on the runway for more than an hour as the planes unloaded and pulled away from a gate where we could disembark. At that point, international flights were still landing, and we thought ours might take off. The monitor showed it as going.

We went to the business-class lounge and waited for a while. Then an announcement came—the airport was closed, and all flights were canceled. The agent in the lounge said to go home and call to rebook. And then the fun began.

We took our carry-on luggage and saw the lines of people waiting for their luggage—once more proving that carry-on is the only way to go. We then looked at how to get to New York City. The Airlink wasn't running. The tracks had frozen. The express bus didn't come. The taxi line was about a quarter mile long, and almost none were visible. We wandered over to the buses and got advice from someone who said to take the number 162 bus. "It will take you to Penn Station in Newark," we were told. "Then you take the Path, which takes you to the Thirty-Third Street station." Our new friend used his metro pass to let us through.

The train let us off at Sixth Avenue and Third-Third Street, and it was absolute chaos. A mixture of freezing rain and slush made it almost impossible to walk. But Stanley somehow threw himself in front of an empty taxi, which took us to Daniel and Catherine's apartment. Stanley got on the phone and was on hold until 12:30 a.m. Saturday morning. We had arrived at the apartment at 9:00 p.m.

There were no flights to Ottawa until Tuesday. What was available was a flight to Montreal Sunday for Stanley and one for me on Monday. We went to bed and, in the morning, decided to call car rentals. None were available. Interestingly, Catherine and Daniel weren't home. Catherine had decided to take the train to Washington to meet Daniel, as the forecast had predicted bad weather. So we had a car to drive back to Ottawa in. We arrived home no problem and then started calling around for someone to drive the car back.

No problem. Jacob Shouldkraut's stepson took his girlfriend along and arrived in New York City at 3:30 p.m. Monday, in time for Catherine, who needed it that evening. We paid him well, and they took the bus back. It was an extraordinary trip for sure!

Necessity is the mother of invention, or if there's a will, there's a way. No matter what the situation in life, sometimes you just have to be lucky!

After you arrive in a place, sometimes "Getting Around" your destination requires luck as well.

Chapter 3

GETTING AROUND

Over the years, we have traveled in every type of transportation—planes, trains, boats, buses, taxis, and a variety of rental cars. We've driven on the right side, the left side, and often on the wrong side and sailed in many oceans. Our favorite type of travel is arriving in a place where we have never been, renting a car, and figuring out where we want to go. Often, getting lost is the most fun and leads to finding things by accident. It can also be frustrating when you find yourself at the end of a one-way street, one lane wide, in a medieval city, with cars parked on both sides. On several occasions when this occurred, a local offered to drive our car to where we could turn around and continue on our way. This chapter is devoted to taxis and rental cars and some of our best getting around stories.

Taxis

Some of my favorite stories have involved fights with taxi drivers. Stanley always feels that taxi drivers are trying to take advantage of him. Many times, this is true, as going one way ends up being twice the cost of going the other. Often, he'd negotiate a deal with a promise of future longer trips, like the ride to the airport when we would be leaving. Sometimes he even made a deal with a perfect stranger who had a car or a truck when a taxi was trying to charge him more for one direction than what he had paid in exactly the same distance in the other (see chapter 8, "Golf and Fishing").

There were two trips on two different continents where a lineup of available taxis was on the street where we were, and the taxi drivers didn't want to take us. One was in Algiers, and the other was in Prague, both in 1988. I wonder if things would be different now.

In Bermuda, the taxi lobby is so strong that it still (in 2016) is impossible to rent a car. And, often, taxis are not available and complain about driving up narrow streets but continue to drive very large vans. So taxis continue to be a challenge. In so many countries around the world, other means of "taxi" travel are now available (Uber, Lyft, Via, to name a few). Recently (March 2016) in Santiago, we waited over an hour for a taxi, and it never showed up. Our host drove us back to the hotel. The next day, we called Uber, and the car was there in four minutes. In spite and because of this, the conventional taxi drivers complain bitterly. From so many experiences we have had over the years and continue to have, they mostly have done it to themselves.

Barcelona (1999)

However, my all-time favorite taxi story took place in Barcelona in September 1999. It has been told and retold too many times to count. We arrived in Barcelona at night and took the bus to our hotel, walking the rest of the way. This often was considered a good way to get our exercise (according to my travel partner) although I would rather have taken a taxi. Our hotel, a nice but modest Best Western, had a printed page of caution. We had traveled in many so-called "dangerous" countries at that point, but never had we received a list in our hotel room of scams perpetrated on tourists. One was on tourists who had rented a car. Another car would drive up and motion that the car had a flat tire and to pull over. When the person did, he or she was robbed, or the rental car was stolen. Being the cautious, experienced travelers that we are, we took careful note of that.

The next day, we had to take a taxi to pick up our rental car. It was a very short distance away, maybe a five-dollar cab ride at the most. Spain still hadn't joined the eurozone at that time, and everything was still very inexpensive. But this time, instead of Stan hailing a cab outside the hotel, the hotel employee said that the hotel would call a taxi. A taxi pulled up to the door with a trailer on a hitch to carry the luggage. I had never seen one like this before; nor have I seen one since. We got in; our luggage was in the trailer pulled behind the car. We asked the fare, and he said twenty-five dollars. Well, we had asked the fare from the airport yesterday, and it was eighteen dollars and roughly ten times the distance. We refused and asked to be let out of the taxi. We had driven several hundred yards from the hotel at that point. He let us out but refused to give us our luggage unless we gave him twenty-five dollars.

Stanley jumped on the hitch, yelling, "Bandito, bandito," and the police walking by completely ignored him while the crowd gathered. At that time, there were several kinds of police, in blue uniforms and in brown uniforms. We had no idea what responsibilities these officers who were differently dressed had, but in any case none of them helped and just strolled by. With everyone watching, the taxi driver got on the hitch and kicked Stanley. Well, not wanting to die, Stanley offered him ten dollars, which he accepted. Following this, the driver took our suitcases and threw them into the middle of a four-lane highway. We retrieved them, hailed a cab, and proceeded to Hertz to pick up our car.

We were on our way to Bilbao and weren't exactly sure where we would stay but wanted to follow one of the Labow travel rules, which is to get to the place where you need a hotel room well before dark. We set out on the throughway and were barely twenty minutes en route when a car pulled up beside us and motioned that our tire was flat. We didn't get it at first but then said to each other, "One of the classic scams." We ignored it.

We had been driving a bit further when another car did the same thing. And then, at this point, Stanley could no longer drive. One tire was completely flat. We limped off the throughway and pulled into a garage, where the attendant reluctantly put on the spare tire. This was certainly an epic beginning to this trip. A scam isn't always a scam!

Good advice is to always ask the fare before getting in. Stanley always does that. Often, it is with a local who happens to be in the airport and knows how much it should be.

Rental Cars

We have rented cars in many places. But regardless of where we are, Stanley is always paranoid (or maybe not so paranoid) that the rental agency, as with the taxis, is out to get him. We have heard stories of travelers giving the rental car back to an agent who turns out not to be with the agency, and the car is driven off, stolen, never to be seen again. Often there is a discussion about the fuel—return it full, return it empty, or return it seven-eighths full. I recently read an article in the *New York Times*, which stated that some agencies have a rule that you must fill up less than five miles from the agency and less than thirty minutes before you arrive. I don't think this is true of all agencies, but certainly Stanley always fills up at the closest gasoline station to where he is returning the car.

Advice—don't just leave the car on the lot. Make sure you get the receipt with what the full cost was. The rental agency has your credit card and can charge anything.

Iguazu Falls to Asuncion, Paraguay (1987)

People always ask us how we decide where to travel. We get that to this day (2017). Often, almost always, my answer is one of three: "Because it's there." "Because Stanley read something in the *New York Times*." "Just because it came into Stanley's head." However, this trip was for a very specific reason. We all loved the film *The Mission*, released in 1986.[1] It was about the Jesuit missions in South America, and some of the most spectacular scenes were filmed at Iguacu Falls. We flew from Buenos Aires in December

---

[1] *The Mission* (1986 film), https://en.wikipedia.org/wiki/The_Mission_(1986_film).

1987. As I read my diary, I can't believe that we didn't have our flight reservations to Iguacu, and for this trip we were with our two sons. We arrived on Christmas Eve and didn't find a travel agent open until Saturday, December 26. Aerolineas Argentina couldn't be reached, and so we made our arrangements with Austral. We had a tourist pass to the other cities we were visiting on this trip, but the flight to Iguacu was extra, and it was to the Brazil airport not the Argentinian one. No problem. All the arrangements made were excellent, and Stanley picked up the rental car and drove to the Brazil side of the falls with the boys. Our hotel, the Internacional, was right at the falls, and we could see them from the lobby.

However, there was a blinding rainstorm the next day when we wanted to set out to see the falls, and so we decided to do our side trip to Paraguay first. Reservations opened up at the hotel in Iguacu for our return on December 29 and 30 to Iguacu. Again, Stanley was determined to see the country, run at the time by Stroessner, one of the cruelest and most ruthless South American dictators and friend of the Nazis[2] (see chapter 16, "Surgical Missions"). We arrived at the Brazil border and had no problem. But then at the Paraguay border, there was a huge backup. We had to stop and take out all our documents and buy tourist cards for seventeen dollars in spite of our visas. The Paraguayan border guards didn't take those but kept our car registration, which needless to say was very unnerving, since it wasn't even our car.

---

[2] "Stroessner, Paraguay's Enduring Dictator Dies," *New York Times*, August 16, 2006.

Our drive to Asuncion was difficult. It continued to rain off and on the whole way, and as we drove into Asuncion the German influence was everywhere—in restaurants (Old Heidelberg) and with German names all around. However, right on the main drag was the Israeli embassy, a true irony knowing the history. We found an extremely nice hotel, the Excelsior, and to our surprise found the president of Texas A&M there celebrating foreign student graduations.

After one night, we had seen enough and set out again in a downpour to return to Iguacu. We arrived at a very low area on the main road, and we saw people out of their cars walking them through water that was halfway up the sides of the car. Stanley said that there must be another way. How he knew and the people living there didn't was beyond me, but by some miracle, he navigated side roads up a hill until we rejoined the main road again at higher ground. I couldn't understand why Paraguayans who lived in Asuncion didn't know to do the same thing. I thought that Stanley was absolutely crazy. We arrived at the border with Brazil, got our car registration back, and returned to Iguacu.

Stan and the boys went over to the falls, and what they did, fortunately, I didn't know. They were swimming in the currents and around the rocks. They had a great time. I think this may have made up for the fact that Iguacu in 1987 didn't really look at all like it did in the movie, which was set in the eighteenth century. There were helicopter rides, people everywhere, and walkways around the falls, and Iguacu was small and seedy, a typical border town. This didn't really take away from the majesty of the falls, however, and it is a trip well worth taking.

Ushuaia, Argentina (1993)

On our way back from that wonderful cruise to Antarctica in December 1993, we were stuck in Ushuaia, the capital of Tierra del Fuego and considered the southernmost city in the world. There were indigenous peoples in Tierra del Fuego, but the first Europeans to explore the island were those who came with Ferdinand Magellan in 1520. These people called it Tierra del Fuego because many fires built by the natives were viewed on shore as Magellan sailed around the island.[3] It was settled by the British when the HMS *Beagle* reached this channel in 1833. The European settlement and displacement of the native population didn't begin until the late nineteenth century during the Patagonian sheep farming boom and a local gold rush. Argentinians settled there later, and a penal colony for reoffending prisoners was established based on the model of the penal colonies of Tasmania, Australia. Tierra del Fuego is still a geographic point of contention between Chile and Argentina, and it was possible to see the Chilean navy boats patrolling around.

For some reason, our flight back to Buenos Aires was not scheduled, and we had to wait in Ushuaia for three days. We checked into a brand-new hotel, the Glacier, and the accommodations were excellent. However, many members of our tour were not happy. We, instead of complaining, decided to explore Tierra del Fuego, a unique part of the world.

One day, there was a bus tour, which proved very interesting. We never knew just how aggressive and competitive birdwatchers can be. Well, we discovered this

---

[3] Tierra del Fuego, https://en.wikipedia.org/wiki/Tierra_del_Fuego.

on the bus tour. We went to Tierra del Fuego National Park and walked around the shores of the Beagle Channel, which formed one side of the park. We continued on, and one of our birders spotted a pair of Magellanic woodpeckers. Not only was he extremely knowledgeable about birds, he was also extremely assertive. These particular woodpeckers were not yet on his life list, and he was going to spot them and photograph them. They were beautiful birds, and we were also happy to see them, but the fervor with which he took charge was something to see. Adding to the thrill for this gentleman, these birds are an endangered species.

Another very odd feature of the park was the beaver dams. Beavers were introduced in 1946 to create a fur trade[4]. However, the quality of the beavers' pelts produced in that part of the world was not adequate for use for fur. Instead, the beavers have wildly proliferated and overrun the island because there are no natural predators there. Beaver dams exist everywhere and the few trees that remained there destroyed for the dam construction. Recently (December 2016) the countries (Chile and Argentina)—which are still not too friendly—decided to join forces against the beavers. "The enemy of my enemy is my friend." The armies set out to kill as many beavers as they could.

When we realized that we were going to be stuck in Ushuaia yet another day, we rented a car with a couple we had met on the boat and become friendly with and spent a day driving around. The car was a beat-up original VW Beetle. We discovered early on that there were no windshield wipers at all. We were fortunate with the weather. There was

---

[4] Beaver eradication in Tierra del Fuego, https://en.wikipedia.org/wiki/Beaver_eradication_in_Tierra_del_Fuego.

no rain. We wandered from town to town seeing very few people and driving on mostly dirt roads. After wandering around all day, we returned in time to change for dinner.

We set out with another couple in their car and got very lost. But as usual, eventually we found the hotel we were looking for. It was Hotel Tolkeyen just off the road to the National Park on the shore of the Beagle Channel. It is still there today. I just Googled it. I describe it in my diary as a real find with impeccable service and food. It was a great last night in Ushuaia. The next morning, we had to return the car. That was not such an enjoyable experience, when it cost each couple US$150. Imagine what it would be in 2017 dollars! This was 1993. For years after, our friend would remind me of that bargain rental car we had in Ushuaia.

Shanghai, China (2000)

One of the most interesting parts of our trip to China in 2000 was touring the former Jewish Ghetto in Shanghai (see chapter 15, "Finding Our Roots"). At that time, nobody spoke English, especially taxi drivers you would find on the street. As a matter of fact, one taxi driver couldn't even read the Chinese writing in our *Lonely Planet* guidebook when we showed him the page and had to find someone who could. We were on our way back to the hotel and hailed a taxi, which was going in the wrong direction. We got in, and the driver made a U-turn, almost colliding with a police officer on a motorcycle. Needless to say, he stopped, and we waited and waited in the back of the taxi. Finally, we asked the police officer, who managed to explain that we had better find another taxi because this taxi driver had lost his license on the spot!

Taxis and rental cars continue to be a source of interesting travel stories. As similar as these types of transports may be wherever you are, there were always different rules and cultural behaviors in different places. Certainly, Stanley always felt that if it were possible to take advantage of him, an ignorant tourist, taxi drivers and rental agencies would try. He always started out with the proverbial "man with a wrench." No one was going to cheat him!

Belo Horizonte, Brazil (2011)

We flew to Rio de Janeiro in December 2011, crazy people that we are; we wanted to incorporate a road trip during part of the traveling in this enormous country. I had found out that in Minas Gerais, the mining area of Brazil, there are three UNESCO World Heritage sites. And so we flew from Rio to Belo Horizonte. As usual, there was a "discussion" about how to get to the hotel from the airport. It resulted in us walking from where the bus let us off to the hotel, in the rain. But first Stanley wanted to find out where the Hertz Rental Agency was. It turned out the downtown location was at the downtown airport, but it was closed at the moment. We had arranged to pick up at the downtown airport and return at the international airport. After two days in Belo, mostly in the pouring rain, we set out for Pempulha Airport and the Hertz office for what turned out to be the car rental adventure of the century.

We arrived at the Hertz Rental Agency, and no one spoke a word of English or Spanish or French. I found it so hard to believe that the agents in the Hertz Agency wouldn't admit to understanding Spanish, and we found this to be the case all over Brazil. My theory about this is that when you are 250,000,000 people speaking Portuguese, you really don't need to talk to anyone else in his or her language. And of course, the soccer/football rivalry with Argentina may be another factor.

We finally understood that the agency didn't have what we had booked and wanted us to pay more for an upgrade. Again, this had never happened to us before; nor did we find ourselves in this situation again. No amount of protesting made the agents change their minds—not even a phone call to the head office.

Fortunately, there was a Localeza agency not too far away, and someone there who did speak English worked out a great deal for us. We set out to find the road to Ouro Preto. She gave us a map, which did no good, and we were hopelessly turned around and lost. We pulled into a gasoline station, and a gentleman came in beside us and said in English, "I saw you at the Localeza car rental agency. Are you lost?"

We said that we were.

"Follow me," he said. "I will lead you to the throughway to Ouro Preto."

We thought, *This is crazy*. But we felt we had no choice, and through narrow backstreets, he led us all the way to the road, telling us to be careful in the pouring rain.

When we told people that we had driven in Brazil, they couldn't believe it. And looking back on it now, I don't know how we did it. I guess with great difficulty. The signage was terrible; nobody spoke English; and the man who led us to the throughway was the exception, not the rule. For the most part, people were not friendly or helpful, either pretending not to understand English or Spanish or actually not understanding enough to reply.

However, with most travel experiences, the problems with the driving were worth it. Tiradentes and Ouro Preto were amazing colonial towns that were well preserved, with beautiful accommodation. It was in these cities that the beginning of the independence movement from Portugal began.[5] It was the wealthy mining district as well and so endowed with incredible things to see. One of the most outstanding sites we saw in Brazil was the museum called Inhotim. It is definitely unique—a privately owned, contemporary art museum and botanical garden founded by the former mining magnate Bernardo Paz.[6]

However, I will never forget the difficulty we had in finding it. After a harrowing day driving the wrong way on one-way streets in Ouro Preto, we were going to hire a driver to take us to Inhotim but changed our mind on the day of and persevered. With much difficulty and by asking whomever we met along the road, we found this incredible museum. The landscape is a beautiful botanical garden with works of art interspersed with pavilions with different architectural themes. In 2008, Inhotim's status was changed from a private museum to a public institute, with an annual budget of $10 million. Although the plan is for the place eventually to be self-funding, at the moment, it is

---

[5] Tiradentes, facts and information, http://www.encyclopedia.com/people/history/brazilian-history-biographies/tiradentes.

[6] Inhotim, https://en.wikipedia.org/wiki/Inhotim.

largely financed by Paz with only 15 percent coming from the admission tickets.

Again, with great difficulty, we found our way back to Ouro Preto and our posada. It just took lots of stopping and asking the right people, and eventually we made it back.

The rental car return adventure was just as crazy as its pickup. This time, we had to find the new international airport for the city of Belo Horizonte. We were on the main throughway heading toward the city, and before we knew it, we were seeing the turnoff to Centro, back to the center of Belo Horizonte, which would have been opposite to where we wanted to go. We got off the throughway and stopped at a gasoline station and sure enough we were told we were going the wrong way. The international airport is one hour from Belo and not off the throughway we were on and had been traveling the last few days to reach all these important tourist destinations. We were told to take the exit that said Brasilia off this throughway. Now Brasilia at that exit is approximately 735 kilometers away. We did that and then kept stopping and asking the directions. There was not a single sign to the airport. Eventually we recognized that we were on the road to the "downtown" airport, Pampulha. How to get there was still unclear so we continued to ask directions. We found that many people spoke no English, French, Spanish, or Yiddish (German)—only Portuguese. This is the first country that none of our languages worked.

Anyway, when we were in Pampulha where we got lost the first day and where we had picked up the car, we finally saw a sign to the international airport. Then there were signs every kilometer as we drove along the road to the airport. We finally saw a very large Localeza dealer, but there had not been a single gasoline station along the way where we could fill up. The agent there couldn't understand the deal we got, and we were even getting a refund. But—yes another but—the agents wanted forty dollars to fill up. Of course, Stanley would not pay that, and about six kilometers from the agency, there was a gasoline station. We filled up and returned the car, ending what was definitely one of our more difficult car rental stories.

Travel is always an education. Not really sure what the lesson here was, except don't be afraid to ask. Unlike the stereotypical male who refuses to ask directions, Stanley will ask every few kilometers. I like to think I know the way.

Nicaragua (2009–2016)

Except for the surgical missions (chapter 16, "Surgical Missions") with the team, we always rented a car when we went to Nicaragua. We used many different car dealers and, for a while, a local car rental agency that was right beside our hotel, the Camino Real. The rental agency always had available a Japanese Camry or a Korean Hyundai or at least some other make that we knew.

There was one time our rental was a make we had never heard of called Mehindra, manufactured in India. It seemed that Mehindra mostly manufactured trucks, but we had a very nice van. We took off on our usual Friday morning schedule, drove to the villa, and then took our family in the villa out for lunch. It is hard to describe the condition of the roads in the villa. Really, the roads aren't really roads. They are large paths with grassy patches, holes filled with water, and rocks scattered around. Really, a four-wheel drive would be advisable, but we had always managed to negotiate the track to the family's house. Once we'd arrived, we went on our usual shopping spree, had lunch, and took the family back to the villa.

The next day, we picked them up and took them swimming and for lunch. Then we drove back to Managua. We pulled up to the Camino Real and unloaded our bags. When Stanley went to put the car in the parking lot at the hotel, it died. Now I should mention that twice Stanley filled up with regular lead-free gas. He always likes to have a full tank. The Hertz dealer at the airport sent someone over. He tried several times to start the car, and then he put his fingers to his nose and called out, "Gasolina."

The car needed diesel fuel. It was hard to understand that it had driven all that time (two days) after being filled up with gasoline. But at this point, we definitely needed a new car. In Nicaragua, you never get to fill up a car yourself. Many attendants come by and fill it up. Nowhere were we advised that this car took diesel feel; the attendants perhaps couldn't read what it said inside the fuel cap or just ignored it.

When we got back to Ottawa, we received a bill for US$5,000. Although it is a big deal to put gas in a diesel car, that was a bit excessive. We offered $500, which the agency accepted.

Another time, we had a car that had a very strange security feature of which we were not aware. We were on our villa leg of the trip, and we were stopped outside the house where we stay. We were with our friend Manuela, and when we went to start the car after leaving the house, it wouldn't start. We tried everything. The guys outside the house were great mechanics, and they tried everything.

Finally, we called the rental agency. The guy asked if we had the little black thing attached to the key chain. Now when I describe the "little black thing," it really was a little black thing. It was about an inch long and sort of an irregular shape. It looked like a piece of plastic that had been left over from some kind of sculpting kit. Anyway, it was missing. The guy at the agency said that the car wouldn't start unless that was close by. Very strange for sure.

We went up and down the path leading to the house. This path was like most sidewalks and paths in Nicaragua, irregular, full of holes and dirt; you name it. Sure enough, there it was on the path. Manuela found it. Always our helper! And the car started.

Advice—Stanley always is the driver, and I feel he never takes enough time to find out how to drive these cars. There were always little peculiar differences. Take the time at the rental agency to find out.

Once you have a vehicle to take you around, you need to find a place to stay.

Chapter 4

WHERE TO STAY

We have no absolute requirements when it comes where to stay. It depends so much on where we are traveling. But if it's not an organized tour on a boat or a camping trip, we do not have reservations in advance, except for the day that we land—a Labow travel rule we follow to this day. It is interesting how people react when we tell them that. They say they could never do it. We have been doing it for fifty-five years and have never had to sleep on a park bench or in our car. Of course, you have to be flexible and not have very specific needs for where you lay your head—a certain size room, a bathtub, a view, a nice lobby. And sometimes having to pay more than you would like. I could go on and on.

On our two first big road trips, (United States and Europe) we had no hotel reservations in advance. That certainly, on occasion, can be a problem. For example, in Brussels on our European trip in 1965, there was an agricultural convention, and we ended up sleeping on top of a Chinese restaurant (Le Dragon, three dollars). But for many other trips, we just arrive at our destination and look around for a hotel. This gives us freedom to actually see where we will be sleeping. Arriving at a place on the day you would like to stay there also allows for negotiations for the price of a room. This may even hold true for arrival a couple of days in advance and booking your room in person. A smart manager would rather fill a room with someone than have it empty and often will allow a significant discount. And of course, the InteleTravel travel agent's card is a big help, both for price and availability.

For many years, we have been members of InteleTravel.com. This company gives its members an IATA number. It has changed slightly over the years and now is an online company with a monthly charge for membership. Often, using your membership card for only one trip will more than pay for the monthly fee of fifteen dollars. For example, we booked our Viking Cruise in Russia through InteleTravel.com and received a check for a 10 percent refund of the cost. That one trip will cover our membership fees for over five years. However, most of the time we just arrive at a hotel, show our card, and negotiate a price. It gives the hotel a legitimate excuse for giving us a discount.

But even more important, if you haven't prebooked, it is possible to leave a place if the weather is bad or if you simply no longer want to stay in that location. I remember on our trip to New Zealand, we had wanted to see Franz Josef Glacier. When we arrived there, the mountains were completely fogged in, with no chance of clearing predicted for the foreseeable future. So we just kept driving.

Of course, this isn't always possible. On a camping safari or on a boat in Antarctica, your accommodation is taken care of, and there are no other options.

We learned early on that one thing you never say when you are desperate for a room because places are quite booked up is "We'll stay anywhere." On camp visiting day weekend in Schroon Lake, New York, rooms were pretty tight. We had taken one of many weekend trips when Stan was interning in Montreal in 1961. We ended up in the loft closely resembling a barn. There were no sheets, and there was straw in the corner of the room. I sneezed all night.

Over the years, we have stayed in both the best and worst of accommodations. First of all, I'll describe the worst—a combination of the worst trips with the worst accommodation. Sometimes it was both; sometimes just one or the other.

Worst Trips and Worst Accommodation

Asekrem, Algeria (1988)

I would certainly have to add this place on our trip to Algeria as one of the worst accommodations. These accommodations could best be described as shelters. There were no windows and no beds. We slept on foam mattresses covered in dust in our sleeping bags. The floors were filthy. We were on the side of a rocky cliff where the hermit Pierre de Foucauld lived. I guess one could get the true feeling of what it would have been like to be a true ascetic monk. The gory details are in the chapter on "Food" (chapter 5).

Vietnam and Laos (2005)

Although most of the time, we have traveled alone, there have been occasions when we have joined tours. Sometimes that is inevitable—for example, when we sailed to Antarctica. Often the fellow travelers you meet while on a tour can be fun as well as interesting. We still communicate with people who were on that trip, twenty-five years later. Other times, it can be awful. This can be the fault of either the leaders of the tour company who have made the arrangements for local guides and accommodation or the members of the tour, who are rude, inconsiderate, or just can't keep up with the pace of the trip.

One of the worst experiences was our trip to Vietnam. We had joined a tour that certainly made us not want to use that company, or any other tour company for that matter, again. This was 2005, and part of our trip that year included Singapore and Malaysia, which we organized ourselves. We joined our group in Bangkok and then flew to Laos. Our accommodation there was fine, except for the fact that it was absolutely freezing since it was high up in the hills. There was ice in our water in the morning when we woke up. We hadn't prepared for this cold weather. We tried to warm up at dinner, where there was a fire. However, this wasn't the worst we were to experience.

After Laos, we flew to Hanoi, and all was good until our stay in Dien Bien Phu. Most of the other tours we had heard of did not include this city. However, it was certainly worth visiting from a historical perspective. The battle of Dien Bien Phu was the climactic end to the French occupation of Indochina, and viewing General Giap's bunker made it easy to see why the French were defeated.[7] The bunker that was occupied by the general and his troops was high up on a hill. Even with all their firepower, the French could not conquer the Vietnamese Army. This battle in 1954 ended the First Indochina War, with the division of Vietnam into North and South, and the French giving up their colonization of Indochina. This set the stage for the second and most devastating American Vietnam War. General Giap was still alive at the time of our trip and only died in October 2013 at the age of 102.[8] This interesting historical part hardly made up for the terrible hotel booked by the local tour agency.

We flew from Hanoi to Dien Bien Phu, and we were warned that this hotel was not up to our usual standard. That was a gross understatement. The hotel, along with this city, was filthy. Although there was a wall between where we slept and what served as a bathroom, the shower was in the middle of the room with no enclosure and the toilet and sink were on opposite walls. There were weird-shaped stairs, glass doors everywhere, and tile floors. On the wall of our hotel room was a list of instructions. Article 8 stated that social evils are not permitted in the room. It became clear that the social evils were to take place in a separate building across the courtyard. It was clearly a house of ill repute, where rates were advertised in several languages. A red light flashed all evening, and young women paraded themselves at the windows. Even worse, we discovered that behind the

---

[7] The Battle of Dien Bien Phu, https://en.wikipedia.org/wiki/Battle_of_Dien_Bien_Phu.

[8] General Vo Nguyen Diap, https://www.theguardian.com/world/2013/oct/04/general-vo-nguyen-giap.

pool there were cages with Malay sun bears cannulated to collect bile, popular in Asia as a very valuable aphrodisiac.

Generally, the entire city was bizarre. We seemed to be a real oddity. The women in the street poked my bum and flapped my bat wing arms, and they all laughed. Then a man with a stick walked by and hit us all on the back. People often ask us how we manage in countries when we don't speak the language. I always laugh and say that Stanley speaks every language in the world. But in Dien Bien Phu, when we went for a walk and wanted to have a cup of tea, we could not make ourselves understood. Finally, Stanley drew a picture, and we were served the most horrible green tea. We knew we were in a tourist-free place when we couldn't get a diet coke or orange juice and people didn't speak enough English to understand that we wanted tea.

The hotel continued to disgust us as one of the waitresses serving this crazy breakfast of condensed milk and a French roll was picking lice out of another waitress's hair at one of the tables.

The last morning, our flight was significantly delayed, so we went for a walk and got a little bit lost. By some serendipitous event, we came upon a hotel. We had to go to the bathroom and so went in. It was spotless, and the rooms were suites with a living room, a great bathroom, and even a blow dryer—all for thirteen dollars, including breakfast. We found our guide and gave her the whole story. She was coming back in four weeks and so was very clear when she spoke to the tour company that she wouldn't stay at the hotel we were staying at again. Somehow her boss had not done his homework and had relied on the local agency that was probably paid off to take us to the hotel where we stayed.

The tour members continued to be annoying, although some became good friends, and we kept in touch for a while, even visiting them in the United States. However, there was one man, rather elderly, who seemed to be slightly demented. He was with his much younger second wife, who had never been on a tour before. It may have been that since he was very deaf he would wander off because he couldn't hear the guide. This would significantly delay the progress of the tour, as we had to find him. He drank every night, which didn't help his inappropriate behavior. But one night, I was sitting beside him. His favorite drink was vodka. After telling a few sexist and anti-Semitic jokes, he removed his hearing aid and said it needed cleaning. He plopped it into his glass of vodka and swished it around and then put it back into his ear. I vowed never to sit beside him again.

That was the last tour we have taken. We had our own guides and drivers on subsequent trips (to Libya, Madagascar, and Bolivia) but we were not part of a group. That Vietnam tour may have done it.

Madagascar via Paris and Mauritius (2007)

Although Madagascar is the only country where you can see lemurs in the wild, the experience may not be worth it. Madagascar is one of the poorest countries in the world. Table 1 has listed a few examples of relative GDP per capita. This was evident when we visited Madagascar in 2007 and 2008. Traveling there from Ottawa was not easy. We took the bus to Montreal, flew from Montreal to Paris, spent a couple of days in Paris, and then flew to Madagascar. We stayed there for a couple of days and then flew to Mauritius.

We spent from December 15 to 25 in Mauritius. The taxi ride from our bed-and-breakfast in Mauritius to the airport to fly to Madagascar was the beginning of trouble, but certainly as I read my diary about this trip, I wonder what were we thinking doing all of this on one trip, even though the trip was a full month. Whatever could go wrong on this trip went wrong—from taxi rides to airplane tickets to terrible accommodations. These events happened in Paris, Madagascar, and Mauritius. So all in all, this trip fits into the worst trips section.

Our first bad experience was with the taxi in Paris. The taxi drivers are never a very happy accommodating lot there, but this guy was out-and-out combative. We drove to Charles de Gaulle Airport but didn't know the terminal. Neither our tickets nor our itinerary say which terminal. Our taxi driver was totally unhelpful and yelled at us. How could he drive us if we didn't know where we were going? We finally asked someone, and fortunately we were at the right terminal for our flight to Madagascar.

We weren't starting our tour of Madagascar until after our trip to Mauritius, so Benjamin, the owner of the agency we'd booked with, said he would meet us on our return trip on December 25. Our first impressions of Antananarivo (Tana) were not good. There were young children begging everywhere, as well as adults. Garbage was all over. A garbage truck went by. The stench was awful, and a rat ran across my feet. Our hotel was near the presidential palace, which was surrounded by guards and police. There were constant uprisings and strikes. But we were on our way to Mauritius for ten days.

When we checked in at Air Mauritius, we received the first hint that our tickets were missing something. The agent said, "Your ticket says Madagascar. Do you have a ticket to Ottawa?"

In those days, we used an agent at a website, which sold other peoples' air miles at a discounted price for business-class travel. Usually the airfare was about half the regular fare. The problem was the routing. It was always difficult to get seats to and from Canada. But this time, at the last minute, two seats opened up from Montreal to Paris. We had been going via Chicago, although that flight was canceled because of an ice storm. However, something was wrong with our last leg, but more of that later on. "Interesting" situations continued to arise.

Although Mauritius is a beautiful island with lots of luxury hotels, we elected to stay at a B and B far off the beaten track. We were met by the owner at the airport and drove over an hour to our place. The next day, we rented a car and got a SIM card for our cell phone. We drove into one of the towns, wandered around, and found the Oberoi Hotel, where we had lunch. The rates even then were over $1,000 a night. We started back to our B and B and got hopelessly lost. As we wandered through backstreets, a young boy said we had a flat tire. We always doubt this after the many rumors that this is a ruse to rob you. (I might add, each time we had previously been told we had a flat tire, we'd actually had a flat tire—in Barcelona and in Nicaragua—and the warning was not part of a scam.) This time was no exception, and we called our car rental guy, whose first reaction was "What are you doing there?" We were at a dead end near the water. He arrived right away, and his friend opened up his repair shop and put inner tubes in all the tires. He guided us back to our hotel, and we arrived just as the sun was setting.

The ten days in Mauritius were a series of wanderings and a bit of frustration. It was extremely hot, and our B and B didn't have a pool. Access to the beach was public and not great. We joined a pool club, which ended up being closed because of Christmas holidays. The owner of our B and B became very ill with chikungunya, a mosquito-borne viral disease similar to dengue. Although there is no treatment, chikungunya most often is not lethal, but can leave serious joint pain. Although relatively unheard of at that time (2007), it is now (in 2017) one of the most prevalent diseases in Nicaragua, as well as other parts of Central and South America.

So perhaps our owner was a bit out of it when he organized the taxi rides to the airport. It was Christmas Day, which probably contributed to the mess. We were picked up as planned for 6:30 a.m. Our taxi had picked up two other guests at 4:00 a.m. but had not been paid. The women he had taken to the airport had said they had paid the B and B owners and that they would pay him. The rather big problem that the taxi driver had was that he had no money and had not been able to fill up his car. We tried several times to wake up the owners but weren't successful. He called his boss (who happened to be his uncle), who showed up with a full taxi and gave him a few rupees. However, at this point, the yellow warning light was on in his car, and the closest gas station was thirty minutes away.

We set out for the gas station, but sure enough the car died. We were in the middle of nowhere, near a beautiful development where we had walked one day. Everywhere there were condo developments, where there had once been sugar cane plantations, although there were still plenty of those. We still get e-mails from this development wanting us to buy a condo, but again this is a place that is definitely not on my return trip list. To continue, our taxi driver called his uncle again, who said he would come. In the meantime, out of nowhere came another taxi. There were some people in it, but the driver stopped and took us in. We arrived at the airport forty minutes later within plenty of time. We had set out three hours in advance. A taxi running out of gas had never happened before and hopefully never will again.

Back in Madagascar, we were met at the airport by the owner of the travel agency, who explained our itinerary. Our guide was Andy, a young Malagasy university student, very knowledgeable about Madagascar's unique wildlife and plants. We also had a driver, Carl, as we set out for Vakuna Forest Lodge. This ecolodge was not really a wildlife preserve. We found this to be true in many places in Madagascar. There was an owner for this wildlife preserve, and on his 850 hectares of forest, he had a graphite factory and what he called a lemur preserve. The lemurs were on an island and, since they can't swim, were basically prisoners or, as our guide called it, "free in their jail." We took a boat to the island and played with the lemurs, which were tame and jumped all over us.

After a few days at the lodge, we went back to Tana and flew to Fort Dauphin. We had a different driver and guide there and were taken on a road that is difficult to describe. Basically, it was not a road but tracks along rows of planted sisal, a plant used in making fibers that have many uses. We arrived at another so-called lemur preserve—this one again privately owned and very expensive, with terrible accommodation and food. It was extremely hot, and after a bad meal, we went to bed, only to have a "power failure" in the middle of the night. We found out later that the owner of this resort/preserve cut the power to the lodge to run his fiber factory. We did see many lemurs, but some were very diseased, probably because conditions on the property were not properly maintained. We returned to Port Dauphin early and had a couple of days in a nice hotel near the beach.

The degree of poverty here was something we have never seen before in all of our travels to third world countries (see table 1). As we walked down to the beach from the hotel, there were many women with babies selling whatever they could. It looked like fruit that had fallen from the trees. Stanley would buy from one woman and give the fruit to another who had less. The street people and kids dressed in rags were everywhere. They were dirty and unkempt.

Even worse, all around the beach in Port Dauphin (which was beautiful, with pristine white sand) there were young Malagasy girls with old white men, mostly French. There were signs everywhere that said that sex with minors was an offense that would be prosecuted by the government in Madagascar and in your own country. In spite of that, the warning was blatantly disregarded—terribly disturbing. This was evident in other places as well, including some rather upscale restaurants. But here on the beach, there were other illegal activities, such as a cockfight, with mobs of people watching enthusiastically and gambling. There was a Rio Tinto mine nearby and many workers were there participating in the fun. Also, there were young people working for the UN. It was one of them who said that Madagascar was the fifth poorest country in the world (table 1).

The next few days were the ultimate in adventure travel. We both were terrified. We flew to Tulear and were picked up at the airport by a driver who didn't speak English or French very well, driving a beat-up four-wheel-drive vehicle. The windows were held together by tape, and there were no seatbelts. We set out on the road to Kirindy National Park, which made the road to Berenty look like a superhighway. Unfortunately, rainy season had just started, and it had been raining for days. We did see the Baobob trees, which are amazing. But in the next stretch to the park, the road got worse and worse, with huge holes filled with water so that there was no idea how deep they went. Doing some searching on the Internet, I found a description of the road from Morondava to the park that said it was considered unpassable during the rainy season. It is only practicable during the dry season. The website suggested that people prefer to make this transfer from Morondava by motorboat or by canoe. We were at the height of the rainy season driving down this road that was described as unpassable.

After three hours, we arrived at Kirindy Park.[9] There was no one there. The cabins were filthy, and it seemed that in wet weather the animals do not appear. We decided, even though it was 4:30 p.m., that we would turn back—at least a three-hour drive. Even more disconcerting, the gas tank in the car was showing empty. We had not seen another car the entire time we drove those three hours. Cell phones were not

[9] Kirindy National Park, http://www.travelmadagascar.org/PARKS/Kirindy-Mitea-National-Park.html.

working on that road either. The car stopping on that road in the pouring rain with no one around would have been the ultimate adventure that we would not want.

However, we arrived in Morondava just as it was getting dark and found hotel Chez Magee. It was New Year's Eve, but fortunately there was a room. The rain was getting worse, along with the roads in town, and it may have been due to the tropical storm Elnus, which was only 390 kilometers from Morondava. The storm was heading that way, but luckily, we were going to miss it, as we were traveling inland the next day.

During our stay in Morondava we met two young girls who had spent one night in Kirindy Park. They said that they had seen some wildlife, but the accommodation was awful. Rats and other things ran over their bodies all night long. Fortunately, we had made the right decision.

The next day we flew back to Tulear and met Andy and the driver. We set out for Isalo Park and found an entirely different Madagascar and a beautiful new hotel called Jardin du Roy. The food was great, as well as the accommodation. But there is always a but in Madagascar in my memory of the place; no Malagasies were permitted in the dining room. There was a large tentlike structure in the distance we could see that housed the guides and drivers. This was very disturbing to us. It was hard to imagine what those accommodations were like. We got some idea when the following night there was a knock on the door at 1:30 a.m., and there stood a couple with whom we had had dinner and their guide. He had been bitten by a scorpion, and even though he had sucked out the venom, he was concerned. He had reached under his pillow as he was going to sleep and was bitten. We gave him an antihistamine, but there was nowhere to get some ice. Needless to say, after this scorpion incident, we didn't sleep too well. The rain continued to fall.

However, what is always interesting on a trip is the people you meet. At our hotel, we met a young couple from New York who knew no French and needed a spoon to eat their dessert. We told them what to ask for and then began talking. It turned out the woman was Zana Briski[10], who had recently won the Oscar for the film *Born into Brothels*. She was photographing insects around the world and spending three months in Madagascar, certainly a place for insects. They had spent time in Kirindy Park and said that it was wonderful. As she put it, after living in a brothel in Calcutta, the accommodation in Kirindy Park wasn't so bad. I just Googled her and found out she had a photographic show called Reverence that was a collection of her insect photos taken over the past ten years.

To sum up, education, medical care, and transportation were all sorely lacking. Our guide Andy's mother was a schoolteacher and earned eighty euros a month. This, of course, was in a public school. There were many private schools, but most of the Malagasy population couldn't afford them of course. And, generally, the rural population wanted their children to work in the fields, so there was no great demand for public education.

The hospital we visited in Ambolaro was in pretty bad shape, with old equipment. There was a variety of patients with one doctor to care for them. There was no public transportation. There were privately owned minibuses, which the drivers didn't own. There were taxis in the big

---

[10] Zana Briski, https://en.wikipedia.org/wiki/Zana_Briski.

cities, but in this town, when we wanted a ride back to our hotel from the hospital, the doctor called a *pousse-pousse* which consisted of a man pulling us, and that was how we got back.

The last park we visited was a true national park (Ranofanama) and although the guide was not great, the spotter who came along was excellent. We did finally see lemurs in their own habitat, chewing on bamboo and calling out to one another.

We had no idea what Andy was paid by the agency owner, but when we tipped Andy two hundred euros. He began to cry and said it was three month's salary. Carl (our driver) earned only two euros a day, and if he wasn't driving, he earned nothing. We also tipped him a hundred euros and Andy another hundred as well.

We certainly were ready to return to Canada. This was one trip where we would kiss the ground when we arrived home. But the difficult travels had not ended. We were excited when we got back to Tana and found a message from our travel agent on the computer that two seats had opened up from Paris to Montreal. But when we checked in at the airport in Tana, the airline agents kept saying that they couldn't issue our boarding passes. When we got to Paris and tried to check in, again no boarding passes could be issued. There was some problem, which nobody seemed able to figure out, and the tickets had not been written.

One agent who seemed to be the head guy at the Air France customer service counter was extremely unhelpful and even rude. He pointed to the sign above his head and said, "Does this say Delta? Your tickets are Delta." We would never have made the flight if we had had to go to the Delta terminal. Fortunately, there was a very nice agent who stayed on the phone with Delta for a very long time and found out that all they needed was a credit card for a change in ticket fee. So simple and yet so hard to find out! We paid and got our boarding passes to Montreal. After ten and a half hours to Paris from Tana and seven and a half hours from Paris to Montreal and two hours from Montreal to Ottawa, I was quite sick but just grateful to be alive. My opinion is that the lemurs, as amazing as they are, aren't worth the trip!

Table 1
National Gross Domestic Product per Capita per Year[11]

Rank (poorest to richest)	Country Name	GDP/capita ($CAD)
1	Burundi	275.98
5	Madagascar	411.82
19	Rwanda	697.35
21	Nepal	732.30
28	Tanzania	864.86
47	India	1,581.59
49	Laos	1,812.33
55	Nicaragua	2,086.90
57	Vietnam	2,111.14
71	Indonesia	3,346.49
81	Albania	3,695.02
86	Paraguay	4,160.61
91	Libya	4,643.31
98	Serbia	5,143.95
101	South Africa	5,691.69
103	Thailand	5,816.44
104	Colombia	6,056.25
110	Cuba	6,789.85
	Canada[1]	50,000

Nicaraguan hotels (2007–2016)

There is now an entire range of hotel accommodation in Nicaragua, but when we first started going there in 2007,

---

[11] The poorest countries in the world, http://country-facts.findthedata.com/stories/22362/poorest-broke-gdp-countries-nations?utm_source=google&utm_medium=search.ad&.

we were part of a surgical mission (see chapter 16, "Surgical Missions") and where we slept was pretty bad. Probably the worst thing about where we stayed was the fact that there was only cold water. Our Nicaraguan friends said they absolutely can't stand hot water for showering, probably because Nicaragua is always so hot. But with air-conditioning being more and more available, it is possible to feel cool in Nicaragua. This is especially true at higher elevations, such as the village where many of our surgical missions took place. Our accommodations were very basic but had some unwanted guests—scorpions. It was necessary to check our shoes especially but other clothing as well, as these guys hid very well. Other problems included water shortages and frequent power shutdowns. When we first started going to Nicaragua, the only place we had hot water was at Camino Real in Managua and then at the "fancy" resorts in San Juan del Sur and Rivas. There is now the ultimate in luxury in several resorts, the most luxurious being one called Mukul. The rates are $1,000 a day, and there are flights now that go directly from the airport in Managua to the landing strip near the resort. It used to be the private estate of the former dictator of Nicaragua, Samosa. Now owned and operated by Flor de Cana, the rum company, it is being marketed in New York City as the place to go.

For our last few trips to the villa when we were just there visiting Mariana and her family, there were very nice hotels where there was hot water as well. Where we stayed on our surgical missions, we never had hot water. Somehow for our North American sensibilities, this would rank as "worst accommodations." Somebody once inquired about going to Nicaragua where we went and asked, "How many stars do the hotels have where you stay?" I answered, "How about minus one?"

Our Best Trips and Best Accommodation

Explora, Chilean Patagonia (1996)

We are always asked what our favorite trip was. I do still answer visiting the mountain gorillas in Rwanda (chapter 9, "Encounters with Wildlife"). However, when it comes to accommodation, the best was Explora in Torres del Paine National Park in Patagonian Chile. We were there in December 1996. Aside from the exquisite beauty of the park, the hotel was unique in its luxurious accommodation while maintaining its minimal ecological impact on the local environment. Every evening as we sat around with drinks and hors d'oeuvres, we met with the guides of the hotel, who described the hikes available the next day. These varied in difficulty, as well as the length of time involved. One time, the guide took Stanley alone the service was so impeccable. The food was also outstanding, as were the rooms. All had a view of the Torres and the lake in front of the hotel. Some had a view of Salto Chico, small waterfalls that ran alongside. This place was definitely ranked as all-around amazing accommodation, with everything included in the daily price.

At that time, although expensive, it was brand-new and a relatively unknown destination. I just priced the hotel today, as we are returning to Torres del Paine in December (2016) and found the cost prohibitive. It was US$3,500 per person for four days. In our Canadian dollars, it was certainly crazy. What was amazing, though, was that the hotel had maintained its ecological mandate, and although a small addition had been made, the change was almost imperceptible. When we were there in December 2016, we visited the hotel and the park, and both had maintained their pristine and unspoiled nature. The roads in the park were still unpaved and the numbers of tourists and accommodations kept at a very acceptable level.

View from the lobby of Explora, Torres del Paine National Park, Chile, December 1996

Four Seasons Hotels, Bali, Indonesia (1999)

Another favorite hotel of mine where our InteleTravel card got us a deal was the Four Seasons in Bali in December 1999. There were two Four Seasons, and we stayed in both of them. One was in Jimbaran Bay, and the other was in Ubud. My favorite was the latter. Our room was a two-floor suite.

The rate we got was US$195, about a 50 percent reduction. The architectural design was outstanding. The entrance to the hotel was a bridge over the river, and then you walked under a lily pond to the lobby. The hotel was on the side of a hill terraced with rice paddies, and the restaurant and the rooms, as well as the spa, had a view of the Ayung River rushing past and the rice paddies. The entrance to our room was from a corridor with concrete-covered moss walls and pillars that had water running down them to a channel, which must have led to the rice fields. This suite also had two bathrooms, one on the main floor and one upstairs where the bedroom was.

Lake Taupo, New Zealand (2001)

Although New Zealand is mainly thought of as a country of extreme outdoor sports, some of the most luxurious lodges I have ever seen exist all over the country. We traveled through New Zealand in December 2001 and found what I called in my diary "a jewel." This was Lake Taupo Lodge. The owner lived in the house, and he'd built it eighteen years prior to our visit. The lodge is situated on the western shores of the lake. It's described as having an "innovative architectural design inspired by Frank Lloyd Wright," and the view of Lake Taupo is breathtaking. There are four magnificent suites in the main house with a villa adjacent to it for overflow. The gardens; the furniture; and, above all, the amazing food made it truly exceptional. We made a deal for NZ$650 a night again with our InteleTravel card.

The other people staying at the lodge made it even more interesting. All six of us ate at one table, and we exchanged stories. Among the group was a pair of honeymooners traveling around the world on a forty-eight-day honeymoon. They were from Mexico City and certainly very wealthy. There were six hundred people at their wedding. They were Jewish, and the other couple from New York City was also. They were both lawyers. Dinner was as follows—hors d'oeuvres of chicken in phyllo dough first, tomato soup, lamb shanks, zucchini fritters, olive bread, nut torte, and truffles. The following night, the meal was just as good—yogurt/cucumber soup, salmon in phyllo dough, and lemon *bavarois* with cookies for dessert. The owner seemed to like us a lot and gave us a glass penguin statue as a souvenir.

Tuomoto Islands, 2003

As I thought of the many places where we have stayed over the years, I recalled that one of the most beautiful and relaxing was in the Tuomotos. In 2003, we went to Easter Island, followed by a cruise on the *Windstar* around the islands of Tahiti. We then took a small plane to Manihi Island in the Tuomotos. We were greeted by the Pearl Resort staff and taken by golf cart to our over-the-water bungalow. There was a glass bottom in the middle of the bungalow, and the display of exquisite fish was nonstop. We could feed the fish through holes in the glass floor and watch them eating. In addition, snorkeling from off our bungalows was amazing. The water was almost hot and crystal clear. It was a truly relaxing holiday, which I paid for on our next stop, Nuku Hiva in the Marquesas—a trip I cannot resist recounting here.

The atmosphere in the Marquesas was totally different when compared to Tahiti and the Tuomotos. The people there do not like tourists. This was explained to us by the manager at our small hotel. I can understand the sentiment, since people definitely change a place. The Marquesas do not want to change from their pristine, natural environment.

Our big adventure on this island was to take a long hike to some waterfalls. We hired a guide, but more important, I didn't have the proper shoes. We bought water shoes because part of the hike was in the river, but mine were a size too small. We took a boat to the beach where one episode of the series *Survivor* was being filmed and then started the hike. I was tired and my feet were sore after only half of the way there. At the falls, Stanley cut the toes out of the shoes, and I felt a little better. But we had a two and a half-hour hike back. I was in agony on the way back, and during the last walk over some rocks and mud, I slipped and fell. Although not very hurt, I was completely wet and covered in mud. I staggered into the boat that was taking us back to the hotel.

It didn't matter that I was wet. A storm came up, and we tossed and turned and were soaked in the downpour and the rough seas. When I got back to the hotel, I threw out all my clothes, which happened to have my sunglasses in the pocket. I was totally dead and not feeling very well but did rally for an excellent French dinner. When I returned home to Ottawa, my surgeon husband had to remove what remained of my very damaged toenail. It has never been the same.

Akasa Peninsula, Cyprus (2005)

When I asked Stanley where he thought our most luxurious hotel was, he said Cyprus. We were in Cyprus in March 2005 (see chapter 13 "Border Crossings"). This was at the end of our stay on the Greek side, and we set out for the Baths of Aphrodite, which were in the Akasa Peninsula. Supposedly the Goddess of Love was born in the Mediterranean Sea and walked to Cyprus.[12] We drove to Polis and found the Anassa Hotel. A Mercedes limo was in the courtyard; I assume it was to drive people to and from the airport. We used our InteleTravel card, and the 300 pounds a day was reduced to 122 pounds. March is definitely off-season, and the manager said that, usually, the rate in off-season was 180 pounds. I did check online recently and found that the hotel now doesn't open until April. In any event, the resort was extremely luxurious and well worth 122 pounds. The grounds were beautiful, with four outdoor pools and two indoor pools, as well as a magnificent spa. Our room had two bathrooms and was huge. I think this hotel was memorable because Stanley will never forgive himself for staying there. The products were Bulgari, and I so loved them that to this day I use the shampoo, perfume (Thè Vert), and body lotion.

So, we continue to travel without hotel reservations. From this chapter, it is possible to see that we can stay anywhere and survive. It may not always be pleasant, but it always makes for a good story!

There are several advantages to not reserving an entire trip. It provides flexibility; it allows you to see where you will sleep; and, most importantly, it gives you the ability to bargain for a room.

---

[12] http://www.greekmythology.com/Olympians/Aphrodite/aphrodite.html.

Although getting there, getting around and where to stay are essential for any trip, probably the most important aspect to any travel is the food you eat. A description of our memorable meals follows.

CHAPTER 5

FOOD

As I began rereading my diaries in order to write this book, I found that there is some mention of food on almost every page of the more than one hundred diaries I have kept over the years. It is clear that food is a very important part of travel for me—some of my critics would say the most important part. From the simplest pizza to the most exotic local dish and from the food that made us sick to the food that was amazingly prepared under the most difficult conditions, there was a description about what it looked like and/or how I enjoyed or didn't enjoy eating it. A description of a few of the special experiences follows.

The trek to Machu Picchu (1984)

This camping trip along the Inca trail was certainly a challenge. However, the food rewards made up for it. It was hard to imagine how it was possible to create such gourmet meals in such remote, underserviced, difficult conditions.

On the first day of hiking, we actually were waiting for the team that was going to look after us. Around 5:30 p.m., two horses came into view, with one porter followed by a small army of men bent in half with the load of stuff, seven porters all together. We had an experience watching them set up five tents which in addition to where we slept were a dining tent/kitchen and a portable latrine (which consisted of a hole in the ground and four canvas sides with a zipper). Then an hour or so later, we went to have tea in the dining tent and watched Fortunato the cook do his thing. Another hour, and our first gourmet meal on the trail was ready. Tomato onion soup, braised meat, potatoes and gravy, and carrots with a lemon butter sauce. Dessert was bananas flambé with chocolate sauce. All was absolutely delicious!

It is not easy to sleep at high altitude, but we managed with several trips to the latrine and 2-222's (aspirin with codeine). The first breakfast was also fantastic. Fried eggs, bacon, and a salami (the latter we had brought ourselves; I'm not sure what we were thinking when it came to food along the trail it was totally unnecessary) and grilled toast and jam with a sort of Bovril drink that fortified us for what lay ahead. We climbed about a thousand feet and then chewed some coca leaves. The coca leaves and the tea did absolutely nothing, and we continued after a light lunch for many hours. We hoped that we wouldn't have too many more days like this. There had been a rockfall, and we had to walk around the easy trail, making it an extra long day. So one would wonder, could the gourmet meals continue?

They only got better. That night we had chicken noodle vegetable soup, chicken tetrazzini, and then corn pudding (called *massapora*) for dessert. And so it continued, day after day, meal after meal. A few more highlights included Chinese ginger soup, beef chop suey, green beans, noodles, rice, and fresh pineapple with hot buttered rum for dessert. Another meal was garlic soup, beef stroganoff, and chocolate pudding. The last meal was minestrone soup, spaghetti, and tomato sauce with freshly grated Parmesan cheese, with cookies for dessert. A typical lunch was pita, guacamole (freshly prepared), tomatoes, cheese, and onion (with or without our salami) in sandwiches. This continued for one full week of meals.

One dessert deserves special mention. It was certainly a highlight. Imagine a crème caramel flan prepared at twelve thousand feet. Quite amazing! The stream close to our campsite was so cold it was possible to gel the flan. We actually had to wash in that stream. When I think of it now, I still shiver. But that's all we had.

However, in spite of all this eating, we all lost weight. The hiking was tough, and with altitude, our GI tracts were definitely overworked.

Camping safari in Tanzania and Rwanda (1986)

Several years later, we were on a camping safari in Tanzania and Rwanda—probably a trip I still rank number one to this day. Our meeting with the mountain gorillas is described in detail in chapter 9 and was a unique experience that has not yet been duplicated. However, we did no physical activity on this trip to speak of, mostly riding in the truck. I guess setting up our own tents involved some work. Aside from that, though, we did nothing except for our hike up to the mountain gorillas in Parc des Volcanes. However, we certainly ate. Again, it was amazing food, prepared from scratch every day, with fresh fruit and vegetables from local markets and freshly baked bread.

Each day we got up very early in order to view the wildlife. So, we started with just toast and coffee. We then came back to a huge brunch/lunch, which typically was fruit salad, granola, bread, sausage, guacamole, and beet salad. Then dinners always had soup, main course, and dessert—for example, onion and tomato soup, lamb, potatoes, carrots, and green beans. Occasionally we would overnight at a lodge, and the food was never as good as our two cooks prepared. Even when we camped in the yard of the prison for the criminally insane, we were served a full course meal of squash soup and spaghetti and meat sauce after we all got settled. When we finally made it to Kigali and checked in to the fancy Meridien Hotel, the food was just as awful as warned by our guide, Clive. He said that someone always got sick from the food at this hotel. We had joked with Clive that the food on our trek to Machu Picchu was amazing and one night we actually had crème caramel for dessert. Sure enough, Clive had tried to prepare it, but it would not solidify. It was hardly cool enough in the Rwandan jungle, although at night, I slept in many layers of clothes.

Our last meal in Rwanda was in Kigali while we were waiting for our flight home. With all our travels, this was the first time that Stan had to cancel patients because we were delayed over eight hours. Daniel was already sick (with malaria we later found out; see chapter 7, "Accidents and Illness") and stayed in the hotel room, but we went to a very nice restaurant run by a Canadian woman, Helene Pinsky, married to a Rwandan, Mr. Lando.[13] Lando was a Tutsi, an often-persecuted minority among the Hutu majority. Lando went off to school at McGill, which was where he met and married Helene. In the mid-'80s they decided to move back to Rwanda, where Lando could play a role in building a democratic, multiethnic Rwanda.

He opened a hotel and bar called Chez Lando. We were served in an open court, marvelous brochettes. Then went upstairs to a dining room where we had broiled chicken and a wonderful pizza. There were also ten rooms, and Clive was thinking of suggesting that Overseas Adventure Travel (OAT) use that hotel instead of the Meridien next time OAT traveled to Rwanda. Of course little did he know what awaited the owners of that hotel and restaurant, as well as the rest of Rwanda.

As anti-Tutsi extremism grew through the early '90s, Lando's name appeared on a number of lists of those marked for death. He and Helene were fully aware of this but were determined to hang in. In fact, they were among the earliest targets. On February 17, 1994, Romeo Dallaire,[14] who was commander of the United Nations Assistance Mission in Rwanda (UNAMIR), received information of a plot to assassinate Lando, who at that time was a prominent moderate member of the transitional government. In his book *Shake Hands with the Devil,* Dallaire claimed that he informed them of this plot. On the day of their assassination, Helene called him to ask for UN protection. To this day, Dallaire suffers from guilt in that he couldn't do anything

---

[13] Lando Ndasingwa, https://en.wikipedia.org/wiki/Lando_Ndasingwa.

[14] Romeo Dallaire, http://www.romeodallaire.com.

to stop the genocide. The family gardener later revealed that Lando, Helene, their two children, and Lando's mother, who lived with them, were executed. We were there in 1987. This occurred in 1994.

At this time (2017) there appears to be a stable government. Chez Lando has reopened, operated by the younger surviving sister of Lando. An article entitled "The conviction of Theoneste Bagasora for genocide in Rwanda – a personal reflection," by Gerald Caplan, in *The Globe and Mail*, December 19, 2008, describes the revival of Chez Lando.

Lamb in the Algerian desert (1988)

I was having trouble deciding to start with the outstanding food or with the food that made me sick. It's sort of a good-news, bad-news thing, and of course the bad news thing may be more interesting. I was a *Seinfeld* fan, and one of my favorite episodes was the time that Jerry went on and on about how he had only thrown up five times in his life. My kids called me laughing because that was something I always went on and on about also. With me, it may have only been four times. And now well into my seventies, I think it is quite an accomplishment. Not once during either one of my pregnancies did I even come close to vomiting. So why I go on and on about this is that the most memorable time that I did throw up was when we were camping in the Sahara Desert in Algeria. The ingredients for our meals were carried along in the four-wheel-drive vehicle with us for a week without any refrigeration. I think that trip is well worth describing in detail.

As was true for many of our other destinations, this was a trip that had been written about in detail in the travel section of *The New York Times* (1988). Stanley thought it would be a great adventure for the four of us. It was not only an adventure but also, in retrospect, our toughest trip either with or without our kids. However, the greatest merit this trip had was to give us travel credibility. I was once at a scientific meeting in Oxford and seated at the conference banquet at Blenheim Palace with other delegates. North Americans were being mocked by some Europeans over how soft Canadians and Americans are. I had just returned from Asekrem, Algeria, and when I casually mentioned it, they were blown away. Detailed description of the trip follows, including one of the most remarkable aspects—the food.

Our route took us from Montreal (Mirabel in those days) to Paris. And I guess as far as food goes, it ranged from the sublime to the ridiculous. Our two days in Paris were amazing, as usual, especially as far as food goes—fresh croissants and orange juice in the morning, profiteroles and frites and duck at night. We flew Air Algerie to Algiers from Orly Airport in Paris. The check-in was in the most remote part of the airport, and the security check was at the gate with all the hand luggage opened.

On the flight, a couple in native dress asked Daniel to fill in their landing cards, thinking he was Algerian. As we were getting off the plane, a woman asked Daniel to help her with her bag. And then when we were clearing customs, an agent cleared Daniel and said to the rest of us that tourists go in lane number three.

Then the many fights with taxi drivers began. We finally found one that would take all four of us. No taxi had a meter, and so the rate needed to be negotiated every time. We arrived at our hotel that didn't have our reservation and had mixed up not only the dates but also the number of guests. We straightened it out and then went for dinner at a great seafood restaurant that piled on the fresh shrimp and prepared them in a hot, spicy, delicious sauce. We had to argue with a taxi to take us there, and then it was even more difficult getting a taxi to take us back. The taxis were lined up across the street from our restaurant; the drivers stood around talking, not at all interested in working and actually looking at us with great hostility. Finally, one did take us to our hotel. The next day, we tried to take one taxi to the airport. They insisted we needed two. We finally got one with a luggage rack and arrived at the airport in time for our flight to Tamanrasset.

We met our French-speaking Tuareg[15] guide, Fodil, who picked us up in a Land Rover that had to be hot-wired to start, no key. As we set out for the desert and our first campsite, we were very surprised by the temperature. It was almost freezing at night, and in spite of our wonderful sleeping bags and my Lifa underwear, I was always much too cold. Another problem was waking up covered in sand, as every night the wind picked up when it was early morning. There was no way a tent could be set up in the shifting sand. We slept *sous les etoiles* (under the stars). The amazing thing about this was the number of tourists (read other crazy people)—all European. Many groups were rock climbing. Our guide communicated with their guides, and they all gathered in a circle at night, but we couldn't figure out how they knew where each of them was. Fodil said something about turning a rock in the

---

15 http://www.bradshawfoundation.com/tuareg/.

sand a certain way. There were no shortwave radios allowed. Only the army was allowed to have them. He knew nothing about troubles in Algiers, which we suspected. By the way, Fodil only spoke French and Arabic and, I guess, his own native Tuareg language. So an added benefit to our trip was that it was a French refresher course. We discovered that only the older generation understood and spoke French. Since the independence from France (around 1962) Algerians did not learn French, and many years later, there was still animosity against France.[16]

The food quality and variety started out very good. The restaurant at the hotel in Tamanrasset was excellent, and our relationship with lamb began. On our first day camping in the Sahara, we were quite amazed at the fresh vegetables for salad and soup warmed on an open fire with wood we gathered whenever we stopped. We were particularly excited by the leg of lamb in the back of the van. Great! Lamb for our first meal! The evening meal was couscous and was outstanding. One of the unique food items was the bread called *galet*, which was freshly baked in the sand buried under the hot coals remaining from the fire where our meal had been cooked. Every meal ended with dates and sweet mint tea.

The interesting thing was that the leg of lamb was not only for our first meal. It continued to be the main course for every evening meal on our camping trip for the next five days, and our concern about the lack of refrigeration grew as each day passed. We assumed that food didn't spoil in the very dry desert. But perhaps we were wrong.

After five days of camping in the desert, we went back to Tamanrasset and stocked up with more food. It was at

---

[16] https://www.britannica.com/event/Algerian-War.

this point that we really had had enough of rocks and sand. However, next on our itinerary was Asekrem.[17] After the most incredibly bumpy, windy road, we arrived at what was supposed to be a cabin/shelter but turned out to be probably the worst accommodation we have ever had before, or since I might add (see chapter 4, Where to Stay). Foam mattresses filled with dust and an absolutely filthy floor. There were no windows. At the top of the mountain was the former hermitage of Father Charles de Foucauld, who was assassinated by an invading African tribe in 1916. He had been part of the French Foreign Legion and left the legion and became a hermit. He was even beatified by Pope Benedict in 2005.[18] Our meal, yes, more couscous, was served with the lamb, which was still around eight days later. I was up all night with dry heaves but was encouraged to come along the next day to a nomad's home. The mother in the nomad's home made me some tea, and I did feel a little better. But, here it comes. Walking back up, it came over me all of a sudden, and I vomited, an extraordinary event. Fodil put cold water on my neck, and I felt better.

Our kids' final assessment was that if we ever tried to take them to sand that isn't near water, they definitely would not go.

Eastern Europe while under Communist influence (1988)

We had a few trips with friends a long time ago. Our first trip together with one other couple was in September 1988.

---

[17] Assekrem, https://en.wikipedia.org/wiki/Assekrem.

[18] Charles de Foucauld, https://en.wikipedia.org/wiki/Charles_de_Foucauld.

It wasn't quite as dramatic as our food experience in Algeria, but it was certainly a challenge. I know things are very different now, but at that time, food was scarce both in Poland and Czechoslovakia, and many times the people serving us food resented doing it. Although it was obvious hotels were empty, the people in charge refused to give us a room without a bribe, stating that the hotel was full. It took a while, but we finally figured that out.

The trip consisted of flying to Vienna and then renting a car and driving to Hungary; through what is now Slovakia; to Crakow, Poland; and then to Prague, which is now the Czech Republic, ending up back in Austria. In retrospect, it was almost at the end of the USSR's domination of these countries and, at this point, at the height of the depletion of their resources; in addition to food and accommodation, diesel fuel was also very complicated and difficult to get. Diesel coupons had to be purchased from travel agencies or banks.

Vienna to Budapest was no problem, but as we left Hungary into Slovakia, there were many problems obtaining diesel coupons and changing money. Each of these countries had its own currency. The ease of travel in the Eurozone now is such a huge contrast and, when you think about it, an incredible accomplishment. So either banks were closed or travel agencies were closed, and hours varied. We decided to push on to Crakow but arrived at the town of Brystica around lunchtime. The hotel flat-out refused to serve us, although lunch seemed to be being served to many people. We found a small deli and literally argued with the woman to buy some food. We were able to buy a small loaf of bread and a few slices of meat and cheese. When we asked for more, we were refused. She seemed angry to have to sell us food. We bought chocolate bars and went and had a picnic. Our friend always preferred sweets and went straight for the chocolate bar. As she unwrapped one corner and broke off a piece, a lovely little white worm surfaced. That abruptly ended the picnic, and we continued onto Crakow. Fortunately, our van took very little fuel, and we made it by dark.

Our food experience in Crakow was also not great, but with the usual bribe, a decent meal could be bought. Near the university there was a pizza restaurant. We stood in line for a very long time but finally could order the one small pizza available. It had very little cheese with some tomato sauce on it. We ordered two each, which were given to us reluctantly. The drink, again one kind, orange, was in one of those fountain containers, and it looked very much like it was going to run out. When it did after two drinks were dispensed to us, the server went to the tap with a pail, filled it with water, and added it to the orange fountain. We realized why as we wandered the streets everyone was drinking and smoking. We were able to get one meal at a restaurant, where we gave the doorman five dollars for a reservation for dinner the following night. He came back, assuring us that we could have a reservation but that the cook also needed five dollars if we wanted to eat. We were told that this restaurant was where visiting dignitaries had dinner. It turned out to be a decent meal. I had lamb shashlik, which turned out to be ground lamb and Bulgarian wine. The whole meal including dessert came to thirty-four dollars for the four of us. We had changed far too many zlotys.

We continued on our route to Prague, and our accommodation and food adventures continued. We had to stay overnight in Brno and did find a reasonable hotel there and a good meal. We asked the woman at the desk to get us a room in Prague, and with a ten-dollar bribe, all she could find was a botel; supposedly everything else was booked. A botel was, as it sounded, a boat that had been converted into a hotel. We had heard about these for the "overflow" of all the tourists. A total myth! With the right currency (US) anything is possible.

A bribe was necessary in Prague as well, and we managed to get two rooms at the Three Ostriches, a hotel supposedly full for the entire next year. We left money on the seat of a taxi around the corner of the hotel, and he somehow managed to get us two rooms. The details of black market money and currency exchanges are the subject of another chapter (chapter 6).

The next city en route was Salzburg and, although only a few hours away by car, another world. Here, food was everywhere, beautiful accommodations were available, and the stores were full of merchandise. It was a trip of contrasts at this time.

We found that to be even truer a couple of years later when we traveled to the same countries but included Bulgaria and the former Yugoslavia. It was 1990, and the tension in both of these countries was palpable. We were six people this time in a rented van, and pleasing all of us even some of the time wasn't easy. We arrived in Sofia in the middle of the tent city. There was no food in the stores. Some just had red Kool-Aid, others just tea and coffee. We were able to check into the Sheraton, which turned out to be extremely luxurious. There was a lot of confusion when it came to currency exchange, but that is another story (see chapter 6). Our rooms were like individual apartments, and dinner was amazing. Chicken wings, shrimp, lamb, feta salad, beautifully prepared white asparagus, and two bottles of excellent Bulgarian wine were all under a hundred dollars for the six of us. It was very shocking to see the contrast. The Sheraton was a show place where the Russians often held meetings. There was always food there. This was just before the breakup of the USSR, and the satellite countries were in the process of decay at that time.

We only realized several months after our travels in the former Yugoslavia that we had been there on the verge of the start of their terrible civil war.[19] This was especially evident in Sarajevo, with the diversity of religions and ethnic origins. We found a restaurant, which was recommended by two of our guidebook sources. There we had an authentic Yugoslavian meal, but it almost killed five of us. We were all sick in succession as we drove from Sarajevo to Dubrovnik. Our travel rule of no reservations was a bit of a challenge this time, being we were there in the middle of summer. There were tourists everywhere, and we learned a couple of lessons. Never travel with six people without reservations in the middle of summer! Or on second thought, never travel with six people unless you are on an organized tour!

Although our food experiences in Eastern Europe at these times was a bit of a challenge, it really is impossible to compare to the horrors of starvation and deprivation of all people in this region during World War II, but especially Jews. Details of our visits to the concentration camps

---

[19] https://en.wikipedia.org/wiki/Breakup_of_Yugoslavia.

(Auschwitz-Birkenau and Theresienstadt) in Poland and Czechoslovakia are described in chapter 15.

A Contrast of Cruises

The *Akademic ioffe*, Antarctica (1993)

Although never being "cruise" tourists, we found that there are destinations that require a boat, and we have visited several. One such destination is the Galapagos Islands; another is Komodo Island in Indonesia. A boat is also required to get to Antarctica, where we traveled in December 1993. Although Antarctica itself was exciting and lived up to its reputation, the food on the boat did not measure up to what one usually expects on a cruise. Usually one expects too much food, with meals and snacks and shops where you can purchase snacks, but this cruise had none of these. The boat was the *Akademik ioffe*, a Russian scientific vessel on loan to our tour agency, Blyth & Company, for a year. This particular tour was handled by yet another travel company called Polar Expeditions. All of these companies no longer exist.

Our trip started in Montreal via Miami to Buenos Aires. We were met by a representative of Polar Expeditions and checked into our hotel for one night. We managed to find our favorite restaurant in Buenos Aires, Papas Fritas Deliciosas once more. Although it had been years earlier when we'd last visited, we were able to find it in the same location, and not only was the menu the same but we were also served by the same waiter. This was the Argentinian version of Le Relais de Venise in Paris—steak, salad, and French fries, all you can eat—of course at a fraction of the price you would pay in Paris. But this time, the cost was ten times what we had paid before, due to our currency being low at this time and the Argentinian currency being pegged to the US dollar.

The boat was nice enough. Our quarters were roomy and fairly comfortable. And the ride through the Beagle Channel from Ushuaia, Argentina, was smooth sailing. However, as we set out after dinner across the Drake Passage, things got pretty rough. I think almost all the passengers were sick, and I promptly threw up breakfast. This probably was number four or five. The Drake Passage had maintained its reputation as the roughest water in the world, ranked that way since 1520—quite a record.[20]

The other reputation that had been maintained is that Antarctica has penguins. We would leave the ship by zodiac and sail to shore, being greeted by all kinds of penguins at every stop. They were very smelly but very tame or, I guess, habituated, and we could sit around in the snow watching them go about their business.

However, one thing that did not maintain its reputation was that cruises have food. Each day consisted of a choice of small portions of either meat or fish for dinner. The staff did not speak English, and if you asked for anything extra, it was never available. We found out later that the staff was still Russian and that the boat had been commissioned in Germany with what appeared to be the bare minimum of frozen food. There was no dessert at lunch, which usually consisted of soup and noodles or salad and noodles. Sometime around two, the staff would throw on a table in

---

[20] http://www.seachest.co.uk/blog/2014/07/29/the-worlds-roughest-seas/.

the lounge a pile of social tea biscuits, which was quickly demolished. There was nowhere you could buy a snack if you were hungry. Sometimes there was a choice of beef or chicken for dinner, but they always seemed to be out of beef. We actually lost weight on this cruise, quite amazing.

On the way back, the Drake Passage was very calm for the most part, and we sailed into the Beagle Channel with everybody feeling pretty good. We arrived at Estancia Haberton, the first sheep ranch in Tierra del Fuego, and after a tour of the ranch we had tea in the Whalebone House. Well, there was an attack on the cookies, cakes, and other pastries as though we had been in prison. It was quite hilarious. However, on the last night on the boat, we were served an incredible meal of turkey, smoked salmon, meatballs, salami, and more. I guess they wanted us to remember the last night with the fabulous food, but I certainly couldn't forget the nightly choice of "Mit or Feesh" we were offered.

In retrospect, we were lucky. It could have been worse. Later on in the season, sometime in 1994, there was a small article in the paper about the *Akademik ioffe* being held in port in the Falklands because the tour company had not paid the parent company. Passengers were stranded in the Falklands and could not get back home for quite a while. We knew this tour company was operating on a shoestring given what we were served but had no idea how close it had come to bankruptcy when we were on it. The *Akademic ioffe* has been refurbished and is in use by an upscale tour company called One Ocean Expeditions.[21] We discovered

---

[21] http://www.oneoceanexpeditions.com/ships/vessel-akademik-ioffe.

that friends of ours had been on a tour of the Arctic on the *Akademic ioffe.*

The Windstar, Tahiti (2003)

Our trip on the *Windstar* was what one would expect on a typical cruise. In December 2003, we flew to Papeete, Tahiti, from Los Angeles. And via Easter Island and Manihi, one of the Tuomoto Islands, we flew back to Tahiti to pick up the cruise on the *Windstar.* The service on this boat, a sailing ship with only a hundred passengers, was amazing, and too much food was always available. Regular breakfast, midmorning buffet, lunch, and then late-afternoon hors d'oeuvres were served (a different national cuisine each night) followed by dinner. And to top off the dinner meal, which allowed for unlimited ordering from both sides of the menu, there was a plate of homemade truffles. The plate was situated on a table in between the entrance and exit doors. Stanley would take one, turn around, go back in, and take one again as he exited. He would repeat this process several times each evening. Needless to say, on this cruise the weight gain was ridiculous!

Aside from the weight gain on a cruise, I wrote this in my diary after the Windstar cruise: "There are several reasons why I don't like cruise travel. You are definitely removed from the feel of the place you are visiting, and you are out of control of your daily activities—a little like camp for adults." I did add, "Unless of course you are traveling to destinations that you can't easily travel to any other way, like the Galapagos, Antarctica and Komodo Island."

Catching your pig for dinner, Viñales, Cuba (2013)

We have been to Cuba twice, and although as the expression goes, "the first and the last time," in my opinion the expression could have been applied to our first journey there, we actually did go back a second time, two years in a row. I would have happily missed the second trip. Our first trip was in March 2012. There was a biomedical research meeting in Havana that seemed appropriate for our research, and so in order to use the remaining funds I had in my account at the Heart Institute before I closed my lab, I registered for the meeting. The meeting was useless. Nobody came to see my poster, which didn't fit into any category at this point, but it got us to Cuba.

Havana is certainly a fascinating city. The colonial buildings are being restored. There is music everywhere, and it was mobbed with tourists from all over the world, especially Russia and Bulgaria. Most interesting was the fact that there are three synagogues still in existence, as well as a kosher butcher, in spite of religion not being part of the Cuban culture since Castro took over. The story goes that it was a wealthy Mexican Jew who helped Castro during the revolution, and he never forgot that.[22] Bequin funded the purchase of the boat that Castro took in 1956 after he was in exile in Mexico City following the failed coup against Batista. We wandered over to the synagogue Saturday morning, and sure enough, there was a bat mitzvah going on. There was no rabbi or cantor, and the service

---

[22] http://forward.com/news/world/355481/the-jew-who-gave-fidel-castro-a-boat-and-helped-launch-a-revolution/?attribution=articles-article-related-1-headline.

was conducted by the congregants themselves. The entire congregation was invited to a sit-down luncheon with a full course meal with typical Jewish food (soup, chicken, challah, wine, and Jell-O for dessert).

However, the best food was in private homes (restaurants in private homes are called *paladars*) and we did have a couple of excellent meals. We walked over to one called Casas y Tal. It was in an apartment building, which looked terrible, but when we went into the apartment where the restaurant was, it was beautiful. It was an incredible surprise. The meal was fantastic, all freshly prepared.

The next night, we went to El Tempete, which was not a paladar but a government-run restaurant. We had met a couple at the synagogue and invited them to eat with us. We had chateaubriand and cheesecake, and the price for the four of us was $120. They were shocked at the prices and had never had these foods before. They were both university professors in their fifties, and she had been to New Brunswick as a guest lecturer. They sang the praises of their government, unlike many of the younger people we had met. They mentioned that there are food coupons, education is free, and no one was starving.

However, we could understand how younger people would be frustrated. Communication was extremely difficult, both by cell phone and by computer. Access to the Internet was still not permitted for Cubans and only the most rudimentary e-mail communication was possible. The two-currency system is also terribly difficult for Cubans. Although extremely well-educated professionals are paid in pesos, *cucs*, the currency that tourists have to use, are required for most imported goods. Professionals, salaried in pesos, find it necessary to work in the tourist industry to gain access to *cucs*. At that time, there were twenty-five pesos to the *cuc*. Although we had traveled in 2012 and 2013, I recently spoke to someone who just returned (2015) and nothing had changed.

Another paladar we went to was La Esperanza. This was in a private home in the exclusive area of Miramar. This area is where all the embassies and government buildings occupy the former homes of the very wealthy Cubans who left many years ago after their property was confiscated. The décor was amazing, with beautiful antiques and exquisite table settings. We had another outstanding meal—eggplant and cheese, tomatoes and cheese, lobster, salad, and fantastic mojitos. This place had been open since 1995, and it is hard to imagine that it was a private home all that time.

Our next destination was Viñales, a small town a couple of hours west of Havana with unique geography. The mountains are called *mogotes* or haystacks. Our bus was greeted by Rosa, a very enterprising young woman who ran a casa particulara—the Cuban version of a B and B. We decided we couldn't refuse her and checked into her home for a couple of days. Her husband was a maintenance man, and her mother helped cook the meals. She had a babysitter for her four-year-old when she went to work in the government. The meals were incredible. There was enough food for more than ten people. We had the best homemade soup, chicken, salad, and rice and beans. The next night, we had lobster tails, along with the usual soup, salad, rice, and beans, and the most wonderful fruits for dessert. We helped the family financially. They wanted to improve their casa. We became good friends and promised to return the following year.

As promised, we flew from Toronto to Havana at the end of February 2013. We found Havana solidly booked (an international book fair) but managed to find rooms for the end of our stay and booked a car. It was very expensive, as is everything for tourists. Our hotel, the Havana Libre, was huge, previously a Hilton. The breakfast buffet was something to see. It offered every kind of food imaginable, and the guests were eating it all. We found La Guarida, the restaurant (paladar) where the movie *Fresas y Chocolat* was filmed.[23] The house was totally dilapidated, but again, when you arrived at the restaurant on the third floor, it was beautiful. However, the shortage of food this time started here. Many items on the menu were not available.

We set out for Viñales and Casa Rosa. Although we had only planned one night, they insisted we stay for two. They had planned a fiesta in our honor. So the first day we drove with Rosa and her husband to pick up a live baby pig, which was going to be the main course of the fiesta. They put the pig in a plastic bag alive in the trunk of our car, and we drove home. They did add some holes in the bag so that the pig stayed alive until we got back to the casa. Then they slaughtered the pig in Casa Rosa's backyard. It sounded like the pig was being cut up alive from the squealing. Then the pig was boiled to remove the hair; sliced open; and seasoned with garlic, orange extract, and salt. The pig was left out overnight on a table in the backyard to marinate. The weather was completely unusual for March, cold and rainy. So their outdoor barbecue couldn't be used.

We drove around to find a place to roast the pig. Several places refused or were not able to accommodate us, but

---

23 http://www.laguarida.com/en/history/.

eventually we found a national park where Rosa's relative worked, and he let us use the oven there. After six hours, we went back to get the pig and prepare for the fiesta. We literally pigged out with crispy skin (my stomach still turns as I write this) and paid the price. I was so sick all night, which lasted for a couple of days.

We left Viñales with me feeling very sick. We set out for the Iberostar in Trinidad, a true five-star hotel, and stayed there for two nights to recover. It was the only place we stayed where there was Wi-Fi. However, the food there was awful also.

It was this trip where we rented a car and drove from town to town that we got a better feel of the country. Although booked with bus tours everywhere, there were definitely shortages of food. Not even La Esperanza had beef when we returned for our second visit, and what we ate was mediocre at best. In Cienfuegos, we met up with a bus tour of Jews from the States. We joined them for dinner in a beautiful building, the Palacio Valle, which was a private home built in 1919 for a million pesos.[24] The food served was acceptable there but certainly not what one would expect in any other country. It was hard for me and still is to understand how a country as fertile as Cuba could not have organized better food production, even though the US embargo was blamed for all the shortages. Hopefully that will change as Cuba opens up its society to the outside world with finally the reopening of the US embassy in Havana.[25]

---

[24] http://www.cienfuegoscity.org/cienfuegos-city-arch-valle-palace.htm.

[25] http://www.cnn.com/2015/08/14/world/u-s--embassy-reopens-cuba-havana/.

Needless to say, food is important, necessary for life itself of course. But it is a lot more than that when traveling. Food reflects the very essence of the culture of the people wherever you are, and although it is possible to see McDonald's, Burger King and KFC in almost every city of a certain size in the world, eating the true local food ranks as one of the most important aspects of my travels.

It's hard to give advice about safety with food. We always ask where we are staying if the water is safe to drink and if it's okay to eat the fresh fruit and vegetables. We assume that no place wants their guests to get sick.

Now next, one of the essential parts of travel—how do we pay for all this?

Chapter 6

CURRENCY CONVERSION AND MONEY TRANSACTIONS

To this day, currency conversion is a challenge. First of all, do you convert to Canadian dollars that no country in the world wants or to US dollars that every country (or almost every country) in the world wants? We always bring US dollars. It is hard to go wrong with them. There are definitely problems, though, unique to some countries. For example, Cuba prefers CAD and charges much more for their *cucs* if you use US dollars. In Dubai, our hundred-dollar US bills had to be printed after 2000. Recently (on a ferry boat in the Caribbean, 2017) we saw a small sign saying that US bills with tears or writing on them would not be accepted. I always laugh at Stanley wanting what we call "crispies," brand newly minted bills. In many European cities, banks do not exchange US cash for euros, and it is sometimes hard to find cambios (exchange houses), for example, in Paris. In Stockholm, cash is a dirty word, and there are many places that only take credit cards. Only three banks accept cash, and only the large department store in Stockholm has a cambio where you can exchange dollars for kroner. So the requirement for cash varies greatly but for the most part some amount of cash is required everywhere.

Sometimes it's a simple case of arithmetic or knowing whether to divide or multiply. For example, if the CAD is worth US70 cents, to buy US$1, you need C$1.49. This can get confusing after a camping trip in the Sahara in Algeria. We had returned to Tamanrasset for our flight to Algiers and were sick and very tired. Fodil, our guide, presented us with a bill for the trip of 12,800 dinars. One dinar was 15 cents at the time, so our bill was $1,920 CAD (6.5 dinar to the dollar). We paid Fodil the $1,920 and then went shopping. It was only when we went to buy something that we realized our mistake. We could have had our trip for $780. We had been offered 1,600 dinars for $100, and on the street, we had been offered as much as 22 dinars for the dollar. We had been multiplying $100 times 15 cents instead of dinars times 15 cents.

However, the most interesting times we had exchanging currency was in Eastern Europe during the two trips we took in 1988 and 1990. We confess. We exchanged in the street with young men anxious to get US dollars. And were we ever challenged there!

On our first trip to Czechoslovakia in 1988, the black market exchange was alive and well. We were followed in the street many times, and it became too tempting to ignore. The legitimate exchange at the time was 9.8 krowns (KCs) to the US dollar, but on the black market it was 29. We walked across the Charles Bridge and spotted the hotel and restaurant that was so highly recommended called the 3

Ostriches. The "word" was that this hotel had been reserved one year in advance. A taxi driver was waiting outside the hotel and struck a deal with us. He made a reservation at the restaurant and then at the hotel as well so that 100 KCs a night became $45. We conducted all this business at our botel, where we were staying that night.

The most hilarious currency exchange fiasco occurred on our second trip to Eastern Europe, this time the country was Bulgaria. This was in 1990, bad times in Eastern Europe when big changes were coming. The currency in Bulgaria was the lev. There was recently a new note released which was ten times smaller than the previous one. There were people everywhere wanting to change money, and we could get twice the amount of levs for every dollar if it was a legitimate exchange. *Legitimate* is hardly the word for changing money on the street, but to add to the illegitimacy of these black market exchanges, there were several scams. The new levs looked very similar to Greek drachmas. One of us exchanged US$50 and got 500 drachmas, the equivalent of $5. After a full day of touring, we needed to change more money. Three of us watched this transaction. We got a roll of bills, and when we opened up the roll after the dealer had run away, there was only one 20-lev note, and the rest was brown paper. So now we were down $100.

Everyone in our group except Stanley had given up. He and I were determined to figure out how the scam had occurred. When did the exchange happen? There were always two guys doing the exchange. One counted out the money in front of us, and then the roll appeared. Stanley said that he wanted to count the roll again, and that's when they ran away saying, "Policia." That was it for the lev and Bulgaria.

We were onto the next country, the former Yugoslavia. It was much later when we realized that we had chosen a pivotal time in these countries' history to be tourists.

On a recent trip to Stockholm (2015) we were surprised to learn that Sweden was well on the way to becoming cashless.[26] There were several locations that refused to take cash. In most countries, it is possible to get a discount for paying with cash rather than credit card. The credit card companies all charge the merchant a percent of the transaction. The banks that own the credit card companies vary in their rate. American Express is usually the worst. However, in Stockholm, we went to a small restaurant in the old city. The owner refused to take cash. He said that only three banks in Stockholm take cash. He has to make a special trip to these banks, and when he takes the cash to the bank, the bank charges him a fee that is greater than the credit card fee. Certainly, that seemed very strange to us. When we went to the ABBA museum, it also had a big sign saying it was cashless. We couldn't imagine a cashless society coming to Canada and the United States. But certainly it would eliminate black market money laundering and bartering. Underground economies so prevalent in other countries would be eliminated.

So many different ways of paying keep appearing—with new apps on cell phones trying to make it easier. However, when we travel, Stanley's favorite way of paying is cash, especially US cash. Stanley actually bought a $1,000=brick of US$1 bills. He hands these out as tips all the time. No matter when or where, the face of the person receiving

---

[26] https://www.nytimes.com/2015/12/27/business/international/in-sweden-a-cash-free-future-nears.html.

them lights up. It was a surprise to us that even on our recent trip to Russia (September 2016) our US dollars got us everywhere. Although English is still extremely rare, US cash is loved. We went to a bank in St. Petersburg and exchanged US dollars for rubles without having to show any identification and without exchanging a word in English or Russian. The old expression that "cash is king" still holds true in most parts of the world.[27]

Sometimes "things happen" in spite of all our efforts to stay well and safe. The next chapter describes some of those "things."

[27] Explanation of the phrase "cash is king," http://www.investopedia.com/terms/c/cash-is-king.asp.

Chapter 7

ACCIDENTS AND ILLNESS

We have been extremely fortunate in most of our travels, considering the number of trips, where we have gone, and what we have done. However, we have had some accidents and illness. Over the years, all of us suffered the expected stomach upsets, nausea, and diarrhea due to changes in diet and of course some contamination. Altitude sickness became increasingly severe as we aged so that we don't travel above nine thousand feet anymore. However, our son Daniel has been the accident victim on our trips covering four continents.

He's endured first, a ruptured spleen (Ireland); second, a dog bite (Peru); third, malaria (Africa); and an anterior cruciate ligament tear in Philadelphia. Although his knee surgery to repair the ligament did not happen while traveling, it was also an "interesting" experience and away from home. Daniel was a student at the University of Pennsylvania at the time, and student health insurance cost was $250. The cost of his surgery with a two-day stay in the hospital was around

US$28,000. We often talk about this "best investment" we made when we purchased the student health coverage.

A ruptured spleen in Ireland (1982)

We ask ourselves the question, from which incident was Daniel closest to death? Although this story is an exception to travels with Stanley, on this occasion, Stanley wasn't there, and neither was I. However, the addition of this story completes the narration of accidents that Daniel had, the rest being with us. At that time, he was traveling with my parents and his brother in August 1982. They were on a boat crossing the Irish Sea when, after the boys were chasing one another, Daniel fell down the stairs on the deck, hitting the steel floor. Fortunately, there was an army nurse on the boat as well, who recognized immediately that he was in shock and started an IV. Even more fortunate was that when they landed at Wexford and checked into the hospital there, the operating room was being renovated so that he was transferred to St. Vincent Hospital in Dublin. He was diagnosed with a ruptured spleen. And although it was an adult hospital, the chief of surgery there, Dr. Niall O'Higgins, had just read an article about not removing a ruptured spleen in children. It is too important for immunity. So instead he gave Daniel four liters of blood to restore his hemoglobin, which had dropped to about 25 percent of normal from the blood loss.

Upon learning of the incident, I immediately left for Ireland and stayed there for three weeks while Daniel recovered. Many years later, Daniel, now a surgeon himself, was at a surgical meeting and met Dr. O'Higgins, who immediately remembered him. The incident was part of Daniel's motivation to become a surgeon, given the empathy he was shown by some but not by others. I always call him on St. Patrick's Day because he is the only member of our family with Irish blood.

A dog bite in Peru (1984)

In December 1984, the four of us set out on our first adventure trip—walking the Inca trail in Peru. We flew Canadian Pacific Airways (no longer around) and as sometimes happened, we were not permitted to take our luggage on board; in spite of a few choice words by our leader, Stan, we were forced to check it. Fortunately, it all arrived when we did in Lima. Next day, we flew to Cuzco (higher than twelve thousand feet) and began to feel the effects of the altitude. We spent several days acclimatizing before setting out on our trek, visiting Inca ruins and rafting on the Urubamba, River while I stayed in the van only able to drink coca tea. Our starting point was Ollantaytambo, at this point only nine thousand feet, and after climbing to the archaeological site, we set out for the first day along the trail, a modest two and a half-hour walk across the Urubamba River. December 26 was day 1. We walked the trail until January 2, when we stayed in a hotel at Machu Picchu, exploring that site in detail the following day. I think of all our trips this was the most strenuous and challenging, both because of the nature of the trail and the climate and altitude. Certainly, sleeping in tents in our "ice mantle" sleeping bags at this altitude was not easy, even though the four Labows had thirteen people (porters, cooks, guides) looking after them. The food on this trip was amazing, and the detailed menus are described in a special chapter devoted to food (chapter 5). On this trip, no matter how much we snacked and ate, at the end, we had all lost weight—not what usually happened when we traveled.

Our guide on this trip was Roger Valencia, probably our finest guide from almost any perspective. A true Renaissance man, he spoke many languages (Spanish, Quechua, English, German) and could speak intelligently about almost any subject. Our first hiking day was much longer than it was supposed to be because of a rock slide on the trail, which we had to walk around. My feet were covered in blisters, which Roger miraculously cured with his first aid kit and tender care. As you can tell, I really liked him.

The trail changed between mountain jungle and plateau as we walked along. Each day was different. Some days there were some Inca ruins, some just scenery. For a few days, horses carried our stuff, but by December 30, only the porters carried everything. They had no shoes, just rubber sandals but raced ahead of us, carrying our stuff and preparing our lunch or dinner and setting up our tents. It rained almost every night and sometimes during the day as well. One morning, our tents were covered in snow. Brian and Daniel had totally acclimatized to the altitude and were always ahead of Stan and me. In my case, it was my GI tract that had trouble acclimatizing, but with Stanley it was definitely the breathing and fatigue. This was our first experience with high altitude, most of the hiking being above eight thousand feet. One pass was even over fourteen thousand feet. The daily hiking pattern was Roger leading and Brian next, followed by Daniel. Then at least forty-five minutes later, Stan and I would show up at the campsite.

Another favorite Stanley quote of mine was very breathlessly uttered as I waited for him at a turning point in the trail. "Who would have thought I'd be stuck back here with you?"

He tried anything to help himself. Tea made from the coca plant was supposed to help. It really did nothing. Another method was to chew the coca leaves. That did nothing. The ultimate was to take ashes from the fire and mix it with the coca leaves (free basing?) and chew it. At the end of all of this, Stanley announced, "I have a numb gum."

On December 31, Daniel raced ahead of Brian, who had stopped to pee. He was behind Roger but on a narrow part of the trail. We had met very few people, except on occasion after we had camped for the night, young boys would appear asking for our soft drink bottles. Somehow, they would find us and retrieve the bottles for the money they could get. There was no denying the extreme poverty of the indigenous people in the mountains. However, on that day, we hadn't met a single soul. Sure enough, though, a young boy with two dogs was coming toward Daniel who had to pass them on a very narrow part of the trail. There was a very big dog and a small one. It was the small one who bit Daniel right through his pants and penetrated his leg.

Roger asked if the dogs were immunized, and of course, the boy said yes. We had just found out that many children in these villages had recently died of measles, so the odds of those dogs having shots were slim or none.

The kid said he would meet us at the hotel at Machu Picchu so we could make sure the dog was well, but of course he didn't. We continued on the trail for another two days, and Stanley gave Daniel lots of antibiotics but that wouldn't affect rabies. This meant having the series of rabies shots. We would be home within the time that would be okay for preventing rabies, which removed some of the panic.

The shots were not as bad as they used to be but still involved multiples—one a week for a month. The first time several injections were right into the wound, which was very painful. I would pick Daniel up at school, and then after the shot, we would have lunch at a Chinese restaurant. And so, this trip was memorable for many aspects.

Brian and Daniel at Machu Picchu, Peru, December 1984

Malaria from camping in Africa (1986)

We were on a camping safari in 1986 (see chapter 9) when Daniel's third trauma occurred. We really don't know exactly where he was infected. At the time, only chloroquine was available for the prophylaxis for malaria, but if symptoms occurred, Fansidar was the new treatment. Unfortunately, it was known to cause severe allergic reactions in some people, so taking it far away from a medical facility that could treat the reaction effectively wasn't recommended. At this point in east Africa, most of the malaria was already chloroquine-resistant. We thought perhaps it was at the prison campsite where Daniel could have been bitten. However, there were loads of bugs as we crossed Lake Victoria. It could have been anywhere. Why did Daniel get malaria instead of any of us? Who knows?

The first time that Daniel felt really sick was in Kigali as we waited for the flight to Brussels on January 5. But, when we arrived in Brussels Daniel was feeling better. We had missed our flight because of the delay out of Kigali and arrived in Ottawa on January 7. The first week back, Daniel's alternating symptoms continued—classic malaria, right? After three days of this, we took Daniel to the chief of hematology at the Civic Hospital. Stanley wasn't going to take a chance with just the community hospital, Riverside at the time. His opening statement was "Tell me it's not malaria. We've just come back from Africa."

And after a blood smear, the chief declared that it wasn't malaria. Maybe it was just the flu. Forty-eight hours later, Daniel's fever was 105 degrees Fahrenheit with sweat pouring off him, alternating with terrible shaking chills.

Back to the hospital, this time to the chief of infectious diseases who said, "If it looks like malaria, acts like malaria, and smells like malaria, it's malaria," and gave him Fansidar and started him on quinine. The blood smear at this point was full of the parasite, and when the slide from forty-eight hours earlier was reexamined, sure enough they were there. It was falciparum malaria, the most dangerous kind but fortunately one that doesn't recur.

Daniel was admitted to the hospital that Friday but called us during the night. The patient in the bed next to him had Legionnaires' disease. Stan told him to get out of there and go into the hall or another room. Sadly, that patient passed away during the night. We brought Daniel home the next day. He had to take quinine for five days. It gave him a terrible ringing in his ears, and he didn't feel well for quite a while. The fact that he had had a ruptured spleen was one theory as to what could have made him vulnerable. Another manifestation of his malaria was a very enlarged spleen, with a very low platelet count.

A very interesting coincidence sort of taught us a lesson. This physician sometimes outsmarts himself when it comes to his family. At that time, Stan was on staff at Riverside Hospital and was on call. When Daniel was in the hospital, Stan went into the emergency room at Riverside, and on the board for one of the cases was written "possible malaria." While he was there the technician confirmed that that is what it was. She was from India and was familiar with what a blood smear with malaria looked like. That patient was treated immediately before the malaria took hold as it did with Daniel.

Fish bones in the throat (1997, 2003)

Although Stanley has the rights to fish bones in the throat experiences, early on, I also had a fishbone in the throat experience. It was 1997, and we met our son Brian and our daughter-in-law Stephanie in Bangkok. We were joining a Wilderness Travel Tour, and Brian was going to speak at a scientific meeting in Taiwan. We met up at their hotel to spend one night having dinner together. We had a recommendation for the Seafood Market Restaurant. It was original then. You could walk around, choose your food and method of cooking, and then it was brought to your table. The food was delicious, and I decided to take one last bite as the waiter was rushing to clean up. I wasn't careful enough, and a bone caught in my throat. I ate some bread. I later found out that it is rice you should eat when something is stuck in your throat. Instead, I went to the bathroom and tried to gargle it up. Finally, and very luckily, just as I was about to panic, I was able to reach into the top of my throat and grab it. Luckily, it was close enough to reach.

However, Stanley and fish bones have a longer, more dramatic history. Stanley got a bone caught in his throat on Easter Island. One of our favorite trips was our first trip to Easter Island in 2003. We flew from Papeete, Tahiti, on one of only three flights a week. It was only possible to fly from Santiago, Chile, and Papeete, limiting the number of tourists that could be there at any one time. The indigenous population was still fighting the Chilean government, which had Easter Island inscribed as a UNESCO World Heritage site in 1995. This certainly would bring many more tourists. This proved to be true, so that by 2009 when we traveled there a second time, there were nine flights a week and many more tourists. We viewed the consequences firsthand on this second visit. The reason Easter Island was created a World Heritage site was due to the existance of Moais. These large stone blocks are arranged all over the island and it is unknown to this day how the inhabitants at the time could carve and move them. We found out on our second trip that one of the Moais had been desecrated and so now all were fenced off, and so it was impossible to wander around on your own as we had done on our first trip.

However, to continue, on our first trip, we rented a car and drove all over the island. We could approach the Moai and even touch them. It was possible to wander on your own into the national parks and often be the only ones there. The spiritual life of the Rapa Nui appeared to be intact. The food was good if it was local, especially seafood. So many other things had to be flown in. One favorite of mine were the cherries, still cheaper on Easter Island in December than in Ottawa. Interesting that one day in our wandering we came across a huge plane with a couple of guys who proved to be test engineers. They were flying the Boeing 777-300ER, testing its range with one engine. Easter Island, being the remotest inhabited place on earth, was a challenge then. This was 2003, and so by 2009, this plane was used routinely, increasing Easter Island's availability to many more tourists.

One night, we went to a restaurant right on the shore. We ordered freshly made fish soup. It was filled with fish and floating bones. Sure enough, Stan swallowed one and felt it lodge in his throat. This time, I didn't doubt him. A while ago in Ottawa, after I had served salmon, he'd complained about a bone being stuck in his throat, and I kept saying, "I'm sure it's just scratched." After about a week of this, he went to his favorite ENT doctor and presented me with the bone in a little vial as a Valentine's Day present. Not wanting to doubt him this time, the next day we went up to the "hospital." It was in terrible shape. No head trauma could be treated there. We had visited earlier that week and heard some terrible stories of accidents, after which it was debated whether or not it was "worth it" to fly the patient to mainland Chile. Could the injured patient survive? The distance to Santiago was 3,700 kilometers.

I thought Stan should wait until we flew out to Papeete (much closer), but on Sunday, we found a young doctor there from Valpariso. We suspected we were in trouble because the mirror he used to look down Stan's throat kept fogging up. Stan suggested running it under hot water so that it wouldn't, something that is a pretty elementary technique. He couldn't see anything. Finally, he took an instrument that is used prior to intubation for surgery and put it down Stan's throat. He didn't find a bone, but after that, Stan stopped complaining.

We asked the cost for that, and since it was a Sunday, after we paid the twenty dollars, the hospital staff couldn't seem to write a receipt, which they really wanted to do. We said it really didn't matter, and we left. We went to have lunch at a restaurant on one of the main streets, and sure enough, while we were eating, someone came up and handed us the receipt. I just found it in my diary that I had written while on this trip. Easter Island really was a small place then and truly remote. Everyone knew everyone and, more importantly, everything that was going on.

There is a brand-new hospital there now, one of the benefits from the island becoming easier to fly to with the introduction of many long-range jets and from it being designated a world heritage site that attracts many more tourists.[28] Of course, it still hasn't solved the problem in the difficulty of enticing physicians to spend time there. As in any place other than a large city, obtaining the optimal medical care is not easy, especially on Easter Island, the remotest place on earth.

Altitude sickness (1984–2009)

A very interesting health phenomenon is altitude sickness or *soroche*. It hits you in many different ways. Its most common symptom is shortness of breath. But altitude sickness also affects both your digestion and sleep and often gives you terrible headaches and nausea, along with dizziness, thoroughly unpleasant. That can occur even if you are doing absolutely nothing. Hiking up and down hills while suffering altitude sickness is a real challenge. So, after our Peru experience, we stayed away from high altitude for quite a while. We were in Quito, Ecuador, for a short time on our way to the Galapagos. It is one of the highest capital cities, and we felt the altitude as soon as we landed. But not much physical activity was required prior to our departure to the Galapagos. After this trip, there were no high-altitude trips with our sons, but we continued to travel to places that fell squarely into the category of high altitude.

---

[28] http://whc.unesco.org/en/list/715; Rapa Nui National Park 1995.

The next high-altitude trip was to Bhutan and Nepal, and although we certainly weren't climbing the Himalayas, the altitude made us quite sick. We had no energy and general malaise. In Pokhara, Nepal, I could hardly move. On our first trip to Chile, we went from sea level in Arica, northern Chile, to Lake Chungara on the Bolivian border. We actually found it difficult to raise our hand to take a photo. Another trip to the Atacama Desert in Chile was also difficult, but we were there longer and acclimatized somewhat after a week. But even after a week, we weren't really feeling totally normal. Although the GI symptoms and headaches are difficult, the worst symptom is the inability to sleep well. When awake, you can breathe more frequently and deeply, but when asleep, breathing is shallower. So, when in need of more oxygen, you are awakened, signaling that more rapid and deep breathing was required.

You'd think we'd learn, and I think now, at this advanced age, we have. Finally, it was after our last trip at high altitude when we were in Bolivia in December 2009 that we decided that we couldn't do it anymore. But what we experienced during this trip, in retrospect, made it all worth it. We started in the capital, La Paz, and booked a hotel at thirteen thousand feet in the upper city. We didn't realize until after we had been in La Paz for a few days that there was an entire lower city at a mere ten thousand. After a few days at thirteen thousand, you feel a lot better at ten thousand.

We never really acclimatized fully when we set off for the Salar de Uyuni (Salt Lake Flats) on December 23. Each day in my diary begins with, "We feel really sick. We didn't sleep all night. We have major bowel issues." One day,

Stanley felt so sick, he took two Diamox. The road was in terrible shape, but fortunately our driver was able to navigate it, even after getting stuck in the mud several times. We stayed at a lodge right in the middle of the salt flats in Tahua that had walls and ceilings made of salt. There was a terrible storm just before dinner on Christmas Eve. Fortunately, the ovens were gas, so we got to eat. But there was no heat, it was too dark to take a shower, and the salt from the ceiling was falling down all around us. In spite of all of this, the unique scenery around was something we could never forget. The rainstorm had left a thin film of water on the salt, making the reflections spectacular and creating unique mirages.

The Uyuni Salt Flats in Bolivia after a rainstorm, Stan "holding" Roz, December 2009

We drove back to La Paz, and the day after (December 27) we left for Copacabana. We were on a bus with other tourists and our guide, but then after one night at the Rosario Hotel, we set out on Lake Titicaca for Isla de Sol, our ultimate high-altitude challenge. Lake Titicaca is the highest lake in South

America, if not the world, at 12,300 feet,[29] approximately the height of La Paz (11,975), although the airport is even higher at about 13,000 feet. For me, 1,000 feet more or less at this altitude really makes little difference if you're doing nothing. But if you're climbing to Inca ruins, it becomes an incredible challenge. After a moderate climb, we met with an indigenous health doctor (shaman) who told Stan his health was "tranquilo" (calm) but that I should be "cuidado "(careful) about mine for the next three years. This was told with water on our heads while we were being sprinkled with geranium leaves. After lunch, our guide gave us a choice, which really wasn't well explained. We could hike about four hours to our hotel, or walk down to the boat, a walk of an hour and a half, and be taken to our hotel by boat. There was one very big problem. Although we were taken by boat around the base of the mountain, we had to walk from the water, where we got off our boat, to the Estancia Ecolodge, which happened to be at 4,065 meters (13,744 feet). The lake is at 3,810 meters (12,500 feet). And although I just said that a 1,000 feet more or less at this altitude doesn't matter, when you are climbing with knapsacks, it certainly does. I immediately gave my knapsack to a young boy who was following us. Stan resisted. "If we can't climb with our knapsacks, we shouldn't be here."

These heroics didn't last long, until he finally gave up his knapsack and said, "I can't go any further." I suggested that spending the rest of his life on that rock wouldn't be fun, and so we very, very slowly worked our way up to the lodge.

The view, when we reached it, was almost worth the agony. It was spectacular. Hot showers were wonderful, but it was absolutely freezing at night. And the pages of my diary

---

[29] https://en.wikipedia.org/wiki/Geography_of_Bolivia.

until January 1 when we left Bolivia repeated that we had little appetite, another symptom of altitude sickness, maybe one that isn't so bad. All we managed most meals was soup. We did have enough energy to walk back to the lake to find our boat back to the bus that would take us back to La Paz, maybe a slight relief to the high altitude where we had spent the night. It was a "never again" motto when we returned to Santiago, Chile, on our way back home.

Not being in the comfort of your own hometown always adds to the suffering of being sick or having an accident. When traveling thousands of miles away from your home or, even worse, in remote areas where there is little or no medical care and you don't speak the language, the feeling of helplessness is certainly exacerbated. It is something to consider carefully when you travel as you age. There are many areas that we have traveled to that we would never go to today. Some of the places we've been to are risky from a health point of view, but so many more are dangerous from a security aspect. I said this to someone at a party the other day, and he asked me to name them. I had to think for just a few minutes and then came up with a list. In 2017, who would consider traveling to Libya, Tunisia, Turkey, or Algeria?

Travel is all about what to see and do. There is no end to possibilities, and of course what you see and do depends very much on the location and individual interests. We have never felt that we have to go through a list of what to see and do and check it off. We see what we see. What have we done when we have traveled? What have we seen? The following chapters describe some highlights.

CHAPTER 8

GOLF AND FISHING AROUND THE WORLD

Some of the most interesting places we have seen during our travels, either with or without our sons, have been the golf courses. The variety in difficulty naturally is as numerous as the differences in the local geography. Although lately when we travel, Stanley never plays golf, on some of our earlier trips, he found the opportunities too appealing. When we traveled with our sons, this was all about the family friendly competition. The competition continued on fishing expeditions with our sons, and Stanley's bad luck with fishing followed him across continents. When we traveled on our own, Stanley never went fishing. My all-time favorite fishing expedition was in Pond Inlet (chapter 10, "Camping Trips and Bathrooms/Outhouses") but there were many others where telling the tale is worthwhile.

Golf in Rhodes (1985)

In December 1985, we traveled to Turkey ("chapter 10, "Camping Trips and Bathrooms/Outhouses" and chapter

11, "Security and Leaving Stuff Behind") but also spent some time in Greece. We chose an interesting way to get across that border. We took a boat from Marmoris, Turkey, to the island of Rhodes. It was a very small boat, and the crossing became very rough. It only held nine people and two vans. A group of dolphins followed us the whole way, which helped distract us from the seasickness. Our passports were taken away from us for the duration, and when we arrived on shore and cleared customs, the animosity between these two countries certainly was evident. The flag the boat flew was changed from that of Turkey to that of Greece as we crossed the border in the middle of the Mediterranean Sea, still an illegal practice, to avoid the licensing red tape. Years later, when we were on Cyprus in 2005 (chapter 13, "Border Crossings") we drove from Greek Cyprus to the Turkish side, still not an easy thing to do.

After we'd cleared customs, our first stop was Olympic Airways to plan the rest of our trip. Although it is great to travel off-season, for a Greek island trip it was way too off-season. There was no way to get to Santorini or Mykonos at that time of year, except by local ferry, and all the flights were booked to Crete, so we decided to make the best of it and spend time on Rhodes. It turned out that there was a lot to see on Rhodes, and it, like all the Mediterranean islands, has a history of being conquered and occupied by Romans, Byzantine crusaders, Turks, and back to Greeks, with the medieval old town of Rhodes a World Heritage Site. Stanley rented a car the next day and purchased our tickets for Athens for three days later. There were flights to Crete available, but we decided we were too tired to add another island to our trip this time.

The first activity was a golf game that seemed to go on forever. I waited in the little golf shack and read my book. It soon became too dark for me to read, and Stanley and the boys were still playing. I am not sure why, but eventually they got off the course.

Once more we mixed up flight times. We thought we were leaving at night since the tickets said 9:55, but if the departure was nighttime, the time on the tickets would have read 21:55. We had checked out of our hotel, and Stanley had returned the car. Anyway, this was just the beginning of the saga of our trip home.

We arrived at the airport to find out that all flights to Rhodes had been canceled because of the wind. It was New Year's Day, and everything was closed. We checked later on in the day, and there were still no planes. We became rather nervous, since we had our flight back to Canada on January 4 from Athens. On the morning of January 2, we made a decision to take the ferry to Athens, even though Olympic Airways had landed. We didn't have tickets for that flight, and it was full. There were only second-class cabins, and we were on top of the engine room. There were families lying on blankets on the deck. Many people got on with a variety of animals, including chickens and goats. We were able to switch to a first-class cabin halfway along and slept on our way to Athens. The upside was we got to see some of the islands.

Golf and fishing in Argentina (1987)

On our trip to Argentina in December 1987 one of our stops was Bariloche. It is hard to imagine that this city surrounded by snow-capped mountains is in South America. It could easily fit into one of the villages in the Swiss Alps. It is situated on a very large lake that lies in between Chile and Argentina. The architecture of the hotels and restaurants and the food, like the chocolate factories, also resemble German Switzerland or even Germany itself. There was a very large immigration of Germans there in the mid-nineteenth century, and many German institutions were founded that persist to this day.[30] There definitely is another German connection, since many Nazi war criminals lived here for a time. Among them was Adolf Eichmann, who eventually was captured, but Josef Mengele never was. The film *The German Doctor*, loosely based on Mengele's life, told how he was protected by the German School there, even while he carried out his experiments on identical twins.[31] He eventually escaped to what people believed was Paraguay. This was in the time of Juan Peron's dictatorship in Argentina, and so his tactics fit in well with Nazi ideology. However, in 1987, Bariloche was a beautiful resort town.

We all set out to the golf course and discovered that there were no left-handed clubs for Daniel to rent, so Brian and Stan played, and after walking two holes, Daniel and I went shopping. The economy at that time was in a tailspin, and the austral kept falling, even while we were there. Everything was so inexpensive. In 1993, we visited Argentina on our way to Antarctica. At that time, the austral was pegged to the US dollar. We paid $300 a day for a rental car which we shared with another couple who was on that trip (See chapter 3- getting around). The ups and downs of

---

[30] https://en.wikipedia.org/wiki/German_Argentine#German_immigration_to_Argentina.

[31] https://en.wikipedia.org/wiki/The_German_Doctor.

the Argentinian economy were constant then and remain so to this day (2017). I have a note in my diary that I had cashed $200 in travelers' checks. I had completely forgotten that we were still using those in 1987. Also, in those days, we always bought gifts for everyone. With that $200, Daniel and I bought gifts for fifteen people. We drove back to the golf course and picked up Stan and Brian to go fishing.

The trout we had been eating was fantastic, and so we thought we would go and catch some trout. The boys went fishing on Lake Gutierrez, and Daniel immediately caught a trout. However, even though it was getting dark, Brian was still trying to catch something. They were about to come in, and it looked like the ultimate on his line, but it got away again! The boys didn't get back until 10:30 p.m.; the days were very long at that time of year.

Golf and Fishing in Costa Rica (1989)

In spite of our usual type of travel, this time, we booked our trip through Fiesta Tours; the owner dealt with Costa Rica Expeditions, the local representative. We had paid for a private tour for several activities in a number of locations, but each time, we were with a large group. The lack of deliverables started in Jaco Beach. Our hotel had not been finished. As a matter of fact, we watched them assemble Daniel's bed as we checked in. There was no hot water and no air-conditioning because there was no electricity at night, and there was no place to eat at the hotel. There were also no taxis and no public transportation. There was construction all around, and after we found a restaurant and were walking home, Stanley fell into a hole, just as he warned me to watch out for them. He was scratched but okay. However, we had great fish for dinner and found out that if you caught fish the restaurant would prepare it for you.

We set out the next day having booked a fishing boat and weren't very far out when Stan caught a dorado (dolphin fish). Daniel's got away that time, but we had enough to bring to the restaurant for dinner. Dolphins, marlin, and sailfish surrounded the boat as we were fishing. We weren't disappointed. The fish that night at dinner was superb.

After five days in Jaco Beach, we had adjusted to the pace and weren't really ready to go to the big city, San Jose. Brian joined us in San Jose, and we were briefed on our activities by the Costa Rica Expeditions rep.

The next day, we went white water rafting with only one other couple, but following that was a bus tour from hell day! We were on a very large and uncomfortable bus, and our tour guide had already lost several people. Some didn't get back on the bus at one of our stops and some had voluntarily dropped out along the way. We set out for the volcano, but it was completely fogged in. We then proceeded to make many stops. We were way behind schedule, and it was 3:00 p.m. before we stopped for lunch. Then we set out again. It was already after four. A suspension bridge, we stopped; coffee beans, we stopped; a weird house carved out of coffee plant roots, we stopped. We started to laugh uncontrollably and did feel bad that we were being rude. But the very annoying guide was going to finish his tour no matter what. We continued on and stopped at a beautiful churchyard. The guide continued to try to engage everyone, although by this point, we were all exhausted. He brought over buds of the impatience flower and had us all pop them;

I'm not sure why. We had recently popped coffee plant buds to look at the beans. We thought this was over. But no, one more stop—a waterfall. It was very beautiful, but it was now getting dark.

We continued to the rain forest at Monteverde, walked in the reserve, and went horseback riding, an experience I don't want to repeat. My horse wanted to go back home and raced as quickly as it could. I clung on for dear life. Then there was the flight in a small plane without a copilot that landed on the beach in Tortuguera in a blinding rainstorm. We all survived, but this tour was getting very wearing. We were picked up the next day for a fishing expedition. We were again in a large group, and after sailing about eighteen kilometers in the pouring rain in an open boat, we watched our guide catch shrimp by stripping them off a water hyacinth. Stan did catch a large drumfish, and the boys each caught a small dorado. I was cold and wet and it continued to rain all night long. I was worried that the little plane wouldn't arrive to take us back to San Jose.

It was a slightly choppy flight, but we made it back to San Jose. We were picked up to be driven to our hotel, and we heard a conversation on the car two-way radio. It was the owner of Costa Rica Expeditions, and he was inviting a passenger from our flight and now in our car to his home. We made a note of his phone number.

Our last night in San Jose was at a lovely hotel, the Cariari. The boys played golf on the hotel course, with a caddy for each player required. The caddies were such good players Stan and the boys let them play also. I had my favorite activity—reading a book by the pool.

But with the very last happening, we did leave this trip with a very bad taste in our mouths. Our flight the next day was sixteen hours late (again Fiesta Tours, operated by Worldways).

Before leaving, we spoke to the owner of Costa Rica Expeditions and went to their office. They apologized and said that it was all their fault. The information from the agent in Toronto for private tours had "slipped through the cracks." We did eventually receive some financial compensation, but once again it has sworn us off tours whenever it is possible. It is very often the local vendors that unfortunately don't always come through for the out-of-country agencies. This has happened to us before (Dien Bien Phu, chapter 4).

Fishing and golf in Cabo San Lucas (1992)

In December 1992, we went to Cabo San Lucas with our sons. Brian came first and left first, and Daniel later. Our first item was to find a car to rent. We found a VW bug that was in terrible condition and bargained for the rate of $650 for two weeks, a true Rent-a-Wreck. When we were all together, we organized a fishing expedition and a golf game. The fishing expedition was on a thirty-foot boat, cost $500, and was for the full day. We left at 6:30 a.m., and after sailing up the coast for one hour and off shore (in other words, in the middle of nowhere) for about a mile, two dorado were caught within five minutes of our stopping. They were too small, the captain said, only 10 pounds. We sailed out another three to four miles, and two more dorado were caught. We trolled for another hour, and it was at this point that I got very seasick from the fumes and the side-to-side motion. Brian wisely had his scopolamine patch on. Just when it seemed nothing was going to happen, Brian's line almost was jolted out of his hands. He had a marlin. The fish jumped out of the water just as the ads show it. All other lines were removed from the water, and Brian took the seat. For almost two hours he reeled the fish in and out and the fish jumped out of the water and finally got close enough to the boat to be released. Stanley was so hysterical laughing that we never got a good photo. This fleet was very mindful of the marlin population and returned it to the ocean, giving the person who caught it a certificate. It was almost a two hundred-pound striped marlin. We ate the dorado, beautifully prepared by our hotel, for dinner.

The next day was golf day. The only finished golf course at that time was in San Jose on a time-share development. It was a beautiful course with views of the ocean from each hole. I complained about the price of the golf, saying it wasn't cheap. Can you imagine? Eighteen dollars a person, plus the club rental and the cart, and we had forgotten the balls in Cabo. By the seventh hole, four balls were gone, but just then kids appeared selling balls at a dollar for two balls. Saved the game!

On our last day, we returned the car and so were obligated to take taxis. We shared a taxi to the restaurant with some people at our hotel, and the fare was five dollars. Stanley started his taxi bargaining to go back when the taxis wanted five thousand pesos more (twenty thousand instead of fifteen thousand). It was the same distance, and Stanley stuck to his guns. We were in the middle of nowhere at this restaurant, except for a Chinese restaurant across the road where we had eaten a few nights before. Stanley spoke to the owner and made a deal for five dollars to take us back to our hotel. We were in a pickup truck with no windows and no handles. The taxi drivers were all in a line outside the restaurant laughing at Stanley.

We have been traveling without our sons for many years now, as they now travel with their children. However, some of the best memories are the crazy golf and fishing expeditions we had when we traveled with them.

Golf in Australia (1999) and New Zealand (2001)

Golf in these two countries was a study in contrasts, although we really only checked out the golf course in the Northern Territory. We traveled to Darwin, Australia, in December 1999. It was a side trip from our sailing trip to the islands of Indonesia. A bit crazy, but this would be our seventh continent. We rented a car and drove to Kakadu National Park. This area of the Northern Territory was considered holy land and was protected territory of the aboriginals. It was the wet season, and many trails were closed, both for driving and walking. The crocodiles came into the park along trails, and when the water receded, they were left behind. These trails were clearly marked, and I insisted we obey them even though Stanley wanted to go past the signs and the barricades across the path. The news that week was that women who were swimming in one of the pools at night against all park rules were attacked by crocodiles and disappeared.

We checked into our hotel, aptly named the Crocodile Lodge. It was built in the shape of a crocodile—quite crazy!

We spotted a golf course, but it was closed. We drove by it again and met someone who said it was no problem to play, even though no one was there to take our money. He said just take any set of clubs you want and put five dollars in the can hanging from the front door. He gave Stanley a ball. Looking at the fairways and the greens, Stan decided not to play. The course was basically straw.

New Zealand (2001)

New Zealand had probably some of the most beautiful courses we have ever seen. In December 2001, we traveled to New Zealand and stayed at some of the most luxurious accommodations. There are a series of privately owned accommodations called Luxury Lodges all over New Zealand. Stanley worked out a deal with the owner of Lake Taupo Lodge since he had one room empty (see chapter 4, "Where to Stay"). The lodge was near the Wairakei International Golf Course. This golf course was designed as a flora and fauna sanctuary, and the layout of the course was a site to see, whether or not you were playing golf. However, it was an extremely challenging and strenuous course. Stanley was pulling his cart up and down hills but gave in for the back nine and took a cart, and we joined another couple doing the same thing. The wives were driving the carts, and the men were playing. So many New Zealanders were so helpful, and even though he was a much better player than Stanley, he was enthusiastic about playing with him and was very helpful in figuring out the course.

We flew to Wellington, took the ferry to Christchurch, and rented a Toyota Echo, an automatic the owner threw in to compensate us for the flat tire we had with the other car; we also paid half the cost. That was typical of the way everyone treated us. The car was a crazy turquoise blue, which the owner's daughter called bubble gum. We checked into another beautiful lodge / B and B and then proceeded downtown. Of course, all this time we were driving on the wrong side, for us of course.

We got very lost on the way back and found the visitor center and decided to ask for directions. We parked on the platform in front of the center and started to back up, not realizing this was a staircase, one of our closest calls. We drove to Queenstown and took an overnight tour to Milford Sound. It finally dawned on us that the reason it kept raining was that Milford Sound is part of a rain forest. On our return to Queenstown, we sat down at a café on the mall. Stanley ordered a chicken sandwich. He hadn't eaten all day because he hadn't been feeling well. He took a big bite, and half of his tooth fell out. We found an emergency dentist who was amazing—did a partial root canal and a temporary filling and charged us next to nothing.

Queenstown is full of touristy, fun things to do, and Stanley checked out paragliding. You don't go by yourself, and they do have a weight restriction. But they put it very nicely, saying, "If you could find a seventy-five-pound instructor, you could go."

We drove down to the ferry to get to Stewart Island. No cars are allowed on the island except for those of residents, and the island is access to the only place that the kiwi bird is still in existence in the wild. The problem is that rats were brought by ships that docked there during the whaling period, and the birds were their food. Now there are major efforts to rid the island of rodents. The residents walk in a line side by side across the island scouring it for any rodent, which is then eliminated.

We walked along many trails and eventually found the six-hole golf course. It was a series of cliffs with rope tows to help you up to the greens, a unique location for sure. Stanley didn't play there, but during one of our walks, we met a very friendly couple who lived in Dunedin, our next stop. He invited Stanley to play golf with him and to call him when we got there. We checked into yet another magnificent lodge called Corstophine House. Each room was decorated in another nationality's furniture and art. There was a mezuzah[32] on the door, and we found out that it was the previous owner who was Jewish. Stan got a call from Steve, who picked him up at our lodge, and I went on a city tour. After wandering around Dunedin, we ended up at the golf course. The highlight of our city tour was watching Stanley playing golf. The course paralleled the ocean, and the narrow fairways were not easy. A comment from Steve that Stanley often quotes is "This course rewards accuracy."

Although the golf courses we saw were totally different in these two countries, the situation with the indigenous populations in both these countries had many similarities. Mostly the similarities were complaints about drug addiction, alcoholism, and mental illness. However, I felt that the Maoris[33] were much better integrated into the population

---

32 http://www.chabad.org/library/article_cdo/aid/256915/jewish/What-Is-a-Mezuzah.htm.

33 https://en.wikipedia.org/wiki/M%C4%81ori_people.

in New Zealand than were the aboriginals in Australia. Hunting and killing the aboriginals was not considered a crime in Australia, and there were thousands of massacres even up until 1920.[34]

---

[34] https://en.wikipedia.org/wiki/List_of_massacres_of_Indigenous_Australians.

Chapter 9

ENCOUNTERS WITH WILDLIFE

I thought I would start my stories for this chapter with the answer to one of the most frequent questions I get, which is "What was your favorite trip?" I enjoy travel no matter where it is, regardless of city or country, but I think that of all things there are to see and do on a trip, interacting with wildlife is probably my favorite. And although there have been many trips involving wildlife (the Galapagos, the Komodo dragon in Indonesia, safaris in several African countries, a crocodile rescue in Namibia, and penguin colonies in Patagonia and Antarctica, all described at some point in *Travels with Stanley*), it still remains that our visit to the mountain gorillas of Rwanda in December 1986 is the trip that stands out in my mind as the "best." The stories from that trip are told and retold by us and by our sons.

The mountain gorillas of Rwanda (1986)

The start was very inauspicious, and we were extremely anxious as we boarded the flight to Amsterdam. Two of us were never confirmed on the flight from Amsterdam to Kilimanjaro. We could have flown to Nairobi and bused it to Kilimanjaro, but we decided to take the chance and go standby. Luckily, everyone made it, and we arrived with the rest of the members of our Overseas Adventure Travel (OAT) tour and our guide, Clive. Clive was an excellent guide, always (well, at least most of the time) maintaining an even keel as a series of problems arose during the trip. He was able to solve every problem, from illness and injury to truck repair.

We checked into a hotel to shower, change, and have lunch before leaving for Arusha. We stopped at the market there, bought some food, and set out on a bumpy road for our first campsite after being en route for almost thirty hours. I think of all the stories our sons tell, this one sends them into gales of laughter every time. Just last month, twenty-nine years later, our son Brian told this story. Of course making fun of your parents is a favorite pastime of most kids, and ours are no exception. It goes like this. Our meals at the campsite consisted of sitting on little camp stools. Stanley, totally exhausted and hungry, carried his soup bowl, plate of sausage and vegetables, and a drink, balancing all very carefully as he took his seat on the camp stool. Although no video was available, since smartphones were still not on the scene, the slow motion backward somersault with the soup spraying over their father's face still elicits hysterical laughter from our sons as we visualize the event in our minds' eyes.

From this campsite in Manyara National Park in Tanzania, we set out for the Ngorogoro Crater. At that time, 1986, it was still possible to camp in the crater. It is hard to describe what it is like to be camping in a giant terrarium, since the distance from top to bottom is over 5,000 feet (8,500 to 3,000). The adventure came as we were leaving the crater. After we'd viewed the flamingos and were following tracks to get out, one wheel fell into a hole, and we were stuck. It was getting dark, and there was absolutely no one else around. Just when it looked like we were going to have to spend the night in our truck, out of nowhere, like in an Indiana Jones movie, a small Land Rover driven by a Masai tribesman appeared. With all of us out of the truck, a cable was attached, and the truck was out of the hole, and we were able to reach our campsite just as it was getting dark.

Next day, on the way to Serengeti National Park, we stopped at Olduvai Gorge, where the Leakeys' archaeological expeditions uncovered the remains of what are believed to be the origins of humankind.[35] As will become evident as my stories unfold, Stanley always comes up with the best questions. This time, to the guide at the gorge, after listening to the explanation of the first excavation and how important it was to the theory of evolution, Stanley paused a moment and asked, "Is this the only gorge you got?" This line has become Labow lore, quoted by his sons many times since.

After three nights camping in the Serengeti, a poisonous snake was discovered in the outhouse coiled around the rafters. Our experience so far was that it was safer just to be in our own tents and use nature's facilities around us, rather than outhouses or toilets. Often what we had to do was separate on either side of the truck, boys on one side and girls on the other. Necessity is the mother of invention!

We set out for Rwanda, and the truck broke down again. We camped in a museum village, one of the worst campsites. Again, the toilets were awful, totally blocked. We had to stay a second night, and some tour members were getting very

---

[35] http://www.livescience.com/40455-olduvai-gorge.html.

restless (panicky?). We finally could leave and drove, without really being able to reach our next designated campsite. It was dark, and we saw a government building that had wood for our fire so we could cook. Thanks to much pleading and negotiating, we were able to camp. As we were getting ready for bed, a long conga line of safari ants was marching by. All of us were bitten alive in spite of trying to avoid the parade, except for Daniel. Did a malaria-carrying mosquito sneak into the conga line of ants, who allowed the mosquito to bite him instead of themselves? Was this where Daniel got malaria? And to add to the interest, this well-maintained government building was a prison for the criminally insane. We kept this fact from some of our fellow panicky tour mates.

All of us with two local children on the shores of Lake Victoria, Tanzania, December 1986

After two more truck repairs (a flat tire and the fuel tank hanging by one nail) we finally crossed the border from Tanzania into Rwanda. We checked into the Meridien Hotel in Kigali and had a meal that was much worse than any of our meals on the road. And, as predicted by Clive, many of us got sick, which hadn't happened during all of our time when our own team prepared and cooked the meals.

Next day, we arrived in Parc des Volcanes. The campsite was in the park, and although there was a toilet, again it was too far away from the campsite and not in great working order. During the night, Stan went to pee and, seeing eyes in the darkness, decided not to go too far. When it was my turn, I stayed very close. Stan called out, "Roz, where are you peeing?" Voices from our kids' tent followed, calling, "Ma, you're peeing on our tent."

That certainly amused the entire campsite and many others, as this story was repeatedly told.

We were hiking in the area where Dian Fossey's camp was and very close to where she was murdered in 1985.[36] The way visiting the gorillas worked was that six people went to view the gorillas at one time. Our group was the second one. Although it was freezing at night, during the day, the sun made it very warm, especially as we were hiking uphill to the gorilla camp. In spite of being warned about eating light, Stan decided to have a big breakfast. There was a large cast iron skillet on the fire, and there were sunny-side up eggs swimming in two inches of oil. Stan decided to eat the eggs.

It didn't take long. As we entered the road to the park, everything he had eaten left his stomach onto the side of the bus.

We reached the spot where the hike began. As the truck let us off, we hired three porters; took our cameras, water canteens, and wet suits to protect ourselves from the nettles;

---

[36] http://www.biography.com/people/dian-fossey-9299545#death-and-legacy.

and set off. We also picked up a guide and a guard with a rifle that looked like something out of a World War I movie. Another famous Stanley quote: "If the gorilla grabs me, shoot me, not the gorilla."

Although a vague trail at first, the path quickly deteriorated into thick growth and vines and leaves on bamboo branches—extremely slippery. The method was to go to the previous day's nest and start from there, following the droppings and hoping that the gorilla family hadn't traveled too far.

It was on a carpet of wet vines on a steep slope that Stanley's shoelaces broke. Fortunately, one of our tour mates had an extra pair of sneakers and used those laces to repair Stan's. The classic line from this moment was "I have no lateral traction." This was said by Stan as he gasped for air and slid along the vines with one porter (read pusher) and the other porter (read puller) helping him up the hill. He had on heavy ski pants and, at this point, was extremely hot. However, two and a half hours from the time we started walking, we arrived at the site of the habituated gorilla family. Although having traveled extensively, when asked which was our most remarkable trip, our encounter with the mountain gorilla still ranks #1.

The silverback was relaxing as we approached, and the females and babies were scampering around. We approached to about three to four feet and sat around and photographed. All of a sudden, a female jumped down from a tree over our heads. I tapped Stanley on the shoulder. "Pardon me. The gorilla wants to get by." She went within two inches of Daniel and me.

Stan, again in spite of being warned repeatedly not to try to touch the babies, extended his hand to a baby who was approaching to touch his camera. It didn't take a minute before the silverback charged us. We buried our faces in the ground and hoped he would stop short of destroying Stanley. We looked up, and he hit the mother across the face, drawing blood. Then he faced us, breaking whole trees in half, while baring his teeth and growling.

Then from this shady clearing, the group moved into a sunlit spot and all of them started eating leaves furiously. Then we had to leave. The hour permitted us was over. It was a fantastic display, one that I will certainly never forget, the highlight of all of our travels, and the experience that remains to this day rank one.

Discovering penguins in Argentina (1987)

Over the years, we had three different encounters with penguins; twice we were on guided tours. There really are many penguins in Antarctica. As cute as they are, they really smell. Another time we saw a few in the Galapagos. But the most interesting penguin encounter was the time we found penguins on our own when the four of us (the boys were with us on this one) were driving in Argentinian Patagonia. We flew from Buenos Aires to Trelew and then rented a car and drove to Puerto Madryn. The agency where we had reserved our car had no representative, but fortunately there was someone else there who provided a beat-up Renault, and we set out for Puerto Madryn about fifty-five kilometers away.

It is hard to describe the desolation of this part of Patagonia. There were no other cars, no people on the entire route. We checked into our hotel and then set out to drive along the Valdes Peninsula, where all the wildlife was supposed to be. We drove about 135 kilometers on a dirt road and saw nothing. Finally, Brian called out for Stan to pull over. He had seen lots of birds, but nothing was clearly visible. There was a flattened area where a truck had stopped. We looked over the edge, and there was a penguin colony. Walking down the side of the cliff to the ocean, there were penguins and their babies in every little hole. They were oblivious to us and not at all disturbed as we walked right by them. A little farther down the beach were enormous sea elephants, who also were completely unperturbed by our presence. This penguin colony was a bonus, but where all the penguins were supposed to be was Punta Tombo, 105 kilometers on another dirt road that was even worse than the one we were on the day before. We arrived at a nature reserve, paid to enter, and drove slowly down a road completely surrounded by penguins.

What follows may be my favorite Stanley trip comment, the "quote of the day." We walked slowly down to the shore and, on our way back, spotted a gentleman taking a photo of one of the most bedraggled baby penguins we had seen. Stanley said to him that there were much better-looking penguins farther down the trail. The man smiled and very politely explained. He was the general director of the New York Zoological Society (now the World Conservation Society)[37] and had been coming to this area since 1964. The society had built this reserve and had been studying the

[37] http://blog.wcs.org/photo/2015/01/20/the-power-of-penguins/.

Magellanic penguins and doing a yearly census. There were actually five hundred thousand penguins in this colony, the largest in South America. But this year, 75 percent of the chicks had died, perhaps due to El Nino and the fish migration. We would have liked to ask more questions but instead quietly withdrew and headed back to Puerto Madryn and our hotel.

Snakes, poisonous or not? In Africa (1987) and Guatemala (1995)

On several trips, we did encounter snakes. One was in an outhouse in Africa on our camping safari in 1986 (described above). But although we had used that outhouse for several days, we hadn't seen the snake. One of our guides found it as we were leaving when he checked out the cleanliness of the outhouse. He did remove it and then killed it in front of us. He claimed that it was extremely poisonous, although it certainly wasn't very large. Although I really don't like snakes, I realize that snakes are equally afraid of us and probably rightly so, as when we see one, we almost always kill it.

The time we found a snake on our own was while walking along a self-guided trail in Guatemala. We were at a resort near Tikal, in a town called El Remate. This was in December 1995. The resort was a Westin Hotel, and this nature walk close by was called Biotopa. This was a well-marked trail up the side of a mountain, with steps, vine hand rails, bridges, and benches for if you got tired; in other words, it was very civilized. We saw many birds and butterflies, and then when we were almost finished, Stan spotted a snake. It wasn't too large (about a foot long), and it was multicolored with an intricate pattern. He said, "I think it's dead."

I said, "Poke it with a stick to make sure." It was directly across the path.

Sure enough, it moved. Then Stan went around it, and it picked up its head. I got slightly hysterical but did manage to walk behind it on the side of the path. There were parts of this path where this would have been impossible. Before I'd chosen my route to avoid this snake, Stan had assured me that the snake wasn't poisonous. I said, "We're in the jungle in Guatemala. It's a real possibility."[38] My usual slow walking pace was immediately quickened. I had had enough jungle.

The Komodo dragon in Indonesia (1999)

In December 1999, we wanted to see the Komodo dragon, and so we booked a cruise on the *Adelaar*, a sailing ship with an incredible history, well worth describing in detail.[39] The ship was built in 1902 in Holland in the Staadskanal Shipyards and was originally a sailing cargo ship without a motor, sailing between England, Sweden, Norway, and Russia. During World War I, she was confiscated by the Germans and, after the war, purchased by a couple who used it for forty years to live in and run cargo through the Baltic Sea. During World War II, it was used to transport war goods and renamed *Heimatland*. After the war, the

---

[38] Poisonous snake in Tikal, https://www.travelblog.org/Photos/7269030.

[39] The Adelaar-http://www.adelaar-cruises.com/the-ship/.

German Captain Thimian sailed her along the Baltic Sea, as a cargo vessel once again. The masts were removed, and her first diesel engine was installed in 1954.

In 1979, the *Adelaar* was no longer in service and was docked in a small harbor in the Baltic Sea between the former East Germany and Poland. Two friends, one from the West and one from the East, attempted to buy the ship's two large anchors from the old Captain Thimian, but instead they walked away with the entire thirty-nine-meter ship! She was taken along the rivers and canals to the former East Berlin.

One of the owners, Ben, on this trip with us, hatched a plan to escape from East Berlin. Ben was an anesthetist and taught at a university at the time in the East. He hid in a special compartment in the ship, and his friend sailed it out of East Germany into the West in 1981. Now "free," Ben and his partner began extensive restoration of the vessel, unknowingly at the very same shipyard in Holland where the ship was originally built. By an incredible coincidence, the original builder's son recognized the *Heimatland* as the vessel *Adelaar* that his father had built eighty years earlier. His original pictures were used to restore the ship to her former state. During the four-year restoration, the vessel received a new yacht-like interior; a forty-ton steel-concrete keel; and a traditional schooner rig, solid wooden masts, and sails.

The *Adelaar* sailed the Mediterranean from 1984 until 1987 and then crossed the Atlantic Ocean to sail the Caribbean. In 1988, the *Adelaar* crossed the Pacific Ocean and sailed to New Zealand, where she won the New Zealand Tall Ship Race. From 1991 until 1992, the *Adelaar* underwent a complete renovation, and a full-service dive center was added. Ben and his wife, Janice, who was on the trip with us, set out to circumnavigate the globe, leaving New Zealand in 1993. However, when they reached Bali, the engine needed to be replaced, and they have remained there ever since, running charters for tour companies like the one we were booked on. When I read the history on the *Adelaar* website and compared it to my diary, I found that it was right on with my notes. However, what we missed when we sailed in 1999 was that the *Adelaar* had received a further restoration from 2008 to 2011 and became, in the description on the *Adelaar's* website, a "showcase classical yacht," sailing charters from Bali to Komodo year-round.

After spending a few days in Bali, before starting the cruise among the islands of Indonesia, we went on a little side trip to get the seventh continent on our list (we had been to the other six) and flew to the city of Darwin, Australia (see chapter 8, "Golf and Fishing") which is only two and a half hours away by air.

Upon our return, we boarded the *Adelaar* and set sail for Komodo Island. There were only five other passengers besides us, four single women, all over sixty-five, and one man. The crew outnumbered the passengers (the two owners, Janice and Ben; Glenn, the manager; Putu, the guide; and the crew of eight). We stopped at Lombok Island first. It was a huge contrast to Bali since it was mostly Muslim, whereas Bali was mostly Hindu. As a matter of fact, Indonesia is the fourth most populous country in the world and has the world's largest Muslim population.[40] We went on a

[40] https://en.wikipedia.org/wiki/Indonesia.

hike through rice paddies, and it was there that we were told to walk on the ridges surrounding the garlic fields. Stanley may not have heard, as he stomped right through the fields, avoiding the ridges at all costs. The origin of the title of this book as an allegory of cultural sensitivity (see the Introduction).

We continued to Moyo Island and Satunga. Snorkeling was a part of most days, and our weather was perfect and the water very calm. Indonesia is the largest archipelagic nation in the world, with a coastline stretching over ninety-five thousand kilometers around more than seventeen thousand islands.[41] An extensive group of coral reefs protect these islands. Sadly, a lot of the coral reefs have been destroyed because of blast and poison fishing. We could see evidence of that from time to time, but old practices die hard. Satunga is famous for the fruit bats, and when we were walking on the island, we could see many hanging from the trees. We were told to stay on deck at sunset because, exactly at sunset, the bats fly off the island. Sure enough, exactly at sunset, the bats flew across the sky directly in front of a full moon; a movie set could not have improved on the sight with the sunset "a sailor's delight," deep red.

The next day, we docked at Rincha Island, part of Komodo National Park. We had seen a movie about the Komodo dragon the night before, quite the terrifying animal. As we were standing at the ranger station, one dragon raced down the hill toward us and stopped just short of the station. It was warm, and so the dragons were active, since as reptiles they can only regulate their temperature by what the current environment allows. Our next walk on

---

[41] https://en.wikipedia.org/wiki/List_of_islands_of_Indonesia

another part of the island was much better, a cooler day. It was cloudy, and it had rained. The dragons were totally immobilized. We could get right up to them safely, although they looked very intimidating even when lying quietly. At the time of our visit, we were told that they kill their prey in an unusual way. Their saliva is toxic so they just bite their victims and wait for them to die. Then they eat them. In actual fact, in 2009, it was discovered that the composition of the "saliva" of the dragon was not saliva at all but venom as poisonous as the most poisonous snakes, containing anticoagulants and hypotensive agents that rendered their victims too weak to escape.[42]

Our food continued to be excellent throughout the trip. The cook was positively a genius. The crew was mostly Muslim, and it was the month of Ramadan, so they only ate at night but prepared and served food to us all day. The meals on Christmas Day started out as usual, delicious and fresh, with lunch being a *salade nicoise* with tuna, caught by Ben just the day before. Freshly baked bread accompanied every meal. However, dinner was special. Glenn had heard Stanley speak about my signature dish, roast turkey. Glenn managed to find a turkey, and I proceeded to prepare it for Christmas dinner. I had given him the list of ingredients for the stuffing and the glaze.

Here it is for those of you who want to prepare the perfect turkey:

Turkey ~12 pounds
Turkey stuffing:
2 stalks celery, chopped

[42] Komodo dragon, https://en.wikipedia.org/wiki/Komodo_dragon.

1 onion, chopped
4 tablespoons oats
3 tablespoons cream of wheat
2 fistfuls cornflakes
12 Ritz crackers
salt and pepper
1 tablespoon brown sugar
Grind all very well and keep cold if made in advance. Then add 6 tbsp vegetable oil before stuffing the turkey. This is the smallest amount, but depending on the turkey size you can do multiples. I usually do at least four times this amount, except for the celery and onion—not too much of that.

Turkey paste

1 tablespoon paprika
2 tablespoons dried onion soup or onion powder (not salt)
2 teaspoon poultry dressing
2 tablespoon apricot jam
Again, I usually triple this.

Add a little water to make a thick paste. Rub the inside and outside of the turkey with the paste. Then stuff the turkey. Use skewers to keep the wings and legs close to the body. Line a pan with foil. Place the turkey on the foil and then make a tent over the turkey.

Roast at 325°F for about twenty minutes a pound. During the last hour or so, uncover

> the turkey and baste frequently until skin is crisp. Test if it is done by slitting the leg joint; the juice should run clear and not be pink.

It was hard to believe, but the turkey came out perfectly, and Christmas dinner was by candlelight with all the trimmings, topped off by an apple pie baked by Glenn in town.

We flew back to Bali and stayed in pure luxury in Ubud at the Four Seasons Hotel (see chapter 4, "Where to Stay"). We relaxed by the pool until it was time to fly back to Ottawa.

Rescuing Sodra from a crocodile, Impalila Island, Namibia (2004)

Many years later (December 2004) we set out on another African safari. This one was in Zimbabwe, Namibia, and Botswana, probably the most famous of all our trips since it was written up in the *Ottawa Citizen*. Although usually I organized and booked all flights and accommodation myself for our trips, this time, we did use a travel agency. It was a great combination of a walking safari in Zimbabwe, where we started, followed by a visit in Victoria Falls, where our guide and his family lived. After visiting the falls and paddling down the Zambesi River, we crossed the border into Botswana. At the dock, we were met by the workers from Ichingo Lodge, who took us by boat to Impalila Island, which was in Namibia. The owner of the lodge was Ralph Oxenham, a former chemist who had sold his company and opened this lodge as his retirement hobby. Our first two nights were spent on a magnificent houseboat, recently acquired by the lodge, which provided a great view of the animals, mostly elephants, coming to drink in the evening at the shores of the river in Chobe National Park. The next two nights were spent at Ichingo Lodge itself. Although mainly a fishing lodge for tigerfish, the ride down the rapids of the Chobe River was exciting. And aside from catching tigerfish, we could view the animals on the shore.

We didn't know how exciting it was going to get when we set out that day to fish and view the animals. Our guide, Anton, heard screaming from across the river and saw many children running along the shore. He realized right away that a crocodile had a little girl in its mouth, taking her to deeper water to drown her. Anton managed to trap the crocodile with the girl between the boat and the shore, and while Stan hit the crocodile on the snout with his fist, Anton grabbed the girl to lift her into the boat. I looked around the boat for something to hit the crocodile with while screaming. I realized then that we had nothing in the boat if that motor should fail. The crocodile let go of the girl's shoulder and then grabbed her leg. With more hitting on the crocodile's nose, it finally let go, and the girl was lifted into the boat.

We came to shore close by and were met by the truck from the lodge after Anton had called. We all gathered at the clinic that we had visited that morning. It was staffed by a nurse with almost no supplies. There was suture material to stitch the wounds but no sterile solutions of any kind and not nearly enough local anesthetic to freeze all the wounds. Sodra didn't say a word as Stanley sewed her up. We found out that, often, the nurse didn't show up, and Ralph had never seen the doctor who was supposed to come to this clinic once a month. There were supplies at the lodge, and Nicki, an American woman who managed the lodge with her husband for Ralph, had often carried out first aid.

Stan brought our antibiotics to Sodra in the village, which was nearby the lodge. As we viewed the mud huts—no floors, no water, and no electricity—we were able to see firsthand the extent of the poverty in that village. As we tried to explain when to take the antibiotics, we realized there were no clocks, no watches. How to explain every four hours? We mostly saw women. Sodra had a mother, grandmother, and great-grandmother. It turned out that she did have a father, who accompanied her to the nearest hospital (350 miles away) after the wounds became infected. Stan knew that this would happen, and it was fortunate that her father accompanied her and looked after her for a month while she healed.

Ralph had offered many times to supply clean water from the lodge so that the people of the village wouldn't have to go to the river to wash, but the men never came. After this incident, the men came to Ralph, and a trench was dug for the pipe from the lodge's supply of water.

This happened to be the same time as the terrible tsunami in Asia that killed so many. Money was raised to rebuild the areas affected, many of them resorts. Stan wrote a letter to the editor of the *Citizen* saying that the numbers of children dying from malaria and diarrhea in Africa every year exceeded the deaths from this tsunami by many orders of magnitude. This prompted an interview, with Stan explaining what had happened. The interview was published in the *Ottawa Citizen*.[43] People kept sending money to us, unsolicited, which we sent to Ralph—funding for water and electricity. A patient of Stan's nominated him for an award, and he was recognized with a commendation from the governor general of Canada in February 2006.

Friends of ours visited the same lodge a couple of years later and sent photos of the progress Ralph had made in the village with the funds that had been sent to him from us. There was now water so that the people in the village wouldn't have to go to the river and also some shared electricity. Sodra healed very well and continued in school until she was sixteen, which we funded ourselves. Although education is supposed to be free, uniforms and supplies are required.

We lost contact with Ralph over the years, but recently (July 23, 2014) there was a post on Facebook that he had passed away.[44]

The Lonely Planet's list of travel categories includes food and drink, adventure, heritage and history, art and culture, and wildlife and nature. Although our trips have included all of these kinds of travel, I feel that my most memorable travels over years included some kind of interaction with some kind of wildlife.[45]

Several of our trips that involved wildlife, both by choice and inadvertently, were camping trips. Although several were described in other chapters, the following chapter describes a few of our most memorable, for the sheer joy or lack thereof, experiences camping.

---

[43] *The Ottawa Citizen*, January 29, 2005.

[44] http://176.32.230.17/angler-reports.com/blog-steve/ralph-oxenham-ichingo-safari-lodge/.

[45] Lonely Planet, www.lonelyplanet.com.

Chapter 10

CAMPING TRIPS AND BATHROOMS/OUTHOUSES

We have had a variety of camping trips over the years in three continents. Our trip to Peru (see chapter 7, "Accidents and Illnesses") hiking to Machu Picchu with our sons was challenging, but we were extremely well taken care of. Our trip to Tanzania and Rwanda and visiting the mountain gorillas was still the most amazing (chapter 9, "Encounters with Wildlife"). Camping in the Sahara in Algeria was not much fun, with freezing cold nights and sand in everything we owned and eating the same leg of lamb every night (chapter 5, "Food"). Another camping trip from hell was our sea kayaking expedition in Belize (see below). However, two trips when we camped in Canada were probably even more difficult. One was right next door, in Algonquin Park, with our friends and their children. The other was in the eastern Arctic on Baffin Island, now known as Nunavut.

One of the most interesting parts of travel but especially camping trips is the variety of bathrooms/outhouses you encounter. When camping, we always found that using nature's facilities was preferable to the outhouses that may be provided. Of course, sometimes you have no choice—a campsite in the Serengeti with a poisonous snake in the outhouse (chapter 9, "Encounters with Wildlife") or squat toilets in developing nations (described below).

Pond Inlet (1981)

One great Canadian expedition that involved camping and fishing was our trip to Baffin Island (now renamed Nunavut) in August 1981. We flew from Montreal to Frobisher Bay (since 1987, Iqaluit). It is the capital of Nunavut and has since had a lot of development. But when we were there, it was lacking proper roads and other important services and had almost no hotels or restaurants. We only stopped there a short while and changed planes to a very small prop plane. This plane made several stops as it flew up the coast to Pond Inlet unloading supplies for each small community, each landing more remarkable than the next. Not only are there still no roads that connect cities in the south of Canada with the Arctic, there are no paved airstrips and no air traffic controllers. So the only means of transporting supplies are ships and planes, making basic food like milk extremely expensive. However, we watched cases and cases of beer being unloaded when we landed in Iqaluit.

We traveled with six business executives from the United States who were going on an Arctic char fishing expedition in the Robertson River at Koluktoo Bay. They were loading up cases of scotch that they had brought with them, preparing for their trip. We landed in Pond Inlet and checked into the small barracks that doubled as a hotel. Since there was room on the Hawker Sidley aircraft that regularly flew from Pond Inlet to Koluktoo Bay and Nanisivik, we went along with them. We could overhear a lot of grumbling that a woman and two kids were accompanying them. We heard the classic misogynistic statement from one guy that "c-nting and camping don't mix." I'll never forget that one, but boy did they get theirs! The story continues.

We flew at five hundred feet the entire trip, approximately eighty miles. We saw narwhales and icebergs all along the way.

Our tents at the fishing camp were permanent structures of strong canvas with gas stoves inside for heat. There were two cots to a tent and not much room for anything else. The first night, I put on layer after layer of clothing, to the point where I yelled out that I couldn't move or breath. Eventually it got acceptably warm, and we could sleep.

We fished all day, and the boys caught enormous fish. I got a very small one but Stanley caught nothing. It was amazing how, with people on either side of him pulling them in, he failed to get any. When we were out on the banks of the river, we saw another two people, a husband and wife. He was using special tackle to be the first to catch a certain weight, specific trophy fishing. His wife was an author for the fishing magazine and was going to write up the article after her husband caught the fish. We had never heard of anything like this before, but evidently our other group members had. They were so unhappy and so unfriendly that they always stood on the opposite side of the river from us and the other woman. We thought we were pretty well behaved and really didn't make too much fuss, but the woman who was writing the article had the most incredibly annoying laugh, which you could hear nonstop. After fishing and a barbecue lunch on the shore of the river, we took a boat ride up to a waterfall and even went on a seal hunt. It was quite the amazing experience. After a few days, we flew back to Pond Inlet.

Brian's Arctic char from the Robertson River, Koluktoo Bay, August 1981

Daniel's Arctic char from the Robertson River, Koluktoo Bay, August 1981

Arctic char barbecue on the shores of the Robertson River, Koluktoo Bay, August 1981

The adventure continued. We walked for hours in Pond Inlet admiring the unique flowers with a "tenuous grip on life"—our favorite saying for plant life up there. Brian found an arrowhead. We brought it to the museum of natural history to identify. When we showed it to a curator at the museum, he gently reminded us that we should have left it where we'd found it, something we have learned over the years of travel.

We also took a ride over to Bylot Island in a glorified motorboat, where there was a huge glacier. The water we were crossing was supercooled saltwater. A few minutes in it, and we would be dead. There were narwhals all around, as well as seals. We walked all over the glacier and then found that a small river was in front of us, with no way for us to cross. Our guide carried each one of us across. We were told later that it was very dangerous to walk on a glacier. It could collapse at any minute. We saw evidence of this in Chile, when large pieces of Grey Glacier calved in front of us into the water below. We returned in time for supper and had a very relaxing evening watching TV movies.

As we looked outside, we saw the fog moving in. It was so thick that we could hardly see our hands in front of our faces when we were outside. We were supposed to fly out the next day, but there was no way that would happen. But the best news was that our six woman haters were completely stranded in Koluktoo Bay with the woman author and her fisherman husband. The twin otter tried to fly in and get them, but the plane had to turn back. We were able to fly back the next day, as the fog lifted enough for us to take off. We have no idea when there would be a flight to Koluktoo

Bay. We couldn't help but smile to ourselves thinking about them stranded indefinitely!

Algonquin Park (1983)

Algonquin Park is the oldest and one of the most popular provincial parks in Canada. One of the ways that it was made famous was with the paintings of the group of seven and the mysterious death of one of the artists, Tom Thompson on Canoe Lake.[46] I have no idea what made us take on this enormous expedition, but in early June, we set out with our two sons and our friends and their children. (I don't remember how old they all were but certainly they were all under seventeen.) We trusted our friend implicitly. He was known to us as tripper Bob, with his knowledge of camping, maps of the lakes, and how to get to where we were going to catch our limit of speckled trout within minutes. Our friends had been camping and canoeing many times. He'd even built his own canoe. They also had a cottage on Canoe Lake in the park and were very familiar with the park's conditions.

We arrived at the park, put our canoes in the water along with our supplies, and set out. We knew that we would have two portages, each in the range of three kilometers. This would involve more than one trip with canoes and supplies. One very important fact we somehow ignored. Early June is the height of black fly season. In spite of literally glowing with insect repellant, we were bitten alive. Our friend was bitten so badly her eyes were swollen shut, and blood was

---

[46] Tom Thompson and Canoe Lake, http://www.canadianmysteries.ca/sites/thomson/home/indexen.html.

running down her face. But, undaunted, we pushed forward. We arrived at our campsite hours later, set up our tents, and cooked our steak dinner. We never did believe in camping type food. Nothing but the best! Of course, the next day, our meal would be fresh fish.

We went to bed, and things were all right for a while. Then the storm started. Stanley never could sleep very well in a sleeping bag on the ground and so always took a little pill to help. At some point during the night, the wind came up, and the storm started. Setting up a tent is not one of our best abilities, and our tent collapsed. The boys were in with us at this point; their tent had given up first. We all said we should call our friend to help put it back up. Stanley, in some kind of semi-comatose state said we should only call him if it was an emergency.

The three of us yelled at once, "It is an emergency!"

And then our friend came over and fixed our tent.

The next day, the weather started out okay, and we set out to fish for those amazing trout. One problem—the trout were absolutely stuffed with all the bugs that were around, and all day long we didn't get one single bite. The weather was getting very threatening, and we decided to abort this mission. We set out in our canoes and were becoming extremely nervous about the approaching storm. I thought about the person who had drowned in that lake the week before. The large lakes in Algonquin Park can certainly be very dangerous.

We reached our cars as the storm let loose and were certainly glad to be alive. We went to a gasoline station close by, and everyone went to the bathroom. We filled up and forgot to remove the gas handle from the car, but even more important, we started to drive away without our friend's daughter. I wonder if our friends have told their daughter yet. We all vowed at that time never to tell her.

Turkey (1985) and (1997)

On our two trips to Turkey, we had the most interesting bathroom experiences. On the first trip in 1985 with our sons, we took the bus from Istanbul to Izmir. It was a nine-hour bus ride with everyone smoking, a crazy decision in retrospect. There was a wonderful, clean toilet on the bus, but it was always locked. We stopped to go to the bathroom at a dreadful cafeteria, which was a terrible mess. So our son who had to go to the bathroom thought, *Why go here? I'll just go back to the bus.* And the bathroom, for some reason, was unlocked.

We took off and the bus driver discovered what had happened. He was beside himself. The toilet on the bus was off limits. We continued on the long journey, and Stanley had to go to the bathroom again. There was an attendant on the bus, sort of like a flight attendant. He handed out treats and aftershave lotion and generally kept order. It took asking many people to find someone who spoke English so that Stanley could explain what he wanted.

Finally the bus driver stopped. He picked a place where the tallest item was a dried-out piece of grass on both sides of the road. Stanley stood behind the bus and tried to pee. Kids were looking out the back window laughing. The pipes froze. Somehow he managed to survive until we arrived at the next stop. Quite a journey!

On the other hand, years later (1997) when we were in Turkey again, we rented a car and were driving around the country with our friends. We had very little trouble driving around, except occasionally being robbed or stopping to use a bathroom. We were always excited when we saw a normal flush toilet, which almost never worked. Most often, it was a squat toilet, which if it wasn't overflowing, wasn't a problem. One time we were in a lovely pottery shop buying some gifts, and Stanley had to use the bathroom for more than just "number one" as we used to say. It was a lovely squat toilet, relatively clean, and he carefully took off his pants and left them beside him. He lowered himself onto the squat toilet carefully, but it was sloped and very slippery white porcelain. He landed right into the hole. He screamed, and when we asked what had happened, he told us to go ahead. He would join us later.

Belize (1995)

My diaries are full of sayings, and the one on the first page of my description of our sea kayaking trip to Belize in 1995 is by one of my favorite travel writers, Paul Theroux: "Travel is glamorous only in retrospect." This could be true of many of our travels, but in spite of the beautiful ocean, fish, coral reefs, and so on, this trip had a lot of torture. We were coming from Guatemala and had flown to and from Belize City to Flores. Our launching point for the sea kayaking portion of our holiday was Dandriga, and we boarded a small twin-engine plane that said on the screen visual flight rules "day flight only." There were many people and tons of luggage, but somehow the plane took off, and we landed on a narrow dirt strip in the forest. We checked into Jungle Huts Motel, a cabin near the water with a bath and TV but very open and noisy. It was near a steel bridge that made a noise like a steam shovel dumping a load of dirt and rocks on your front yard every time a vehicle went over it. Not a good night to begin with, but it got worse. I wrote in my diary, "I was very cranky about this whole trip."

We set out from Dandriga in an open motor launch, which held about twelve people, and the ocean was really choppy. As soon as we left shore, it started to pour. We were soaked by the time we made it to the barrier reef, where we stopped for a while and then continued another eight miles to Glover's Reef.

Our arrival on the island was not too great—in a downpour with wind blowing so hard we could do nothing but rest. Our accommodation was a tent. It started out to be a small one. We were slow to grab the four-man tents, which our other tour members got. But another four-man tent was found, and our guide put it up for us. It was large enough so that we could stand up in it. It had excellent screens and a window flap. Our air mattress was a double and started out to be very comfortable.

We were with eleven other people—a family of five with three young boys and a few couples, two young, one older. We were expected to wash our dishes, and at breakfast the first morning, Stanley did everyone's. A note in my diary used the word "amazingly" and noted that when not at home, things are different.

The toilet was also quite amazing. There was a dock with a walk out to a little house high up over the water, with a toilet seat with a hole. Everything just fell in and floated away. The paper went into a plastic bag, and there was a can on a string that you were supposed to place on a hook as a sign that you were in there.

We all seemed to be getting along really well so far and the sleeping was really not bad. Of course, this was only day two.

We had a very good morning snorkeling. The water was beautiful, in color, clarity, and temperature. But since this was a sea kayaking trip, we had to have a lesson. So after a few brief verbal instructions, one of our guides showed us what to do. Each kayak has a rudder and a trap door to keep it afloat when it tips, a sort of air pocket. You wear a kind of skirt, which essentially seals you into your compartment. You had to try to get in without tipping, and it wasn't easy. So we paddled a little and had to deliberately tip it in deep water and get in. After you tip it, you hold your paddle and flip off your skirt, which is attached to you and the kayak. That part went okay. Then trying to get back in was a disaster. Stanley made it on the third attempt, but then I couldn't get in. My arms were too weak. Finally, Stanley said to the guide who was with us as I was draped over the kayak with my bum in the air, "Just push her in."

By now I was black and blue and bitten all over. There really are bugs called "no see 'ems." You do not see them no matter how hard you try. Now supposedly the easy part—back in the kayak, we had to paddle back to the dock. The wind was still quite strong. It had not let up for two full days. We started out, and everyone had decided to walk their kayaks back. Not Stanley! Stanley had decided to go around the outside of the buoys, and we started getting pulled out to deep open water. I kept saying, "Stay inside the buoys."

Anyway, one of our guides kayaked over and helped us back.

We then had a shower, which I should describe. It basically was a big plastic bag filled with water. Upon pulling a plug, the water came out, and it sprinkled you. Water was very precious, mostly rainwater and some well water, which may only last until January, they said.

The food was always amazing, however. Fresh fish caught a few hours before being cooked.

Sleeping was always a bit of a challenge. There was a downpour almost every night. For some reason, on day four in the middle of the night, our mattress collapsed. Once more I got hysterical. Were we having fun yet? One of the guides tried to give us another double mattress, but it didn't even stay inflated for an hour. We made a deal with the young boys to give us their single mattress in exchange for unlimited cokes. Their parents made a limit of six cokes, and the deal was sealed.

As I went to the bathroom at 1:00 a.m. after my mattress was flat, I saw the lights from the beautiful, large boat docked off Manta Resort (a well-known scuba diving location). I thought of the Wayne and Shuster skit of the first- and second-class passengers on Air Canada. We were in the rain, with a deflating mattress and an outhouse with a monster in it, with all our clothes hanging outside in the pouring rain, bitten alive.

The wind stayed strong for almost the entire time we were on Glover's Reef, but finally we made it to Middle Caye, although it was still very windy. We were able to sail there and it was a terrific ride. Our guide was hanging on to us but then saw that another couple was having more trouble. We finally had been promoted to above the worst level.

We had a tour of the most amazing toilets. There was a conservation area there, and we got a tour from someone who was working for the New York Zoological Society. The toilets were on a second story, and waste entered a liquid broth, which contained just the right mixture of bacteria to dissolve, digest, and produce a fine black ash. This ash could then be used as a fertilizer—a wonderful ecological bathroom! We sailed back in under an hour and were the third kayak back.

On our way back to Dandriga, we stopped to snorkel at the barrier reef. When we thought back about this, it was not too safe. We were completely alone, or at least a very long distance from any kind of help. Certainly the snorkeling was outstanding. We saw many sharks, and I was wondering what my mother would think if she knew where I was. Fortunately we made it back to shore without a problem.

We still had one more day in Dandriga and had another very interesting ride on an inner tube in a couple of caves. From there, we were driving back to Belize City on this terrible jungle road when the van we were in died. I think back to the borderline equipment we either drove or flew in. We weren't too far from Belize City, and the Biltmore Hotel picked us up. Stanley had arranged for our New Year's Eve dinner at a great restaurant where we had eaten the first night, and many members of our group joined us. So many times, Stanley has organized a group that we are with for meals together. We almost always ask people to join us, especially if we are not with a tour group and the people we meet are dining alone. These group meals never fail to be interesting and are, for us, one of the most entertaining aspects of travel!

Also, Stanley had organized the tip. He left a bag outside our tent on the last day, and people could anonymously put in whatever they wanted. It was a great idea, since our group was very diverse economically.

I remember one young woman who had a meltdown one day. She was crying as she told us that they had saved up for this dream trip (right!) and it turned out to be so hard, and she was bitten alive, and her clothes were a mess. Although I felt the same way, I was used to the fact that, often, travel fits that quote I mentioned at the beginning of this story: "Travel is glamorous only in retrospect."

Other parts of travel that are certainly very far from glamorous are what security and border crossings have become. The next few chapters describe some of our serious and less serious interactions with police, security, and border crossings.

CHAPTER 11

SECURITY AND STUFF LEFT BEHIND

One very important part of security is how to handle money and other essential articles for each trip. As much as we think we are careful and check and double-check often, we forget stuff. Of course, this often makes for some of the best stories. However, at the time it is never amusing, to say the least. I have to admit, it is mostly I who leave stuff behind. I have left things behind in hotel rooms, restaurants, and airport bathrooms. However, I recently recalled that Stanley was the first to leave something very important behind on our very first trip together. In 1962, we drove from Montreal to Chicago and then on Route 66 to LA. Stanley would hide our money in our motel room in various locations, since the places we stayed in on that trip didn't have a safe in the room. On our very last leg of the trip, we were driving from Mitchell, South Dakota, to a small town in Minnesota (can't remember exactly where) and Stanley hid money in the telephone book. When we reached our next location, we realized what we had done. The absolutely hilarious thing was, when we called the motel, they said, "Oh yes. We found the money in the telephone book." That was before we told them where we had hidden it. We believe that we are much more careful now. But judge for yourselves after you read the following stories.

As far as security goes, the most important Labow rule that has evolved over the years is never to carry a purse or money pouch around your neck, waist, or anywhere else. The money or wallet or passport or boarding passes *must not* be visible. Over the years, Stanley has acquired pants that are not only like the regular cargo pants you see in every store these days. His pants have a pocket at the bottom of the leg that can be closed so that this pocket is not visible at all. He also has a shirt that has a pocket that runs the full length of both sides of his chest and closes with a Velcro patch. A passport with a boarding pass fits in and again is invisible. A wallet fits into the pocket in the front of the pants. Another security measure is what we call a fake wallet. This contains some cash and outdated credit cards. This would be a first line of defense if mugged. The bulk of the money and the major wallet are well hidden. For colder weather travel and for security clearance, all these items are not placed in the trays at security. There is a jacket made by Scottevest that has thirty-two pockets. So prior to going through security, all items (phone, money, wallets, and glasses) are removed and placed in the pockets of the Scottevest or the special shirt that also has the pockets. That way, they don't lie loose in the trays going through the scanner, making them much harder to steal. We have heard stories of money going missing after travels have gone through security, and although you try to keep an eye on your stuff, more often than not, you are told to move along, and you can't watch the trays containing your valuables. We had a phone disappear when our bags were opened and scanned at Logan Airport.

We recently purchased pants from a company called Pick-Pocket Proof Clothing. Although the pockets are amazing, with zippers and buttons over the zippers, the pants didn't have a large pocket at the bottom of the legs. We have not been able to find replacements for these very old pants, which look terrible. However, after all these years, on our last trip to Houston, we purchased a shirt for me similar to one Stan has had forever. Prior to that, Stan always carried my passport and boarding pass. I love that shirt, and I will never travel without it again.

Although I consider myself a very organized and careful person, when I travel, somehow things happen. Although the incident on our Turkey trip in 1985 may be the first documented time I left something behind, my diary notes said, "I pulled my routine trip performance." I can't recall exactly what I meant by that, although I did have a history of being robbed and/or leaving things behind. The robbery part fortunately never included being aware of this happening. It was always due to carelessness in retrospect. The earliest I can recall is being in Macy's in New York City buying shoes and leaving my purse draped over the back of the chair behind me. The purse disappeared. Then in O'Hare Airport in an elevator, a guy handed me back my wallet. I was carrying a huge purse with a not very secure closing. The robbery was foiled by a man in a wheelchair getting out of the elevator, so there was no easy escape for the pickpocket. Then I left behind a wallet in FAO Schwartz in Palm Beach, Florida. The people at the store said they had found it, but when I went to get it, nobody knew where it was. Our lawyer friend wrote a letter, and the store sent me a check for what I knew was in it. One time, I was at a meeting in San Diego, California, with my lab mates and Stanley. I left my passport and wallet in security, and Stan had to run back to the other terminal to get it, and on and on.

Stanley was only robbed once. It was on the Metro in Paris when he had to reach to hold on while standing, and francs were taken out of his back pocket. Now of course he never has anything in his back pockets. All is on his body in the well-secured front pockets. In all our trips to Nicaragua, only two personal items were missing, and they were both Stanley's. On one trip, his Bose earphones were missing. We have no idea where or when they were taken. And on the next trip, his iPhone was missing. We only noticed these robberies on the very last couple of days of our trips. We have no idea where or exactly when it happened.

Turkey (1985 and 1997)

We went to Turkey twice—once in 1985 with our sons and once with our friends in 1997. One time, it was a "left behind" story, and the other time, it was a robbery. Anyway, the "left behind story" was from the trip in 1985, when we went with our sons to Turkey and Greece. At that time, the movie *Midnight Express* had just come out, and to go to Turkey was falsely considered extremely dangerous. It turned out to be an amazing trip, and the people were very helpful and honest. In those days, I was trusted with all the valuables. I carried all the passports and airline tickets and boat information for the ride to Greece and also had travelers' checks (common at that time) and cash for the four of us in my purse. In retrospect, I see it was a completely crazy idea, but I continued to carry a purse for many years afterward. I had my purse looped over the back of a chair, and after afternoon tea in a lovely little restaurant in Kusadasi, we all left and walked quickly away. We looked behind at one point and saw a young boy running furiously after us carrying my purse. So much for danger and dishonesty in Turkey!

The robbery incident we had was in Istanbul on the trip in 1997. I was carrying the same purse as I had in 1985. I still hadn't realized that this was not a very good idea! We were standing in line at the Topkapi museum, and when I went to purchase the tickets, I saw that my wallet was missing. I couldn't remember if I had taken it with me. I knew that I had it in Zurich duty free and noticed at one point that my purse was open. It was hard to say where it happened, but six hours later when we got back to our hotel, there was no wallet in the room. In the purse were the following—a Visa credit card, a calling card, my driver's license, the InteleTravel card (our independent travel membership card), an OHIP card (Ontario government health insurance card), a bank card, a prestige Air Canada card, a Met Life insurance card, and $300 cash. We called Visa international, and we found that about $4,000 worth of merchandise had been put on my card. We didn't know the details until we returned home and received our Visa statement. All items were purchased in Istanbul, most from a sports equipment store. So it must have been stolen in Istanbul, most likely at the Topkapi Museum.

We had our American Express card, which many places didn't want to take. Visa did send us a replacement card a couple of days later, but it hadn't been properly activated and didn't work. Lesson learned. Two questions: Why wasn't my wallet in the hotel safe? And even more important, why was I even carrying a purse with my wallet with every single valuable in it? Now, Stanley and I take different credit cards and, when traveling, carry them separately. If there isn't a safe in the room, we leave the irreplaceable articles with reception in a secured spot.

LAX Los Angeles Airport (2003)

Another time I was rather careless was on a return trip from Easter Island to Los Angeles. Whenever I go to the bathroom in an airport, I think of the time I left the passports and boarding passes on the toilet paper dispenser in LAX. Stanley was being searched as we went through security, and so he handed me the passports and boarding passes for our ongoing flights. This was 2003, and already I had been relieved of my duty of carrying all the important documents.

As soon as I left the bathroom Stanley asked, "You have the passports, right?" And of course, at that moment, I knew I had left them in the bathroom. I ran back into the bathroom, and sure enough, someone was in the stall where I had been. It turned out to be a little girl with her mother waiting outside the stall.

She didn't want to give it back to me until her mother said that it was okay. "Please pass it under the door."

A little hand reached under the door and handed me the passports while Stanley outside the entrance was screaming, "Are they there? Are they there?"

This will never happen again because the passport and boarding pass are next to my heart in my special Royal Robbins shirt.

Mallorca (2012)

One of my favorite "left behind" stories happened recently on our first trip to Mallorca in 2012. We did a lot of driving around on that trip and stayed at the small town of Porto Cristo for two nights. It was an old style hotel, meals included that were very bad but very cheap, since it was off-season. But the view of the Mediterranean was beautiful.

In spite of being off-season, the weather had been amazing, and we set off for our next destination town, Soller, a one and a half-hour drive. Soller was up a very winding mountain road from that sea level port and had some of the most amazing homes and a beautiful cathedral. There was a tunnel through the mountain that greatly cut the time to get there. We stopped at the entrance, and Stan said, "You pay."

I said, "I don't have my wallet." I had asked before we left Porto Cristo, "Did you empty the safe?" But I should have asked, "Where is my wallet?"

We turned around and found ourselves before long on a road that went alongside a farm and was barely one lane. A woman guided us out, and we drove back to Porto Cristo. At this point, we were quite frantic. Our friend at the front desk took us back up to our room. No one had checked in there yet, and it hadn't been cleaned. Sure enough, the safe was left open, and my wallet was there. We decided to stay a third night in Porto Cristo, not our favorite place in Mallorca. As a matter of fact, we went back to Mallorca twice more but never returned to Porto Cristo.

Heathrow Airport (2015)

More recently "left behind" items involved technology advances. I left the adapter for electrical outlets in Europe in the outlet when I pulled out the charge cord in Stockholm. Stan left a charge cord for his phone in a hotel in Madeira. And on the same trip, on our way back to Ottawa, I left behind my cell phone at an airport hotel at Heathrow. Sometimes we get lucky and are able to retrieve the items left behind. We did go back and retrieve the charge cord in Madeira but not the outlet adapter in Stockholm. However, the left behind cell phone at the hotel in Heathrow is the beginning of a great security story.

We had called a taxi to take us from the hotel to the airport, and just as we got on the throughway to the airport, I realized I didn't have my cell phone. The driver said he couldn't turn around. So, we went all the way to the airport and then turned around. The chambermaid was waiting at the door with my phone, and we proceeded back to Heathrow. Fortunately, we had loads of time, but our taxi driver was not at all accommodating. Not only did the driver triple charge us (ten pounds to get to the airport, ten pounds to drive back to the hotel, and then another ten pounds to go back to the airport), but he kept complaining that he didn't have much time and had to get to his next customer. We paid it reluctantly and proceeded to go through security.

Stanley went through one lane and I went through another lane. I had a lot of little shampoos in my one-liter bag, but each one was less than ninety milliliters, all within the regulations. I was through the line and was waiting for Stanley. Recently, in many airports we had not been asked about liquids, so Stanley never bothered to take his out or put them in the one-liter plastic bag. On a previous occasion in Heathrow, when asked if he had liquids, he'd said that he didn't. Sure enough, he was pulled aside, and the agent very kindly took his liquids and put them in a plastic bag. Realizing that in Heathrow you don't try to slip through, Stan had his liquids in a proper plastic bag. However, this agent, a middle-aged woman, took him aside. She said that he had too many liquids and took them out and discarded them. Stanley said that perhaps his wife had room in her liquids bag. So I handed over my liquids bag. She proceeded to remove liquids from my bag that had already passed security. She said that the bag was too small. This was a plastic bag that had been issued by our airport in Ottawa, as was Stanley's. We argued a little, questioning how it could be that what one agent had passed was now considered unacceptable. She was in essence saying that. She was unmovable.

Having lost half our shampoos, we carried on. We were very annoyed and agitated to say the least. Interestingly, Heathrow had little red and green buttons you were asked to press as you left the security area in order to rate your experience in security. We pressed the red button several times. We continued on to the Air Canada lounge. The new terminal where Air Canada was now located was a very long walk away, and early on, I couldn't locate my passport and boarding pass. I went hysterical. The experience in security had totally unhinged me, and I was sure I had left it there.

We went back and asked if anyone had found it. No one had, and the manager was extremely rude, even mean. He said that if we didn't lower our voices he would call airport security. We were nervous. My knapsack was a black hole, and when I removed everything, sure enough my passport was buried under everything in it.

When we returned to Ottawa, I wrote customer relations at Heathrow. I did receive an e-mail back, saying that the agent had been totally inappropriate and that the e-mail writer would report the incident to the head of security. Nothing much happened after that, but at least we got an answer. The avoidance of Heathrow when traveling to Europe is a top priority when booking our flights.

Madeira (2015)

One of the funniest left behind stories was a bathing suit in Madeira, not left behind on purpose. We were staying at a beautiful hotel called Belmont Reid's Palace Hotel in Funchal in 2015. There were two swimming pools and a spa and many places in the resort where a bathing suit was what you would wear. Stanley went down to the sauna in the terry cloth robe provided by the hotel and his bathing suit. He put the bathing suit in a locker along with his robe and went to take a shower after his sauna. When he returned, he found his robe but no bathing suit. We immediately reported this to housekeeping, the pool, and the manager and assumed that the bathing suit would be found. After a few days, we left to go home with no bathing suit, a mystery for sure since the robe had remained in the locker, but the bathing suit had not. One day about a month later, a big, brown envelope appeared in our mail. The bathing suit had been found and was mailed all the way from Madeira to Ottawa—without getting lost. Quite a surprise!

In summary, although we seem to have developed a method for not getting robbed, the leaving stuff behind has continued to this day. The "losses" might not be life-altering—recent items have included my new nightgown on a road trip left in a motel room in Scranton, Pennsylvania, or extra batteries and a currency converter on our Viking river cruise in Russia—but they're left behind nevertheless. The most recently left behind item was Stan's cell phone on our last trip to Chile. We called our friend, a former Air Canada pilot, who called the pilot on our flight whom he knew well. No one in the lost and found department at Santiago Airport had found it. Sure enough, he found the phone, buried in the side of the seat. The pilot of that flight took our phone back to Toronto. Then our pilot friend flew to Toronto and brought it back to Stan. Wouldn't it be great if we could do that with all our left behind items?

We have developed a method for not forgetting anything before we travel. One of the worst items we forgot to bring on a trip was our driver's licenses, and so we couldn't rent a car. This was on our first trip to one of our favorite countries, Chile, where we have been five times. We managed with public transportation, but it's not our favorite way to travel. There is always a solution. However, now we have trip meetings, where we check items off from a travel checklist

I prepare in advance. People laugh when we say today we have a trip meeting after we answer that it's just the two of us. That's our tour group. It just came to me that where and when we need the checklist is when we leave a hotel room, to make sure we leave with what we came with.

Aside from the unpleasantness of dealing with airport and other security, we have had police encounters, both pleasant and unpleasant. One would think that the best way to deal with police in a foreign country when you don't speak the language is to pay the fine and go on your way. Not Stanley! He would use any argument he could to get out of a fine. Some are described in the following chapter.

CHAPTER 12

POLICE ENCOUNTERS

We have driven rental cars in many countries, and often we have been stopped by the police. Sometimes Stanley has talked his way out of tickets, claiming he did nothing wrong and being an ignorant tourist. This would be in response to what he thought was just being targeted as an easy way for corrupt police to get some money. It is very difficult to tell and maybe a little dangerous to decide whether or not to resist and whether or not to pay or even whether you've genuinely committed an offense, especially if you don't speak the language.

I remember one time in Malta a car was following us closely. We were forever getting lost between the two towns on the island and, in frustration, were driving slowly. Stanley gave the guy following very closely behind us the finger, and he turned out to be a cop. He stopped us of course, and Stanley convinced him that it didn't mean the same thing in Canada. We got away with it that time. Another time in Lisbon, Stanley stopped on a very busy street; it had multiple lanes with streetcar tracks. He ran into a store to get directions. There were signs everywhere saying not to stop, and a cop pulled up immediately and handed us a huge fine.

Stanley said, "This isn't the way we treat our tourists in Canada."

The cop accurately answered in perfect English, "Stanley, this ain't Canada!"

Motor trip to Mexico (1965)

One of our earliest trips driving to and in a foreign country was in 1965, when we drove to Mexico from Ann Arbor, Michigan. At the time, Stanley was a resident in surgery, and I was a graduate student in biological chemistry at the University of Michigan. Stanley got one month of vacation a year, and I could usually organize my courses and research to go along. On this trip, the month was January, and we decided to drive to Mexico. We were very young and foolish, but the trip proved to be full of great stories. The day we left, snow was forecast but I had never before and have never since been on a road trip in such terrible conditions. We were on the thruway, hoping to make it as far as possible south. But after about an hour, we couldn't even see the sides of the road and ended up in Dayton, Ohio. At this time, we were driving the car that, of all the cars we had, I loved the most—the Alfa Romeo Spider, hardly a car for winter driving. That car belonged on the Italian Riviera.

The next day, conditions improved. But at some point in Tennessee, something hit the fan blades, and one broke off. We were in the middle of nowhere, but the garage attendant knew to cut off another blade to make a symmetrical fan. We hobbled into Little Rock, Arkansas, and a fan was ordered, the closest dealer being in Wisconsin. The fan arrived in a day, and we were on our way.

The next great adventure was the border crossing. I can't remember why we chose this particular crossing into Mexico. However, the closest city was Brownsville, and we ended up at the Falcon Dam, crossing where there is a bridge over the Rio Grande. It is now (2017) known to be a very dangerous location, with rival drug cartels often having gun battles there. We arrived at the border, and at that time, Canadians needed visas to enter Mexico. We showed our visas, but the agent at the border said that those visas were not good at that border, our first introduction to corruption. We paid what he wanted and went on our way.

We drove through Cuernavaca on our way to Mexico City. I remember that we paid $2.50 for that room, and when we told the owners that the toilet was blocked, they handed us a plunger. It worked.

We continued from Mexico City to Acapulco, where we met our friend from Ann Arbor. He had been to Mexico many times he said and took us to his favorite restaurant. Although we were eating everything, I drew the line at Caesar salad, where they still were preparing the dressing with a raw egg. Bill got so sick that he said he had to count the steps from where he was to the nearest bathroom. He didn't recover for weeks after he was back in Ann Arbor.

I don't remember the road we were on, but it definitely had more than two lanes. Traffic was merging from all sides, and Stanley was honking his horn. He was pulled over by two police on motorcycles. At this point, our Spanish was less than nothing. But we made out eventually that Stanley was honking his horn twice, and only once was allowed. Now, talk about a phony violation!

In those days, the police wanted the equivalent of twenty-five dollars. Stanley absolutely refused, saying he was "estudiante Canadiensis" and that he would call the Canadian embassy. The police officers took his driver's license and told him to follow them to the station. We started to follow, and I was hysterical, imagining my young life and brilliant future wasted—in a Mexican jail forever.

After about five minutes, the officers stopped, and we stopped. They returned Stanley's license and said adios!

Shoplifting in Spain (1983)

Our first trip with our sons was to Spain in December 1983. For some reason, we decided to drive to New York and fly from there to Madrid. At this point in time, we were still checking luggage. Maybe we thought by taking a nonstop flight, we would avoid any lost baggage, but no way! My suitcase, and only mine, was lost. We went to Iberia the next day, and the airline gave me US$100 to go shopping. In the meantime, I was wearing some of the boys' clothes, like sweat pants. I wasn't totally upset about it, which, when I think about it now, amazes me. I went to El Corte Ingles and shopped. In those days, Spain was still so inexpensive. The country was not in the EU, and the currency was the peso. I bought a warm jacket, a sweater, and pants—all of which I wore for years after. I paid and proceeded down the escalator.

Stan and the boys were waiting for me at the bottom of the stairs, and I couldn't figure out why they had such crazy looks on their faces. I was being pursued by several plainclothes detectives who apprehended me for shoplifting. The sales clerk had forgotten to remove the security tag from the coat. I showed them my American express receipt, and they let me go. First, though, I had to return to have the tag removed.

Although there was security in the department stores, robbery was rampant among tourists. We met a couple who had had their car window smashed and everything taken. They were without clothes for three weeks. And as we drove along the highways, they were littered with clothes and suitcases left open.

We kept checking with Iberia for my bag, but no luck. What we saw in the lost and found in Madrid was amazing. There were hams, cheeses, and every kind of suitcase and bag. But not my bag!

We arrived home and, after all these trips together, very happy to be back in our home, in our separate rooms. Six weeks after we returned, we got a call from the airport. They had found my bag. We tried to decipher from the tags where it had been all this time. Aside from the last one, which was Mirabel Airport, which no longer exists, we couldn't tell how it had missed getting on the plane from New York to Madrid. We believe that there are two kinds of luggage—carry-on or lost!

Driving in Nicaragua (2007–2016)

Aside from the Nicaraguan drivers that obey no laws, the biggest hazard driving in Nicaragua is the police. On almost every trip over the ten years we traveled in Nicaragua, we were stopped by the police (See chapter 16, Surgical Missions). We either touched a line or passed when we shouldn't have passed. Or one time, supposedly, we had gone through a red light. But at the time we were stopped, we were miles away from any traffic light. Usually we had done nothing. Stanley always used his line about operating on Nicaraguan children, and once he'd showed his business card, the police officers would let us go. Sometimes it took a little more talking and actually showing the papers signed by Daniel Ortega and the ministerio de salud (Ministry of Health).

One interesting tip we learned from someone who also ran an NGO was to make photocopies of our driver's licenses. When police stopped you, they demanded your driver's license. You had to surrender it and go to the nearest town that had a bank and pay the fine. Then you had to drive back to where you were stopped and, hopefully, find the cops that had your license. I should add that, after making the photocopies, we never did have to give away our license. But one time when we were driving with Manuela on our way from Managua to our family in the villa, we were stopped by the police, and no argument worked. Manuela spoke to them in Spanish. We thought that wasn't a smart move. He took Stanley's driver's license, and we had to go to the bank in the next town, pay the fine, and then return to where we were stopped. There was a time deadline in order to find the police officer who had given us the ticket while he was still on duty. That would be the only way to get Stan's license back. We did make it back in time, and the officer was waiting at the spot of the so-called violation with Stanley's driver's license. This never happened again. Not speaking Spanish too well and saying you are a surgeon volunteering has always worked. These police officers are paid next to nothing, and the bribes they receive so that you don't have to pay the fine are a very good source of income.

The only time we actually bribed a police officer was when we had our granddaughter Hannah with us. We were on our way to the airport, and Stanley missed the entrance. He just went a short distance into the entrance directly before the one we wanted, which was for service vehicles. Immediately realizing this, he pulled out. A single policeman was right there, and this time I said to just pay! So five dollars on the clipboard that he handed to Stanley sufficed. We were on our way. A clue to when the bribe and not a fine will work is when a young police officer is alone. That other time, there was a large group of officers.

There was, maybe one time I recall that we weren't stopped. We had a very nice car, and the rental car agency label was not on the car. That seemed to help, but there was no sure way to avoid getting pulled over.

The contrast to Cuba was very interesting. One time we rented a car in Cuba (March 2013) and were on a thruway. There were four lanes and almost no traffic. Stan liked the outer lane because it looked less worn. A police officer stopped us and very politely pointed out that that lane was only for passing. No fine and no bribe!

Over the years, there were many other encounters. There were lots of parking tickets. On occasion, the rental company would just charge the credit card they had. Other times, we just kept receiving the bill. Most of the time, when it was clear that you were a tourist, the police were friendly and didn't impose the fine. Play the ignorant tourist. It usually works, and often, it is the truth.

One of the very few occasions that Stanley doesn't argue or joke is when we are crossing from one country to another. The immigration officer has total control over whether you get to where you want to go. It is best to be polite but, more important, submissive. There are some great border-crossing stories in the next chapter.

Chapter 13

BORDER CROSSINGS

Contemplating the news at this moment in history (2017) when Britain voted to leave the European Union and President Trump's ban on travel from seven countries in the Middle East is pending, I think back to the difficulties we have had over the years crossing borders. It still involves a variety of steps to cross the border between Canada and the United States. Fortunately, there are programs in place like Nexus and Global Entry that facilitate it. Recently, when we've traveled between countries in Europe, it has been such a pleasure to just drive from country to country and not have to stop for administrative details. In addition to border crossings, currency was different in each of these many countries prior to the EU, and there wouldn't always be a money exchange at the border. The bordering country wouldn't necessarily take the currency of its neighbor.

The vision of a united Europe started right after World War II, including such illustrious founding fathers as

Winston Churchill and Konrad Adenauer.[47] Gradually, economic agreements were made, and more countries joined so that, at this time, there are twenty-eight member countries, nineteen of which use the euro. By 1995, the Schengan Agreement allowed travel between all EU countries without checking passports.

Border crossing in Eastern Europe (1988) and (1990)

However, during our two trips to Eastern Europe in 1988 and 1990, border crossing was definitely a challenge. We took both of these motor trips with friends, starting in Vienna and driving through the countries that still were communist. At the time, we didn't realize that there were huge changes about to occur just before and just after the fall of the Berlin Wall. Our first crossing in 1988 was between Austria and Hungary, and it only took ten minutes. We went on our way to Budapest the next day, viewing the famous synagogue on Doheny Street that was under repair. Budapest was one of the last cities to lose its Jewish population, and many were saved as the Russians entered the city. Aside from two traffic violations at ten dollars each, we had no trouble crossing into Czechoslovakia.

The problems occurred with buying coupons for diesel fuel, which were only available at travel agencies. They were never open when we wanted them to be, so we decided to proceed into Poland. We had read in some guidebook that cigarettes were a great commodity to facilitate border crossing, but as we handed out cigarettes, we never noticed any effect.

---

[47] https://europa.eu/european-union/about-eu/history_en.

Although not exactly easy, we arrived at the Polish border at 3:30 and were on our way by 4:30, not bad. We spent a few days in Poland (see chapter 15, "Finding Our Roots") and then had to cross back into Czechoslovakia. We arrived at the border at 10:30 a.m., and it appeared that everyone was waiting for the border to open. However, we found out that there was a method involving processing the people in groups. It again took an hour. We had a very interesting time in Prague (see chapter 15, "Finding Our Roots") and had to account for our minimum spent when we arrived at the Austrian border and crossed after forty-five minutes. So, on this trip to four countries, we had to cross the borders five times and change currencies each time. Now, none of this would be necessary because all of these countries are in the EU, and two of them use the euro as their currency.

Our first border challenge was between Hungary and the former Yugoslavia (Serbia) on our way to Belgrade. At that time, it was just before all hell broke loose in that country. We found that people weren't helpful and seemed very unhappy. There were demonstrations all over, and when people found out we were from Canada, they always mentioned our separatist movement between Quebec and the rest of Canada, probably because all of these loosely held together ethnic groups were looking for a model system on which they could base their desire to become independent. There were huge lines at the border crossing. Stanley surveyed the scene and made a third line, and we got through to Belgrade in half an hour.

After a couple of nights in Belgrade, we decided to proceed to Sofia, and again, since it had worked so well on our way to Belgrade, Stanley made a third line. We drove right through to Bulgaria. After a few days in Sofia, where they were running out of fuel and food, we left and had no trouble crossing back into Yugoslavia and arrived in Sarajevo after a full day of driving, half of which was in the wrong direction.

The last border crossing was back into Austria. But now (2017) Hungary, Austria, Bulgaria, Slovenia, and Croatia are all members of the EU. Most of our border crossings would not exist now.

Israel and Jordan (1996)

On one of our trips to Israel (1996) we traveled to Jordan through the Allenby Bridge from Jerusalem.[48] It was early in the treaty with Jordan. This strategic bridge was destroyed and rebuilt many times. It is now the only way that Palestinians living in the West Bank can cross to Jordan in order to go to another country. They must travel through Amman's airport, as they cannot use Ben-Gurion Airport in Tel Aviv. The original bridge was built in 1885 during the Ottoman Empire, but at the end of World War I in 1918, it was reconstructed by the British general, Edmund Allenby. It was destroyed once by the Palmach in 1946. The Palmach was the elite striking force of the Hagana—the underground military organization of the Jewish community prior to the establishment of the State of Israel during the British Mandate of Palestine. It was destroyed again during the Six-Day War (1967), but was replaced in 1968 with a temporary truss-type bridge. This bridge is still called the Allenby

[48] http://www.iaa.gov.il/en-US/borders/alenbi/Pages/About.aspx.

Bridge by Israelis, although it is also known as Al-Karameh Bridge to Palestinian Arabs, and the King Hussein Bridge to Jordanians. In the late 1990s, and subsequent to the Israel-Jordan peace treaty in 1994, a new, modern, paved crossing was constructed adjacent to the older wooden one. However, it was that one lane, very rickety, wooden bridge that we crossed on our visit in 1996.

When we wanted to organize our trip from Jerusalem to Amman, a taxi ride was negotiated by our Israeli friend, which saved us forty shekels. We got four different prices from four calls to four taxi companies. We were picked up at 6:30 and arrived at the Allenby Bridge. Although it was only forty minutes from Jerusalem to where we were staying at our friend's home, the process of crossing the border was neither easy nor short. Although Heathrow Airport security personnel think they have the best security in the world, in my opinion and those of many others, it is the security in Israel that is probably the best, while still maintaining personal freedom for most if not all of its citizens. It involves a combination of intelligence gathering as well as physical surveillance. Before boarding a flight, you are always asked a series of questions that seem irrelevant. The only other place we experienced this was in Bogota. For example, we were asked, "Did you go to Cartagena?" "Where did you eat?" Our truthful answers were all that the border guard needed.

Certainly, the security at this crossing was very tough. The bridge opened at 8:00 a.m., and traffic had already piled up. First the workers at customs and immigration went through all the cars. They checked underneath with mirrors. Then an Arab taxi pulled up, and the Israeli guard told us to get in. He took us to the Israeli passport control.

Our bags were taken away and left outside. We then paid an exit tax and waited. While we waited, two soldiers walked around the room, continuously checking ashtrays and garbage pails. We then picked up our bags and got on a bus. We stopped and picked up a Jordanian border guard who took our passports. This was particularly unnerving. The guard got off the bus with them. We crossed the bridge, which was one lane and the water below, the Jordan River, was barely a trickle. We arrived at yet another building, which was Jordan customs and immigration. Two hours after we arrived at the first point, a guide carrying our names appeared, and we were off in his car.

We arrived at our hotel in Amman, the Hotel Forte Grand, and were greeted in the lobby by a very enthusiastic employee. He asked us, "Are you Jewish?"

Not ever wanting to lie about that but being very intimidated, we answered, "Yes."

He put up his hands and yelled, "Welcome to Jordan."

Unfortunately, borders between countries seem to be more and more desired, and walls are built instead of bridges.

Cyprus (2005)

In March 2005, we traveled to Cyprus. I had a colleague in the biomaterials world who was from the Turkish side, and he had made arrangements with his family to greet us once we got across from the Greek side. This border crossing had a lot of history. We flew from Ottawa to London and then onto Larnaca. We picked up our rental car at the airport and set out to find our hotel. We passed it a few times. I had the wrong name, Golden Bay, not Golden Tulip. The next day, we decided to set out for the mountains, and we found the ski hill. There were people in all kinds of outfits; it really wasn't that cold, but it was certainly cold enough to maintain the skiing.

We witnessed something at the base of the hill that we had not seen before nor have we seen again after. A gentleman lifted up his shirt, took out an IV bag of fluid, and proceeded to connect a tube coming out of his abdomen to it. He was carrying out peritoneal dialysis on the slopes of a ski hill in Cyprus. He was totally nonchalant about it, not at all anxious or even slightly embarrassed. A blizzard started shortly after, and although there was a group of Scotsmen in kilts walking bravely around, we decided to descend to the beach, where it was warm and sunny, and checked into a hotel on the beach. That's travel! You never know what education you might receive.

We started trying to call our friend's sister in Turkish Cyprus early the next day and couldn't get through. It seemed that they were answering but couldn't hear me. We had all kinds of clandestine theories, but it turned out that the phone needed charging. We decided to cross over anyway and set out for Lefkosa or Nicosia. We arrived at the Hilton Hotel, which is on the border, and went in to get instructions on how to cross. All the information we got there proved wrong.

The crossing at the Lydia Palace was only for pedestrians. We were told at the border that we had to go to Aros Demetrios, wherever that was. We started talking to two men who were also there, and somehow we trusted them to know where to go. They were from Jordan and said to follow them. We went through areas of the city that didn't seem to have any relevance to a border crossing, but eventually we did come to a crossing. The border was very crowded. We filled out a visa application and paid ten pounds for three-day insurance. We had to return by March 14; we were crossing on March 12. The border between Turkish and Greek Cyprus had only been open two years at this point.

The history of Cyprus is very long and very tumultuous, as is the case with most of the islands in the Mediterranean and the countries surrounding it.[49] As early as the tenth millennium (Stone Age) there was evidence of civilization, followed by a series of conquering nations (Greece, Assyria, Egypt, and Persia) until it became a province of the Roman Empire under Cleopatra's rule. The struggle between the Judeans and the Romans occurred in many places between 66 and 136 CE, including Cyprus, and in the Kitos War (115–117 CE) supposedly a small band of Jewish Cypriots massacred 240,000 Greeks. This revolt was defeated by a small Roman army, and from that day on, no Jews were permitted to live on the island.

Cyprus continued to have many more conquests. In 1192, Richard I of England conquered Cyprus, and there is a site we visited in Luminissol where supposedly he was married. The big turning point in Cypriot history, which is still felt today, was the invasion of Turkey (the Ottomans) with the fall of Nicosia in 1570 so that Cyprus became a part of the Ottoman Empire. This ended after World War I, and Cyprus eventually became a British colony in 1925. However, in 1974, the invasion of Turkey led to a divided Cyprus, which continues to this day (2017). Cyprus (Greek) is part of the EU, and the currency is the euro. The

---

[49] http://www.lonelyplanet.com/cyprus/history.

northern third of the island is Turkish and operates as a separate country recognized only by Turkey. The UN has had a peacekeeping force there since 1964 and monitors a buffer zone between the two regions. Britain also still has a military base there, protecting its interests. Since the border between the Greek and Turkish regions had only been open two years when we crossed, the tensions between the two were still very evident.

So after crossing into the Turkish side, we found a small shopping plaza and were able to get through to our friend's father. Our friend's sister, Feza, was in Istanbul that day, and so we checked into our hotel and explored on our own. We met many British tourists who had invested in villas in the Turkish sector, being much cheaper of course than Greek Cyprus or other Mediterranean locations. Many of these locations were left behind by Greek Cypriots, who fled south during the invasion by Turkey in 1974. It may be a risky investment if reunification ever occurs.

The next day, we finally connected with our friend's family and had a wonderful time. They were very excited to have us visit and picked us up and took us out for lunch, where we met other members of the family. They pointed out that there was a big distinction between the immigrants from Turkey and the resident Turkish Cypriots. The Turkish Cypriots are well educated and are more European than Asian. There is definitely a problem with the influx of immigrants from Turkey, who are poor, uneducated, and are Muslim and not Greek Orthodox. There are differences in their rights as well. We found out that Turkish Cypriots have citizen keys for the Republic of Cyprus and can cross the border for free health care in the south, which is denied to the Turkish immigrants.

We easily crossed back and continued on our exploration of Cyprus. We headed for Polis, looking for the Anassa Hotel (see chapter 4, "Where to Stay"). According to Stanley, it still is the most luxurious and beautifully located hotel we have stayed at. Definitely an island of contrasts!

Although our favorite way to travel is to wander on our own, over the years we have had guides who have been memorable. They deserved a chapter of their own, the next one.

Chapter 14

GUIDES

Although our favorite way of travel is just to wander, there are many places where guides are essential. Sometimes you need a guide for the entire trip, like on an African safari. Sometimes you need one just for a day or two, if part of a trip involves a place that requires a guide locally, as in Agra where the Taj Mahal is or in Marrakech for a tour of the market. Some are excellent, like our guide Clive in Tanzania and Rwanda or Joe in Zimbabwe (see chapter 9, "Encounters with Wildlife"). Another perfect guide was Roger Valencia in Peru, when we walked the Inca Trail (see chapter 7, "Accidents and Illnesses"). Our guide in Israel on our very first trip when our son was Bar Mitzvah there many years ago was also very special (see below). But one of the most remarkable stories was the life of our guide in Libya, and although it was difficult deciding what chapter to put this trip in since it was unique in so many ways, I decided to tell of the trip through his story. Probably the story of our guide's situation exemplified life in Libya in the time of

Gaddafi and maybe even today (2017) in Libya and other countries where there is no religious freedom. It is hard not to get involved with your guide's life, since on a trip, your guide is your lifeline. Guides can make or break a trip, and we have had our share of both. Many are described in this chapter.

Israel (1979)

No matter to whom you speak, it is always their Israeli guide who was the best. In Israel, the guides are especially well trained and knowledgeable, and there certainly is always lots to know, the political situation forever changing. The guides need to know about the history of Israel, in addition to all the religions that embrace Israel as their own. It isn't easy to know more than ten thousand years of history. The walls of Jericho, which we saw on one of our trips, are believed to have been constructed in 8000 BC, making them somewhere around that old.

So far, we have been to Israel four times—1979 for Brian's Bar Mitzvah, 1984 when Stanley led a United Jewish Appeal (UJA) fundraising mission, 1986 when our friend led a UJA mission, and 1996 for a friend's daughter's wedding. We had the same guide in 1984 and 1986. She was certainly excellent but, on occasion, excitable. Our bus driver took the wrong road she thought somewhere around Ramallah, and she felt we were in danger. Now it would be impossible to go to Ramallah without special permission or access with someone on the West Bank who could travel across the wall from Israel to the occupied West Bank. Certainly, Jericho is off limits. Due to the current political situation, so many of the sites that we have seen on our earlier trips are no longer accessible. So much has changed since our last trip.

I would have to pick Eli as the ultimate Israeli guide. Eli drove us around Israel in 1979. It was after the Yom Kippur War and was probably the largest geographic area that Israel occupied in modern times, maybe at any time. At this point, Israel included the Sinai Peninsula. This was before the treaty with Egypt, when it was given back. Eli had a Mercedes taxi that could seat all of us. Stanley, Brian, Daniel, our friend and his son, and I fit comfortably. He had a pistol in the glove compartment and was totally cool at all times. He was a typical (or what we think of as a typical) Sabra—tough on the outside and soft on the inside. He knew everything about everything and told it well. He not only knew what each site meant to Jews but also to Christians and Muslims. And when asked, for example, if this was really Rachel's tomb, he would say, "If a site is important to all three religions, then it must be true."

Before setting out on our tour of Israel with Eli, we had the unique experience of Brian's Bar Mitzvah at Yochanan Ben Zakkai synagogue in the old city of Jerusalem. It was very difficult to arrange. The principal of the boys' school (Hillel Academy at the time) helped us, and it did work out. The rabbi wanted us to sleep in his home the night before services, and we had a typical Shabbos (Sabbath) meal for Sephardim.[50] First course was a bright yellow fish head, the sauce being made with saffron. Needless to say, the boys didn't eat it. We managed to get down our meal. The challah was home baked and delicious. The Muslim call to prayers in the old city woke us up, and the rabbi wanted Brian to

[50] http://www.jewfaq.org/ashkseph.htm.

drink some scotch with a raw egg so that he would have a strong voice. The services were very short. Brian's chapter in the Torah reading for that Saturday included the Ten Commandments in Deuteronomy, and the rabbi said that someone else would recite that part. Aside from that, Brian did the whole thing. The women were behind an almost solid wood wall. We could barely see Brian. Afterward, we had lunch at the Jerusalem Plaza hotel with my parents, Stan's mother, and my aunt and uncle and some cousins. We were happy it was over and were ready to start our tour of Israel.

We covered Israel, from the Lebanese border in the north, the Syrian border in the east, the Egyptian border in the south, and everything in between, from top to bottom. One of our biggest surprises was the size of the Jordan River. The source that we saw was a group of babbling brooks that ran over some rocks in the nature preserve of Tell Dan. Years later (1996) we saw firsthand just how small that essential river is (see chapter 11, "Security"). However, one of the most interesting places on this trip was, in this case, the bottom, Sharm el Sheikh. We drove from Eilat through the Sinai Desert. It was definitely very warm in August, and we checked into our hotel and immediately hit the beach. It was interesting to see that the people on the beach were young northern Europeans who had come to deep-sea dive in the Red Sea. What an incredible underwater view of the fish and corals. It was possible to simply walk out into the sea and look down and see the most exquisite varieties. Our sons, then ten and thirteen loved the view on the beach, with nude women sunbathing, just as much.

It is quite amazing that this very small country continues to occupy the news almost daily (2017). We want to visit Israel again, always identifying this unique place in the world as partly our home. When in Jerusalem, I always had the feeling of immortality, as though the thousands of years of history of this city have made time stand still.

Zimbabwe (2004)

On our trip to Africa in 2004, we visited five countries (South Africa, Zimbabwe, Zambia, Namibia, and Botswana) and each one had its own special story, most worth retelling. The story in Namibia was on the Chobe River (see chapter 9, "Encounters with Wildlife"). In South Africa, it was meeting the Jewish community in Plettenberg Bay (see chapter 15, "Finding Our Roots"). In Zimbabwe, we camped and walked with Joe, an amazing South African who continued to live the life of adventure protecting the animals in the national parks that were constantly under threat from poachers. Zimbabwe, formerly Rhodesia, was a British colony but declared independence in 1965.[51] There were years of turmoil until Mugabe became president in 1980, when the minority white rule was overturned. However, under Mugabe's authoritarian regime, there was economic ruin and widespread human rights violations. The white population now is less than 2 percent.

We flew from Johannesburg to Victoria Falls and were picked up by Joe and his crew. There was one other member of our group, but he wanted to train as a guide, so he was

---

[51] Zimbabwe history, http://www.bbc.com/news/world-africa-14113618.

hardly another tourist. It was a long drive to our first camping spot in Hwange National Park. We were able to walk into our tents and had a double bed inside. Our bathroom facilities were a latrine and a portable shower—a bag with warmish water. We had a large crew who prepared our food, set up and took down our tent, and did our laundry. Our routine was to be awakened very early, at dawn about 5:00 a.m., have a very light breakfast, and drive to an area where we parked. We then walked for two to three hours tracking the animals. Our tracker, Albert, was amazing. He was tracking a rhino mother and her baby. He picked up their tracks, could tell exactly where they had eaten and where they had left their dung and urine. He sighted them, but just then the wind changed, and they ran away. I missed seeing them. After this morning walk, we drove back to the camp for lunch, had a rest during the heat of the day, and then set out for another drive/walk in the late afternoon. This was more or less our routine for a week. We saw all kinds of wildlife, were charged by an elephant, followed lions killing a buffalo that was pregnant, and watched them eat the buffalo and her unborn baby completely. It was an amazing experience. We also were fed very well, with great food and unlimited Diet Cokes. The tally was seventy-two Diet Cokes during our camping week.

Even more amazing was our guide, Joe's, story. Although he had many problems with the Zimbabwean government, he continued to live there and protect the wildlife. On one of our walks, we came across an elephant carcass. It was one that was shot by Joe because it had charged him. However, he also had shot a poacher. He was telling us this story just as our tracker knew that two poachers were just ahead of us. He said that one was wearing car tires for shoes, and the other was barefoot. Most of them were local, and they killed the animals for their meat. They usually hunted with spears and snares, but in the case of the poacher Joe had shot, he had a gun and wouldn't lower it. It seems it was perfectly all right to kill poachers—true in other African countries as well.

Joe was full of stories. My favorite was the one about a tourist who wouldn't listen to him. It seems that whenever the laundry was done, it was necessary to iron it immediately in order to kill the larvae of the putzi fly.[52] Damp clothing hanging to dry makes for a perfect spot for the putzi fly to lay its eggs. The larvae hatch in two to three days, and as soon as one sweats while wearing the garment, the maggot buries itself in the person's skin, creating terrible cyst-like boils that contain the maggot inside, making it necessary to remove each maggot individually from each cyst. It seems that one woman tourist wanted to wash her underwear herself. She felt awkward having the Africans wash it and didn't listen to the warning. She didn't iron her clothes and, sure enough, got at least twelve horrible boils that were clearly visible. Hopefully there weren't too many more where you couldn't see them.

One of our day trips when we were in Victoria Falls was a canoe trip on the Zambesi River. Two guides arrived in a truck at 7:30 a.m., and we set out for our entry point through the back entrance of Zambesi National Park. We started with a breakfast served on the shore of the river and

[52] Putzi fly, http://www.dailymail.co.uk/health/article-2377761/Woman-28-squeezes-infected-insect-bite-stomach-discovers-infested-14-FLESH-EATING-MAGGOTS-visiting-Africa.html.

then set out. I was a little concerned when I saw the canoes. They were sort of rubber zodiacs, and they had a double paddle for each canoe. I thought, *Perfect, one guide for each canoe.* But then they set off together in one canoe and put us alone in the other one. There were rapids, and at the first set of rapids, Stan and I did a full 360-degree turn. I almost lost it.

Even more frightening were the hippos. Our guides were very afraid of them, which didn't inspire much confidence in us. There were hippos everywhere, and most of the time, they just looked like rocks. We knew the answer to the question "What is the most dangerous animal in Africa?" It's the hippo—extremely territorial, and how could they know I certainly didn't want their territory?

After a while we got the hang of the rapids and stopped for lunch on the Zambian side of the Zambezi River, which divides Zambia from Zimbabwe. The view of the animals from the water provided a very different perspective for the hippos and crocodiles all along our route, and we could relax a little and enjoy them. After lunch, we switched canoes. This time, we each got a guide. It was a good thing because we were very tired, and even though the area of the river we were traveling on was calm and flat, it seemed to take forever to get back to the truck that was picking us up. Stanley kept asking, "Where's the truck?"

We were exhausted by the time we arrived at the pickup point, but we were happy that we had done it and survived.

The next day, we had Christmas dinner with Joe. There was an eclectic group of tourists, expats, friends, and family, and we certainly had a great time meeting all these very different and interesting people.

Stanley continued his adventure the day after Christmas, white water rafting on the Zambezi after Victoria Falls. I decided I needed a day at leisure and worried about Stanley all day. The ride was extremely rough, and often one or more people were thrown out of the raft, where they were recovered by kayakers who picked them up.

Although we had already seen Iguacu and Niagara Falls, Victoria Falls is called the largest waterfall in the world. Viewing these falls was overwhelming and certainly defied description. Although, they are not the widest waterfall or the highest, when all dimensions are taken into account, including the flow rate, they are considered to be the biggest curtain of falling water in the world, surpassing Niagara and Iguacu Falls. Seeing them was definitely one of the highlights of this trip, which had so many unforgettable moments.

Libya (2006)

The decision to go to Libya was Stanley's, and again if I was asked why, I really couldn't answer. In order to go to Libya, you had to book with a Libyan travel agency. Stanley started to e-mail travel agencies and found one who said that his relative was coming to work in the embassy in Ottawa. So, Stanley went to the Libyan embassy and met with our travel agent's relative. He turned out to be a very friendly man, Ahmed. He was a Berber. This nomadic tribe still exists, and many still live as they did centuries ago. The Berbers were not considered true Libyans by Gaddafi and never rose to the top levels in his government.[53] Ahmed had a daughter, Salma, who was a physician trying very hard to enter the Canadian medical system. Stanley became very good friends with them, and we invited a group of men from the embassy, as well as Ahmed and his family, to our home for dinner. We danced around the religion issue from the very beginning. The steak we served we said was Halal from a different direction, and Ahmed laughed. He wasn't terribly religious as far as we could tell. His English was pretty good; Salma's not bad but improving. So we managed to communicate.

We helped his family get settled in Ottawa. We gave them lots of furniture that we no longer needed. Over the years, we continued to keep in touch with Salma. She completed her training as a physician and got married. Recently, we met Salma and her husband, her baby daughter, her parents, and her brother, who were all living together in the city where she now was practicing medicine as a recently naturalized Canadian citizen. It took ten years from when she first arrived in Canada. A wonderful immigrant success story!

On arrival, we were met by our guide (Ali) and a driver (his cousin) for the entire trip. Our hotel in Tripoli was adequate, and our first dinner very good. We set out to Sobrata, Roman ruins that rivaled anything we had seen in Europe, except maybe Rome itself. The Italians occupied Libya for many years in the twentieth century, having conquered it from the Ottoman Empire in 1911 and held it until World War II, when the Allies defeated Italy.[54]

---

[53] Demographics of Libya, https://en.wikipedia.org/wiki/Demographics_of_Libya.

[54] Italian colonization of Libya, https://en.wikipedia.org/wiki/Italian_colonization_of_Libya.

During that period, extensive excavations took place, but about 75 percent still remain buried. It is hard to know now what the state of these magnificent ancient structures is. Hopefully, a good amount remains and will eventually be restored.[55] Even at that time, there were almost no tourists, which made the ruins all the more interesting. Travel from North America was at a virtual standstill, although some still occurred from Europe. Cruises still stopped to tour but never stayed overnight. This was the way throughout our trip. During our first two days, we may have seen a total of a dozen tourists. The interesting events that continued throughout the trip made this trip exceptional.

At our choice of a restaurant for dinner the first night, an amazing coincidence occurred. We drove from our hotel, near Green Square, the center of Tripoli, through an upscale area. At the time, the Libyan flag was green, all green. There were no distinguishing letters, insignia, or drawings of any kind; it was the only flag in the world that was a solid color. It had to do with Gaddafi's *Green Book*, his interpretation of the color of Islam. We arrived at an Italian restaurant, where the Canadian ambassador was entertaining the "wardens." These were a series of volunteers who monitored events in different areas where Canadians lived for a variety of reasons, most being the oil industry. They reported on any unrest or threats of violence and/or demonstrations. We listened to the ambassador's speech for a while, and then he asked what we were doing there. When we said we were tourists, the entire crowd stood up and cheered. We were asked to join the dinner as guests of the Canadian government. Even at

---

[55] Berbers, http://www.aljazeera.com/news/middleeast/2014/12/libya-berbers-fear-ethnic-conflict-2014123065353199495.html.

that time, Canada considered Libya a hardship posting. So a posting extended only two years. Most company employees worked for six weeks and were off for four. There were no movies, no nightclubs, and no English anywhere. There were no alcoholic beverages available either, but people made their own beer and wine. Internet was available here and there, but all were dial-up. Land phones hardly worked.

The next day, we headed to Leptis Magna, a Roman city about a hundred kilometers from Tripoli and one of the most spectacular sites in the Mediterranean, even more impressive than Sobrata. The size of Leptis was overwhelming—it was maybe even larger than Ephesus in Turkey—but garbage everywhere detracted from its beauty. The restoration, only 25 percent complete, ended in 1974. Even at the time of our trip, it was in bad repair, but since 2011 and the civil war its existence is in danger. However, when I Googled Leptis Magna recently (2016), I found out that a group of vigilantes have banded together to protect it from ISIS.[56]

We drove back to Tripoli, and the experience of a lifetime was dinner at Ali's home that night. Our guide, Ali, was a university graduate and spoke English very well. He said that he was not an Arab but also a Berber like Ahmed. He smoked and was afraid that someone would see him and report him to his mother. Smoking was considered a sin. She was an extremely religious woman who taught religion and during the evening never appeared because men were

[56] ISIS in Libya: The New Centurions Protecting the Ruins of Leptis Magna from Militants Cultural Jihad," http://www.independent.co.uk/news/world/africa/isis-in-libya-the-new-centurions-protecting-the-ruins-of-leptis-magna-from-militants-cultural-jihad-10298153.html.

present. I went back to say hello with one of the women whom Ali had asked to join us. We sat on the floor, and food was delivered by Ali and his brothers. Everyone ate with his or her hands, but they did give us spoons. His father was in a wheelchair and was wheeled out to say hello.

Ali invited his friends who were teachers. The school used to be run by the oil companies, but the Libyan government took it over. We started to hear stories about human rights. One story they told was about a girl who wouldn't get up to give her brother tea in the middle of the night. He stabbed her, and she died, but the story was that she fell on glass. Another story was that if a girl was violated sexually, she was locked in her room with only a slit in a cement wall to see out.

We continued to talk to the teachers and found out their connection to Ali. They had taught him English, but more importantly, they had converted him to Christianity. It meant execution if he was discovered. He told us he had a terrible secret. He was Christian, and we told him our secret was that we were Jewish. He had studied for his conversion in Egypt and the Sudan but was baptized in the Mediterranean off the coast of Libya. The teachers employed by the oil companies were missionaries as well and carried out the conversions at the risk of death for their converts. We got an e-mail from Ali when we returned to Canada saying that his mother had found a Bible in his luggage and had had her brother who was a policeman beat him up.

We continued with our tour. Whenever we were on the road, Ali had to stop frequently to show our documents. It was both annoying and frightening.

The next part of our trip was a flight from Tripoli to Benghazi, a hotbed of resistance to Gaddafi and what still seems to be in the news all the time was the attack on the American Embassy, where the ambassador was killed. It was and is hard to know where the attackers' loyalties lay and whether the danger was adequately warned. At the time that we traveled there, it was clear that this was a very different part of Libya. There was a very large hospital, which was totally empty. Gaddafi was not popular here, and the population was predominantly Berber, not Arab.

The flight from Tripoli to Benghazi was an interesting experience. There were assigned seats, but when we boarded, barely able to fit our carry-on bags in the overhead compartments, we found someone in our seats.

No problem, he said, "There are other seats. We all arrive at the same time."

So on arrival we picked up a new driver but continued with Ali as our guide. We proceeded to drive east, the main objective being the cemeteries in Tobruk, although there were other Greek and Roman ruins on the way that were amazing sites as well. We stayed overnight in Appolonia and were supposed to get to Tobruk and back to Appolonia in one day. However, there were things to see along the way, and the traffic was bad.

One of the amazing highlights was the Greek city of Cyrene, dating back to 600 BC, after which the Romans took it over. This city, set in the beautiful Green Mountains, was restored during the Italian occupation from 1911 to 1941. It was another incredible site that, in my estimation, rivaled Agrigento in Sicily and is probably in jeopardy of survival at this time in 2017.

Next, we stopped in Derna and went into a hospital there that was not in very good shape, although there were rooms filled with great equipment that wasn't being used. We found out why none of the Libyan residents in the Ottawa Hospital ever showed up to our dinner with the embassy staff. They didn't want to return, even though the Libyan government was paying big bucks to the Ottawa Hospital for their training. We spoke to a doctor from Jordan who is paid $4,000 a month. However, the Libyan doctors are only paid $250 a month. Crazy like so much else in this country! The wealthy go to Egypt for medical treatment, and the very wealthy go to Italy.

When we were at the cemeteries in Tobruk, our guide said that minefields from World War II still exist outside the cemeteries, and just a few days earlier, a woman had been injured by a landmine. Sure enough, the young doctor took us on a tour of the hospital there, and in ICU was the poor woman whose face had been blown up, her vision lost. The public hospital in Tobruk, surprisingly, was very well equipped and very clean.

The cemeteries in Tobruk were in the most amazing pristine condition and beautifully landscaped. There were signs there, which said that if you saw any damage, you were to report it to the British War Commission that maintained the graves. There were many Jewish young men buried there, and if there were two or more men shot down together, their tombstones were attached. We went around to all the Jewish graves and put stones on the tombstones. It was so tragic that these very young Jewish men were buried where most, if not all, of their families could not visit.

With the current situation in Libya following the death of Gaddafi, there has been news that some of the graves near Benghazi were vandalized. The tombstones were pushed over and crushed with sledgehammers. Currently, there are two Libyan governments, one in Tripoli and one in Tobruk, with a third unity government trying to unite the two. None really has the power to govern.[57] There is limited control over the many Islamist extremist groups, and it is unclear what the security at all these sites will be able to do.

So, after touring the hospital in Tobruk and having dinner, it was clear that we would have to stay over in Tobruk, although originally, I believe that the plan had been to return to Appolonia. The one hotel there was about to undergo renovations, and its condition was questionable to say the least. It is hard to say whether this may have been the worst accommodation we have stayed in. Although Algeria may have been worse, there were no bed bugs there. The room looked nicer than many other accommodations we have had, but fighting off bugs all night was not fun. The next day when we examined our arms and legs, it was clear that we had been bitten, Stanley a lot worse than me.

The next morning, we set out for Sousa, retracing our steps. We went to see a beautiful waterfall in the Green Mountains, but there was garbage everywhere—not just pieces here and there, but piles of garbage like you would find in a dump. It was hard to understand the lack of pride in one's country. But when I thought about it more, I determined that maybe it was not. When people are living under terrible conditions, when they feel that the

---

[57] https://www.pri.org/stories/2016-03-31/libya-now-has-three-governments-none-which-can-actually-govern.

government doesn't care at all for its citizens, then nobody cares about anything but survival.

That evening, we were invited to dinner at a good friend of someone else we knew at the embassy. I ate with the fourteen-year-old daughter of the host, in his mother's home. There were many other family members. His mother had thirty-five grandchildren. Sarah, my hostess, was one of eight. She was quite amazing and, after only one year of high school, spoke perfect English. I wonder what has happened to her. Her father had wanted to send her to Canada to study, but she never did arrive. Interestingly, none of the women were covered, probably because they weren't going to see any of the men.

After dinner, we drove back to the hotel in Appolonia to fly out the next day to Tripoli. Before that, our host was there with his friend who had a bad hand infection. Stanley gave him our antibiotics and some Advil. We certainly wondered about health care, but we were going to get another picture soon after.

First, however, we had a very long drive to Ghadames, about five hundred kilometers from Tripoli.[58] This area was Berber country, and Gaddafi wanted to eliminate Berber culture and language. There was an old city that dated back to the fourth millennium BC. But, in 1982, Gaddafi forced the inhabitants to leave it and move to a badly constructed new city. The Berber language was banned, and although our local guide in Ghadames denied this, it had become clear to us that the Berbers were second-class citizens.

---

[58] Ghadames, https://www.temehu.com/Cities_sites/Ghadames.htm.

On our way back, we stopped in our guide's hometown and had lunch at our driver's home. His sister made a fabulous meal—as usual much too much food—while his mother was out in the fields gathering olives that had fallen from the trees. Our guide lit up a cigarette but was terrified that, in his hometown, someone would tell his mother. Sure enough, as soon as he lit up, someone he knew appeared.

Our next stop was at Ahmed's hometown. After asking anyone we met where his family home was, we located it; there were no road signs of course. We had tea and then continued on our way, already twelve hours on the road. The drive back to Tripoli seemed to go on forever.

We reached Tripoli in the dark and set out to find Ahmed's brother, in order to bring him greetings from Ahmed. Ali kept asking where Ahmed's brother lived, and eventually we parked the car. We saw a man walking down the muddy street, in the dark, and asked him if he knew where Ahmed's brother lived. He said that he was Ahmed's brother and that Ahmed was in his house down the street. We said, "You don't understand. We're bringing greetings from Ahmed. He's in Ottawa."

We finally reached the family home, and sure enough, Ahmed was there. He had decided the last minute to surprise us and show us around his Tripoli. It was already very late, and so we arranged to meet for dinner the following night.

During the day, we were picked up for a tour at a big public hospital for the most part, which also had 170 plastic surgery beds. We had a royal tour of the facilities with loads of modern equipment, which seemed to be in use. Things looked great until we gowned and went into the ORs. One doctor went from one room to the other and didn't scrub—in other words, didn't remove his gloves from one case to the next. Nobody wore their masks over their noses for some reason. At one point, they removed their masks to talk and laugh. We also visited a private clinic. Patients pay to go there, and there is a split of sixty/forty as in the clinics here in Ottawa, except it was sixty for the clinic and forty for the doctors.

Our next few hours before lunch with Ahmed, Ali took us to the former synagogue, which was in ruins, chickens nesting, in the oren kodesh (the area where Torahs would have been stored). He repeated that he would be in serious trouble if his mother knew he was here. We met Ahmed for lunch. We walked through the old city back to our hotel because he wanted to show us where he grew up. We were exhausted at this point but were able to have a short rest before the final evening in Tripoli, and what an evening.

Ali picked us up, and we went back to the "fancy" area of Tripoli, where we had eaten with the Canadian ambassador on our first night. When we arrived at the restaurant, there were loads of people, photographers, and flowers everywhere, and we were asked to cut a ribbon opening the new restaurant. There were people there from the tourism industry, many women with no head covering. And halfway through the dinner, they called me up to cut a huge cake. I officially opened the restaurant!

Our last day in Tripoli, we continued sightseeing with Ali. We went to the antiquities museum but then, more interesting for us, the site of a former Jewish school. This was used as archives of material for PhD students from what we could understand from the guide explaining what we were seeing. There were a few tombstones and our guide described the artifacts we were looking at being from a people who no longer existed. There had been a very large Jewish population from early Greek times. During the Italian occupation from 1911 until 1931 there were approximately twenty-one thousand Jews, 4 percent of the population. In the '30s and during World War II, conditions deteriorated for Jews, and many left for Israel after the state was founded in 1948. The few that remained were de facto expelled by Gaddafi when he took power in 1969, but the last Jew left in 2003.

We made it to the airport with Ahmed, who expedited our exit. We boarded our Emirates Airlines flight to Dubai. When we landed, it appeared that we had entered not just a different planet, but a different universe.

The situation in Libya is something that exists in so many places. Jews were there, but are there no longer. It was not only interesting from our perspective being Jewish, but also from a historical perspective—how, from time to time, the ethnic populations for a variety of reasons are discriminated against and often eliminated. The next chapter describes how this has been perpetrated, specifically on the Jewish population, in many locations.

Chapter 15

FINDING OUR ROOTS AND THERE ARE OR WERE JEWS EVERYWHERE

Jewish Sites in Europe

While on many of our European trips, I thought so often of the undeniable fact that both Stanley and I would not be here today if our grandparents had not immigrated to North America when they did, at the beginning of the twentieth century, prior to both world wars. This certainly was concretized in the two trips to our grandparents' birthplaces when we visited memorials to the Jews who were massacred there. However, it was certainly evident in so many other places we have traveled to over the years.

There were trips to see the concentration camps, where the Holocaust took place. We have visited several concentration camps—Auschwitz-Birkenau (Poland), Theresienstadt (Czechoslovakia), and Natzweiler-Struthof (France). When in Berlin, we went to the Villa Wannsee, where the Final Solution was orchestrated. I remember wondering how such evil could be discussed in such a beautiful place. It is always very difficult, if not impossible, to understand how and why this systematic attempt at elimination of Jews was perpetrated, but I always come back to the question of our survival.

In spite of World War II, there are still many Jews all over Europe, although greatly diminished in numbers. Whenever we travel on other continents, we also look for Jews or the possibility that Jews were once there. In addition to where we came from, this chapter will describe some of the more interesting locations we found on our trips where you might never expect to find Jews.

Prague-Theresienstadt (1988)

One of the most memorable Jewish sites was in Prague. We were there in 1986 on a UJA mission and again in 1988 with our friends. Czechoslovakia was still Communist during those years, and so negotiating our way around was always a challenge, especially when it came to money exchanges (see chapter 5, "Currency Conversion and Money Transactions"). On both trips, we visited the Alt Neue Shool, a thirteenth-century synagogue still in use with the few members of the Jewish community still there at that time. There was an old cemetery near the Jewish museum where we could see the graves of scholars from the fifteenth and sixteenth centuries. The museum had a collection of the art of the children in Terezin, all of whom died. Our tour of the concentration camp, Terezin, was overwhelming. Terezinstadt was a fortress built by the son of the empress Maria Theresa and named in her honor in 1780. It never served its original purpose and became a prison for political prisoners. However, during the German occupation in World War II it was a combination ghetto and concentration camp. Many of European's elite Jews were sent there. One famous woman who died there was Sigmund Freud's sister.

There was an organized Jewish council and a rich cultural life. Music and art flourished there somehow. With great preparation of fake shops, homes, and schools, late in the war, after D-Day and the invasion of Normandy, the Nazis permitted representatives from the Danish Red Cross and the International Red Cross to visit Theresienstadt in order to dispel rumors about the extermination camps. Somehow, they managed to fool the Red Cross representatives into thinking this was a model city designed to protect Jews. Bottom line, 144,000 were imprisoned there, and only 17,000 survived.

We visited in May and as we watched a film about the liberation of the camp, lilacs flashed on the screen. I realized it was at this very moment in time in 1945 that Terezin was liberated. Another historical fact recounted by our guide was that the first execution in the small fortress occurred on January 10, 1942. I was born on January 8, 1942. I was thoroughly shaken by the experience of this visit.

Auschwitz-Birkenau (1988)

The trip to Auschwitz was with our friends in 1988. We had started our trip in Vienna and then drove to Budapest. We drove through Czechoslovakia and arrived very late in Crakow, Poland, and had a terrible time finding Hotel

Francuska, which ended up being closed. We did find a hotel, the Krakovia, and booked in with great difficulty. The clerks emphasized that the entire town was booked and we were lucky to find rooms. The next day did make up for it. We set out in a taxi to the old Jewish quarter and by chance met a group, two couples from Montreal. The former president of the Shaar Hashomayim synagogue in Montreal, where my parents were members and where we were married, was with two others and a guide from Warsaw. They were walking around to find where he used to live. It was his first trip back since he left as a young man. We were with him when he found his home, his high school, and the restaurant that didn't allow Jews. They invited us to join them, and we continued on to the Jewish museum, the Jagellonian University, and the old market square.

The next day in our trip to Krakow, we set out for Auschwitz-Birkenau, which is about sixty kilometers away. Auschwitz began as one of the labor camps set up by the Germans as they systematically occupied countries. Auschwitz, until 1942, consisted of mostly Polish prisoners, and it was only in the final years that Auschwitz became the execution camp for the Jews. The final death toll was more than 1.1 million. Birkenau was a few kilometers away and was the site of the gas chambers and crematoria. We walked around both of these camps and the scale of them boggled the mind. The barracks were solid brick structures in Auschwitz, more wooden barracks in Birkenau. In the museum, piles of shoes; glasses; and, the most horrible, a room full of hair, were exhibited behind display windows. The film shown in the museum at that time concentrated on the Red Army's liberation and the fact that there were many other prisoners besides Jews. It is clear from the website now that, in 1942, these two camps became death camps for all the Jews of Europe. Now for everyone, as well as for Jews all over the world, Auschwitz has become a symbol of terror, genocide, and the Holocaust.

There has been a renaissance of the Jewish community in Krakow, and my cousin participated in a Ride for the Living in 2016, a ninety-kilometer bicycle trip from Krakow to Auschwitz. This annual bike ride raises money for the Jewish Community Center there. The event in that year started with a tour of the concentration camp with an eighty-year-old Auschwitz survivor while he told the group his story on the train platform overlooking the barracks that served as his "home" at the age of ten. Another event highlighted the seven Krakow synagogues that survived World War II and were opened to the public with exhibits so that thousands of Polish citizens could learn about Judaism.

Romania (2013) and Latvia and Lithuania (2014)

We went on two trips to the cities where our grandparents were born. Stanley's father's parents were born in Tecuci, Romania, and my father's parents were born in Daugavpils, Latvia. Both of our mothers' parents were born in Ukraine, near Kiev, but we have yet to make that trip. Our trips to the cities where our paternal grandparents were born were amazing from both a personal and historical point of view.

In October 2013, we traveled to Romania where Stanley's father's parents were born. We flew to Bucharest on Tarom Airlines and took the bus from the airport, which just happened to stop right outside the Intercontinental Hotel where we were staying. It was a lucky break in this case, when of course I argued about taking a taxi rather than the bus. Our usual plan on a trip such as this was to have hotel reservations in advance for the first two nights and then either drive to find hotels for the remainder of our stay or drive to our next stop. We wandered around Bucharest, found the Jewish Holocaust Memorial, which was closed for renovations. We walked in Carol Park, and the old city, which was filled with restaurants with loads of people sitting around drinking on this beautiful, sunny day. On the third day, we picked up our rental car and got excellent instructions from the car mechanic and a great map from the Avis desk hostess; the Avis station happened to be right at the hotel where we staying. We had no problem finding our way to Tecuci, the town where we knew Stanley's grandparents were born.

We checked in to the Matrix Club Hotel, adequate but with a bar with everyone smoking. There was smoking everywhere, and only a few places had a nonsmoking area in their restaurants. This was only in the better restaurants in Bucharest and Sibiu but certainly not in the small town of Tecuci. We have met many Romanians who have immigrated to Canada over the years, but none have been to that small town. There was almost no English spoken at the hotel, but somehow the manager knew enough to call the owner, who did speak perfect English and was in London at the time. After speaking to the owner, she explained to the manager that we wanted to go to the Jewish cemetery and which taxi driver to call to take us there. He of course spoke no English.

We arrived at the Jewish cemetery that had recently been restored (2001), but it was locked, and the woman who had the key was not home. A woman in the neighboring farm came over, and our driver got a ladder from her. We proceeded to climb up the ladder and over a cement wall. First we had to sit on top while the ladder was lowered to the other side. I was sure I was going to kill myself, but I thanked my fitness classes for helping my flexibility. There were dogs in the cemetery, but they were tied up and we could walk among the tombstones. We did see one that looked like Lachsman, Stan's father's mother's maiden name (Lackman). That tombstone was dated 1901. That was probably a few years before Stan's grandmother came to Canada and may have been a relative, but it was more just seeing where our ancestors lived that was the objective of this visit. We didn't have enough information to go back that many generations and find exactly where they may have lived. Stanley's grandparents came to Canada more than a hundred years ago.

Roz climbing into the Jewish cemetery in Tecuci, Romania, October 2013

After one night in Tecuci (more than enough) we set out for Sibiu, a long drive through many cities with difficult traffic. When we were on the outskirts of Brasov, there was so much construction that we couldn't figure out how to get through. Luckily at a roundabout there were policemen, one of whom spoke some English. He actually drew us a map, and we made it out of there. Sibiu was a charming town and heavily booked, but as usual, even without reservations, we managed to find a very nice room. We went to what was supposed to be a lovely restaurant, and it was empty. When we asked why, the waitress said to come and look. Everyone was jammed into a room where everyone was smoking. We were in the nonsmoking room. Sibiu was named the eighth most idyllic city to live in in Europe and is in Transylvania.[59] That area is supposed to be the home of Dracula, the fictional vampire character. There is a supposed connection between the Transylvania-born Vlad III Dracula and the fictional Dracula. During his reign (1456–1462), "Vlad the Impaler" is said to have killed from forty thousand to a hundred thousand European civilians, mainly by impaling them on long wooden stakes. However, he is revered as a folk hero by Romanians for driving off the invading Ottoman Turks; from this group, his impaled victims are said to have included as many as a hundred thousand.[60]

We returned to Bucharest without much difficulty and set out the next day to visit the Jewish museum. A woman there gave us a quick summary of the Jews in Romania. At the beginning of World War II, there were eight hundred

---

[59] http://www.thelandofdracula.com/158/draculas-legacy-tour-sibiu.

[60] https://en.wikipedia.org/wiki/Vlad_the_Impaler.

thousand. After the war, there were still five hundred thousand. However, this was not because Antonescu, the president at the time, wanted to save the Jews. He waged a war against the Jews that was as brutal as Hitler's.[61] The murder of three hundred thousand Jews was only second to the number annihilated in Germany. But because Hitler wanted Romania to fight against Russia and also for the vast oil fields Antonescu had control of, he left him to his own devices. In 1942, Antonescu changed his policy toward the Jews in order to preserve his economic position for bargaining power in a peace conference at the end of the war. He was convinced that Hitler would lose, even at this early time. So Antonescu began to moderate his Jewish policies; the program of extermination that had been perpetrated by the Romanian Army in Bessarabia, Northern Bukovina, and Transnistria throughout the summer and fall of 1941 was not extended to the rest of Romania's Jewish population. Today there are only eight thousand, four thousand in Bucharest. Most immigrated to Israel during the years following the war and during the repressive regime of Ceausescu. Romania is still recovering from years of one of the most repressive and brutal regimes in the Soviet bloc. Nicolae Ceaușescu was the president from 1965 to 1989 and was removed from office by revolution, the only one in the collapse of the USSR. He and his wife tried to escape but were caught, tried, and executed. However, a synagogue still exists, and we were able to see the list of many Leibovicis

[61] Christopher J. Kshyk, "The Holocaust in Romania: The Extermination and Protection of the Jews under Antonescu's Regime," *Inquiries* 6 (12), 2014.

(Labovitch? Stanley's family name) who disappeared during the war.

Latvia and Lithuania (2014)

In October 2014, we traveled to Latvia, where my grandparents were born. My grandfather and grandmother, my father's parents were born in 1890 in Dvinsk, now known as Daugavpils. Dvinsk and all of Latvia in those days were in Russia. Although the Baltic peoples settled there early in the second millennium BC, the area was often in conflict between Germany, Sweden, and Russia. In 1922, it declared independence only to be occupied from the end of World War II by Russia. However, in 1990 after the collapse of the Soviet Union, Latvia became independent and joined NATO and the EU. When we were there Latvia had already converted to the euro.

We flew from Ottawa to Frankfurt to Riga and took a city bus from the airport. This is always an argument between Stanley and me. I would rather take a taxi when I have no idea where I'm going. However, for one euro, we were able to get downtown, and with a bit of a struggle, we found the Old City Boutique Hotel by asking many times. It was a most interesting hotel that had been converted from an ancient site with some of the original walls preserved.

Early the next day, our rental car was delivered, and again with many instructions from the front desk, we wandered for a while before finding the highway to Daugavpils. The best instructions came from a gas station attendant, who said to keep the river (Daugava) on our right side all the way. Sure enough, we had a beautiful and easy drive to

Daugavpils, which turned out to be a very poor, rundown city close to the Russian and Belarus borders. We saw signs to Moscow all the way along the highway—"Moskoa (RUS) 900 km." It was clear that outside of Riga there had not been the same investment of money by the EU. The only hotel we could find was the Park Hotel. It reminded us of Tecuci in Romania and some of the smaller cities in Cuba.

We found the synagogue, and someone was leading a tour with a group from Belarus. He took a long time, explaining the Hebrew language and Torah in great detail to a group that really didn't seem to care. We gave up waiting for him to switch to English from Russian and instead went for a long walk to the arsenal where an art gallery and a memorial sculpture was built for Mark Rothko. When we were in the synagogue, we saw a plaque, which said that the synagogue had been restored with funds from the Mark Rothko (Roskovitch) family. There were less than two hundred Jews remaining in the city at that time, so it was not hard to understand that all the other Jewish sites had been converted into other uses.

When we arrived at the arsenal, we found a large crowd. It was still open, and there was a wedding taking place there. It was a beautiful museum, with artwork on loan from Mark Rothko's children. He was born in Daugavpils (then Dvinsk) in 1903. My grandfather and grandmother were born thirteen years earlier. I got the feeling that they may have known each other. Rothko left Dvinsk when he was thirteen. The following year, when we were visiting our cousins in Houston, we went to see the Rothko Chapel at St. John's University, commissioned by the de Menil family. The chapel included a series of black paintings that incorporated other dark hues and texture effects of brown and mauve. A typical question raised by us and other visitors viewing the massive black canvases that lined the entire walls of the chapel included some variant of, "Are these actually paintings?" The dark canvases in the darkened room made it very difficult to make out any images. The chapel is supposed to be a place of meditation, and these paintings reflect a very dark period at the end of Rothko's life. Just before the official opening, he took his own life in 1970. The town of Daugavpils was also a dark and dingy place, and one night there was enough.

The next morning, we set out for Vilnius, Lithuania, and found another vibrant restored city in a Balkan country. Lithuania was also in the EU and NATO and was just about to convert from the lita to the euro. The city was filled with many Jewish sites. We checked into the beautiful Kempinski Hotel, a former palace. The hotel was situated in the main square of the city, although again we wandered for a very long time until we found the synagogue.

It was closed, along with the Jewish Community Center since it was Sukkot, the festival of the tabernacles. There was a plaque on the wall as we walked through the streets where many Jews had been slaughtered. In 1939, there were two hundred thousand Jews in Lithuania. After the war, there were less than two thousand. We were so tired from all our walking in the morning we decided to take a city bus tour. The most interesting part was meeting an Israeli couple on the bus. Her grandfather was born in Vilnius and was a partisan and survived by living in the forests that surround the city. They moved to Israel in 1972.

Across the river from our hotel, there was an abandoned sports stadium. It had been built by the Russians in the '50s on top of the Jewish cemetery, and so, not knowing what to do about it, the city of Vilnius has so far just left it. There was another older Jewish cemetery where the Gaon of Vilna, the Talmudic scholar in the eighteenth century was buried. This cemetery was well preserved and filled with many other well-known Jews of those times, and recent ones as well.

As with Latvia, Lithuania was part of the Russian empire from the eighteenth century until the 1920s, when it gained independence very briefly. After 1922, it was assimilated into the USSR until World War II when the Nazis occupied the city, using USSR buildings for Gestapo headquarters. After that, the same buildings were used by the KGB, and once again Lithuania became part of the Soviet Union until 1991, when it gained independence again. We kept missing important sites and found that these KGB headquarters, now the museum of genocide, was closed on Tuesdays when we tried to get in.

We headed back to Riga without a problem. However, finding the Old City Boutique Hotel became a problem again. We decided in advance to hire a taxi to lead us back. This was a technique we had used several times. One taxi gave up after wandering up and down one-way streets. So many streets also were pedestrians only. We hired another taxi driver who managed to find the hotel, and we parked the car, never to use it again.

We arranged for a taxi to take us to Rumbula and Bikerniecki memorials to the Jews executed by the Nazis. Our driver didn't know where we wanted to go exactly, and we ended up at a memorial to Latvians killed in World

War II. We realized this after a while and encouraged our driver to call and find out. Finally, we arrived at Rumbula. The massacre that occurred there was the second largest two-day Holocaust atrocity, Baba Yar being the largest.

About twenty-five thousand Jews were killed in two days. About twenty-four thousand of the victims were Latvian Jews from the Riga Ghetto, and approximately a thousand were German Jews transported to the forest by train. The Riga Ghetto had been emptied in order to make room for Jews from Germany and Austria. The memorial was beautifully designed, and there was a printed list of all the twenty-five thousand names. I did see some names that resembled my grandmother's maiden name (Feldman) as well as my maiden name, Fisher.

Another well-designed memorial was in the Bikernieki Forest, the biggest mass murder site in Latvia during all of World War II. There are fifty-five marked mass burial sites in the forest, and as you wander through them along a trail, the cities in Europe from which the Jews were taken are listed. The memorial was built by the German War Commission.

We continued our tour of the Holocaust sites after lunch in the new city, which is across the river. We got the directions to what we thought was the Holocaust museum. It turned out to be the KGB[62] museum instead. It was kept in its original state; the building very run down and, because of that, extremely disturbing and easy to visualize the atrocities carried out there. The documented stories of torture were hair-raising—no trial, simply a shot in the head.

The next day we managed with great difficulty to find the holocaust museum. Unfortunately, as I suspected, it was

---

62 http://kgbbuilding.lv/.

closed because it was Simchat Torah.[63] However, we saw a car parked inside the grounds, with a worker on the roof. There was a padlock on the gate, but it was simply looped through the gate and not locked. We opened the gate and went in. There were panels of the names of Rigan Jews evacuated from the ghetto and executed at both memorial sites, all alphabetically listed. These included many Felmans, Fischers, and Magidsohns, the maiden name of a friend of ours. The worker on the roof said nothing as we took photos.

What amazed me along with all the well-restored buildings and memorials was the quality of the restaurants in Riga and the architectural design that preserved the outside of the old structures while providing the most modern redecorated interiors. We ate at Locale, a Latvian tapas place, several times. Another favorite was Muuzu. We had eaten there the first night and started talking to a couple from the States. They were spending much of their time traveling. After talking for a while, he disappeared. Sure enough, he had paid for our meal. So Stanley wasn't the only one who did things like that. We exchanged business cards, but our paths have not crossed again.

Another restaurant that we discovered on one of our walks along the river was the 3 Pavarous. The dinner went like this: First of all, we each got a white piece of paper that doubled as a place mat. Then the waiter spread different colored sauces with different seasoning in lines across the paper place mat, very reminiscent of a Mark Rothko painting. After creating this work of art, a bread basket of the best bread was delivered in order to mop up the sauces. The rest of the meal was also excellent.

---

[63] http://www.jewfaq.org/holiday6.htm.

This trip was everything we had hoped for but much more, a most interesting, emotional, and above all enjoyable experience.

Crete, Greece (2014)

In March 2014, we traveled to Crete. We flew to Heraklion and spent our time traveling west of the capital and have yet to explore to the east coast of this very large and very interesting island. We rented a car, and here was one of my very few errors in navigation, telling Stanley to follow the coastal road. Stanley wanted to take the thruway, but I suggested the coastal road. We kept going farther and farther inland. Finally an hour later, we asked some guys in a small town how to get to Chania. They laughed and said to go back to Heraklion and start over. We found a very nice hotel, the Kydon, on the main street, and after Stanley gave his travel agent talk to the manager, we got a junior suite for a great price.

We set out for the old town and eventually found our objective in this ancient city, the one surviving synagogue in Crete after 1944, Etz Hayyim. This unique synagogue dates from the fourteenth century. The remaining 263 members of the Jewish community in Chania were arrested by the Nazis on May 29, 1944, and loaded onto a ship. Ironically, the ship was hit by torpedoes fired from a British submarine. The ship sank, and there were no survivors. The Jews were almost certainly on their way to Auschwitz. In 1999, Etz Hayyim was rededicated after five years of reconstruction, and although there are now no Jews living in Crete, this synagogue has become a center of Jewish culture for all denominations.

We spent two nights in Chania and then drove on to another small town called Rethymnon. We found the old city where no cars were allowed and parked our car. We checked into a lovely boutique hotel and then started walking through the old city. After lunch (the food in Crete is amazing and the portions crazy) we still found room for gelato and were sitting outside in a small square when we saw a couple taking pictures of each other in front of a Venetian fountain. Stanley always asks if a couple would like their picture taken together. Most answer yes. On occasion we get a suspicious reply of, "No." This couple answered, "Sure," and we started to talk. We asked where they were from and first came Canada and then Ontario and then Ottawa and then finally the name. It turns out this emergency room physician had been referring to Stanley for thirty years but had never met him. Then an even further connection was that their son was also a plastic surgeon and trained with a plastic surgeon in Ottawa. What a crazy small world story! We spent the next day with our new friends visiting some ruins and vowed to get together in our hometown of Ottawa. We ended our wanderings and returned to Heraklion.

I did something very bad just before we were leaving. I viewed our Amex bill online and proceeded to pay. Not only wouldn't the bank pay, all our passwords were shutdown. The desk manager at our hotel was wonderful, and we called and set everything straight. I will never do that again. We had excellent weather and, aside from being difficult to get to from Ottawa, Crete is a wonderful destination.

Jewish Sites in Africa

Aside from South Africa, where there are still many Jews remaining, especially in Johannesburg (sixty-six thousand), there are very few Jews on the African continent. There used to be many Jews in North Africa—Libya (see chapter 14, "Guides") Egypt, Tunisia, and Morocco)—but now Jewish numbers have greatly diminished, and those who do remain are mainly very elderly people.

Morocco (1991)

When we visited Morocco with our sons, we discovered some young Jews at a Bar Mitzvah, but most were very old. On another trip many years later to Tunisia, there were remnants of a Jewish community in Djerba, again mostly very old senior citizens. By now there are less than 10 percent of the original populations left.

The first Jews of North Africa originated from the destruction of the temple in Jerusalem, followed by a second wave following the expulsion of Jews from Spain in 1492. In actual fact, Queen Isabella and her right-hand Torquemada wanted the Jews to remain and gave them the option to convert in order to stay. However, most left, which eventually proved a detriment to Spain. The Sephardim (see chapter 14, "Guides") have customs that are totally different from the other European Jews, the Ashkenazi (from whom we are descended), which we discovered when we visited Morocco with our sons in 1991.

Our prearranged driver/guide met us at the airport in Casablanca in spite of the fact that we were on a different flight. (That was a very long story; see chapter 2, "Getting

There.) We drove to Meknes the next day and visited the old Jewish quarter. There was an old age home and a residence for chronically ill patients, but then we heard that, in the Jewish Community Center in the new city, there was a Bar Mitzvah celebration going on. Our driver found it, and when we arrived, we were greeted by the parents and relatives of the Bar Mitzvah boy who immediately asked us to join the party, and we were seated at a table with the brother of the Bar Mitzvah boy who lived in Paris. Our French came in very handy again when he talked to us about Jews in Morocco. He said that most have gone to France or Israel. There were twenty thousand in Meknes, and now there are only twenty thousand in the whole country, two thousand in Meknes. The king was and is still kind to the Jews, and on the surface anyway, there seemed to be peace between the Arabs and Jews in Morocco at that time.

Even now, Morocco is a very diverse society, with the Jewish population that remains regarding themselves as Moroccan. The Bar Mitzvah boy was smoking and immediately offered us cigarettes. Everyone was smoking as a matter of fact. There was an incredible amount of food. The parents of the Bar Mitzvah boy had daughters and were ready to promise them in marriage for our sons. There was dancing and singing with both Jewish and Arab songs. It was an incredible, serendipitous experience!

South Africa (2004)

With a population of 120,000 Jews in South Africa,[64] it was inevitable that we would find some on our trip to South

[64] https://en.wikipedia.org/wiki/History_of_the_Jews_in_South_Africa.

Africa, although with the situation evolving continuously, there is an exodus of Jews to Israel and North America. We drove from Cape Town to Port Elizabeth along the Garden Route and stopped in Plettenburg Bay, one of the towns along the way. Little did we know that this was the place for the Jews from Johannesburg (which still has a population of approximately fifty thousand Jews) to go for their holidays, and this happened to be the week of Chanukah. We found a local synagogue and participated in the candle lighting on the last night of Chanukah and met the rabbi, who had spent a year in Ottawa. Small world!

Jewish Sites in Asia

Shanghai Ghetto (2000)

One of the most unusual places that Jews lived was in Shanghai. We were on a smarTours trip in February 2000. This was for the ridiculous price of $899, which included airfare and two internal flights, from Beijing to Xian and from Xian to Shanghai. The trip also included one tour in each city, which we took. But then we met up with friends of my graduate student, Yiwen who showed us around privately. Even in 2000, there was terrible pollution, and I woke up every morning with a blocked nose and burning throat. Shanghai was already very westernized, with Pudong's skyscrapers facing the Bund, the area occupied by the British around the turn of the century. It is now one of the tourist areas with outstanding shops and restaurants.

There was another Jewish couple on the tour, and she had done extensive research on the Jews who had lived in Shanghai and organized a tour with Mr. Wang, an international treasure and a walking history book. He spoke perfect English, which he learned while living in the ghetto. He told us what life was like there in the '30s and '40s[65] and explained that there were immigrations of Jews long before World War II, in the 1830s. There were the wealthy Baghadi Jews, including the Kadoorie and Sassoon families from Persia and Iraq. They made great fortunes, perhaps in the opium trade. Their huge mansions are now the Children's Palaces, where wealthy talented children study art, dance, and music.[66] At the end of the nineteenth century, Russian Jews came to avoid the pogroms. They were helped by the wealthy Sephardi Jews already there. And then following the Battle of Shanghai in 1937, the city was occupied by Japan, which, until Pearl Harbor, allowed the Jews escaping Hitler to enter.

However, the wealthy Jews who had been there for many years left and went to Hong Kong after 1941, so there was limited help for the refugees from Europe. Those Jews came by boat from Italy or overland via Siberia. The conditions in the Shanghai Ghetto got increasingly bad as the war intensified. The ghetto occupied one square mile for twenty-three thousand people, and food was scarce. However, when Hitler wanted those Jews handed over, Japan refused, and those lives were saved. We have good friends in Ottawa who were saved in Shanghai and then immigrated to Canada at the end of World War II. Most of the Jews left for North America or Israel after the war. Mr. Wang commented that

---

[65] Shanghai Ghetto: https://en.wikipedia.org/wiki/Shanghai_Ghetto.

[66] The Ghosts of Shanghai, http://www.gluckman.com/ShanghaiJewsChina.html.

very many Jews intermarried and only a few remained. However, the last Jew remaining died in 1981.

Mr. Wang walked us up and down the streets showing us what does remain from that era. The government has preserved the one synagogue called the Ohel Moshe Synagogue, and it is now the Shanghai Jewish Refugees Museum. A new synagogue was built in 1941, and despite the terrible conditions in the ghetto, a vibrant cultural and religious life flourished. Two other synagogues were demolished; a third is in the department of education. It was interesting to see the old houses that still had fading letters where signs had been, Jewish names like Goldenberg comes to mind. And then on many buildings, we could see the remnants of where mezuzahs[67] had been nailed.

There are many expat Jews living in Shanghai now. There are so many companies with branches in Shanghai that the need for services arose. There was a Bar Mitzvah in the Ritz Carlton Hotel where services were taking place. The rabbi, who had come from Hong Kong, was invited to stay, and at that time he lived at the Ritz Carlton. The mother of the Bar Mitzvah boy worked at the Israeli consulate. Relations between China and Israel were established in 1992, and Israel bestowed the honor of the Righteous Among the Nations to Chinue Sugihara[68] (the Japanese consul in Kaunas, Lithuania) in 1985 and to Ho Feng Shan[69] (the Chinese consul-general in Vienna) in 2001, both of whom

---

67 http://www.chabad.org/library/article_cdo/aid/256915/jewish/What-Is-a-Mezuzah.htm.

68 Chinue Sugihara, https://en.wikipedia.org/wiki/Chiune_Sugihara.

69 Ho Feng Shan, https://en.wikipedia.org/wiki/Ho_Feng-Shan.

were instrumental in facilitating the rescue of the European Jews during World War II.

The Jews of Latin America

With the exception of Brazil, which was Portuguese, and the northeast coastal region of South America, all of that continent, as well as Central America, Mexico, and some of the Caribbean islands, were part of the Spanish colonial empire from 1492 to the 1820s.[70] Along with this colonial imperialism, the Spanish Inquisition was initiated in 1480. The explanation is controversial at this point, but many books written about that period paint it as brutally anti-Semitic. The forced conversion of Jews and Muslims led to the expulsion from Spain of Jews in 1492 and Muslims in 1502. It remained in effect until 1834 and was the reason that many Jews came to South America at that time. It is believed that many even came as early as Columbus's expedition in 1492, although disguised as converts.[71] Jews continued to come to Argentina, Chile, Uruguay, and Brazil for many years following. The Jews from Spain were Sephardim, whereas a great influx of Ashkenazi Jews came from the rest of Europe during 1880-1914, mostly to Argentina, Uruguay, and Chile. Many escaped the Nazis in the '30s when they were given sanctuary in those countries and not in other countries like Canada, where our minister of Foreign Affairs said when asked, "How many Jews should

[70] *The Inquisition in the New World*, http://sefarad.org/lm/037/6.html.

[71] https://en.wikipedia.org/wiki/List_of_Latin_American_Jews.

we admit? And he responded, "None is too many."[72] On the other hand, a true paradox, Nazi war criminals were also given sanctuary in Argentina, Paraguay, Chile, and Brazil after the end of World War II.

Argentina (1987)

Although there are some Jews in many of the South American countries, the Jewish population in Argentina is the largest in Latin America, the third on the continent, and the world's seventh largest outside Israel. The immigration began early in the sixteenth century and waves of immigration followed from Europe during the pogroms in the nineteenth century in Russia. The Jews settled on agricultural properties encouraged by the Argentinian government. Argentina kept its doors open until 1938 so that many Jews fleeing Nazi persecution came there. This was a prime example of the paradox facing the Jewish population. Although freely accepted many times over the centuries, Argentina under the dictatorship of Peron became a haven for Nazi war criminals, the most notorious of which was Adolf Eichman. Eichman lived near Buenos Aires until 1960, when he was captured by Israelis and brought to trial.[73] However, Mengele never was (see chapter 8, "Golf and Fishing").

On our first visit to Argentina in 1987, we were with Brian and Daniel and hadn't made plans for the rest of

---

[72] Irving Abella and Harold Martin Troper, Harold Martin, *None is Too Many: Canada and the Jews of Europe, 1933–1948*, University of Toronto Press, 2012. ISBN 9781442614079.

[73] https://en.wikipedia.org/wiki/History_of_the_Jews_in_Argentina#World_War_II_and_antisemitism.

our trip. We found a travel agency open and made our reservations on Austral Airlines to visit Patagonian Argentina (see chapter 9, "Encounters with Wildlife"). We became friendly with our travel agent and her family, members of the Jewish community for many generations. We had traveled to Iguazu and Paraguay and returned to Buenos Aires on December 31 for New Year's Eve. They invited us to join them at the Sheraton for the party. It was a formal affair, and ties and jackets were necessary.

They outfitted the boys, and we set out for the festivities. As usual, the event was overpriced and not great. Many times, traveling at this time of year has meant we have had to succumb to the cost of New Year's Eve in order to find a hotel room. Although the austral to the US dollar was falling daily ($4.78 when we arrived to only $5.09 when we left) the event price that night was US$65.

Chile (1996)

On our first visit to Chile in 1996 and on many subsequent trips (see chapter 2, "Getting There") we met with a prominent member of the Jewish community and a relative of people we knew. The community is not very big and, in this case, mostly Ashkenazi. The ancestors of our friends came from Germany around the same time as our grandparents came from the Ukraine, at that time Russia. We were shown around the Jewish community center and day school, the Israeli embassy, and the Jewish country club. All of these had heavy-duty security, and we would never have been able to tour these places without her clearance.

The dictators in many of the Latin American countries during and after World War II, who themselves were fascist in their tendencies, supported fascists escaping from Europe so that anti-Semitism continued for many years until democratic governments were established in many countries (Chile, Argentina, Uruguay, Paraguay, and Peru). It is hard to know what the future may bring to the Jews in Latin America. At this time (2017) many occupy important leadership positions in many countries and certainly consider themselves "at home," as most Jews do in the diaspora.

It is interesting that the migrations of Jews in Europe to North and South America followed similar waves, due to the conditions in Europe. However, in Canada, we know very little about our neighbors to the south, whether Jewish or not.

When asked about our favorite countries, they are, without doubt, in Central and South America. One time on a trip to Uruguay, we met a political science professor. When we asked him what he thought caused instability and the rise of dictators in so many Latin American countries, he replied "Do you remember the Cold War? You (meaning the western governments) fought the hot war in our countries." And inevitably, the Jews suffered whenever there was a "hot war."

Panama (2007)

When we were in Panama (see chapter 2, "Getting There") we were introduced to a descendent of a Jewish family (David) that had left Spain hundreds of years ago. David's ancestors went to Holland at the time of the expulsion of the Jews from Spain in 1492. Then from Holland, they went on to Curacao and finally to St. Thomas. His father was the first Jewish governor of St. Thomas.

We had arranged to meet for dinner, and so we left Panama City for the mountains. We got a phone call from David; he and his wife couldn't make it back in time for our dinner date and could we change that. They then asked where we were at the time. When we told them, they couldn't believe it. We were about five hundred meters from their country home where they were. We went over and had a wonderful evening with them and their guests.

The next day we went to their apartment in Panama City. Their apartment was very beautiful with a view of the canal in the distance. David talked about the problems in the Jewish community. There had been a large influx of Jews from Venezuela who were very religious, leaving because of the fear of Chavez. The old Jewish community in Panama was mostly Reform and assimilated by that time and so very different. The Venezuelan immigrants were Lubovitch and did not want to associate with the established Jewish community.

The dinner was most elegant and served by two helpers, one of whom had been with the family for forty-two years. The most remarkable item in the apartment, aside from the beautiful furniture, china, silver, and artwork, was David's family tree, going back four hundred years. We can barely trace ours one hundred.

Nicaragua (2008–2016)

On one of our earliest trips to Nicaragua in November 2008, we asked the manager at Camino Real about the Jewish community. He said that there was a family who held services in their home. He owned a store in Managua, but when I called his home with the number I got, I understood that he was in Miami. Although there had been a Jewish community up until the Sandinista revolution in 1979, all the Jewish community had left, being accused of being Samosa supporters. Their property was confiscated, and the synagogue burned. This was true not only of Jews, but also of many Nicaraguans who were financially successful. There were many Nicaraguans whom we got to know personally over the years of going there that had left for the United States during the revolution (1979–1990)[74] but returned to Nicaragua after the Sandinistas were defeated in an election in 1990.[75] Daniel Ortega regained power in 2006[76] and remains the president to this day (2017). These families lost their money and, in some cases, their property as well, which many never regained. At that time, Ortega was anti all religion but mostly any financially successful businesses.

When the Sandinistas were defeated in 1990, although many families did return, there were very few Jews among them. Some families acquired American citizenship so that they returned periodically, especially for the Jewish holidays,

---

[74] The Nicaraguan Revolution, https://en.wikipedia.org/wiki/Nicaraguan_Revolution.

[75] The Sandanista party, https://www.britannica.com/topic/Sandinista.

[76] President of Nicaragua, Daniel Ortega: https://www.britannica.com/biography/Daniel-Ortega.

but kept their homes and businesses in Miami. Others were not in the States long enough and so lost that flexibility.

When Ortega was reelected in 2006, he found religion and was allied with the Catholic Church.

On another trip, we met with someone who called himself the "head" of the Jewish community. I don't recall how we found him, but we had dinner with him at Camino Real. He was British and had married a woman in the British Foreign Service, who had been posted to Nicaragua. That marriage broke up, but he remained in Nicaragua because he had started a business there. He then married a Nicaraguan woman and had made Nicaragua his permanent home. They arrived an hour late, not sure if this was what we call Latino time or if we hadn't communicated the time correctly. He said that there were around thirty Jews in Nicaragua at the time (2008). He said they were not observant, and he always invited the archbishop to the seder[77] that he threw every year. We lost contact with him but found another very active Jewish community.

There is still no synagogue or permanent rabbi in Nicaragua, but on our last visit, February 2016, we found a brand-new Chabad house in the beach resort of San Juan del Sur. In the 1950s, Rabbi Schneerson started the worldwide expansion of the Chabad-Lubovitch movement.[78] It is the most widespread Jewish movement in the world, with a network of more than 3,600 institutions that provide

---

[77] http://www.myjewishlearning.com/article/the-passover-pesach-seder/.

[78] http://www.chabad.org/library/article_cdo/aid/36226/jewish/About-Chabad-Lubavitch.htm.

religious, social, and humanitarian needs in over a thousand cities, spanning eighty countries.

We first heard about Chabad in Nicaragua on our trip in November 2013. We had just arrived in the town where the medical clinic was that we operate in and after setting up our clinic as usual (see chapter 16, "Surgical Missions") we went for a walk. Like something out of a science fiction movie, we heard Hebrew songs. Could we possibly be hearing this in this small town in the middle of nowhere? We followed the music, and sure enough, in the city hall, there was a group of men wearing *kippahs* (skull caps) and a full room of Nicaraguans singing and waving their arms in religious fervor. They were dressed up in long, silk dresses, almost in costume. We spoke to one of the men, who spoke English and said that now there were more than a hundred Jews in Nicaragua, mostly in San Juan del Sur and Corizo. He said that he was born in Nicaragua and that both his parents were Jewish. I asked if they were converting all these Nicaraguans. He said, "Yes. They all want to be Jewish." I don't think that any of these people had any idea what being Jewish was, and I questioned him again. Very strange to say the least!

However, in February 2016, when we went to the Chabad house in San Juan and spoke to the young man in charge there, he said that this was brand-new, and they served Kosher meals three times a day and had a variety of Jewish programs and activities. He was a recent recruit from Israel. He confirmed that, at this point, there were a hundred Jews in Nicaragua. Certainly, they had financial support because this was a brand-new Chabad house located on the main street in San Juan. The young man was anxious to be photographed with us and was extremely welcoming, as was definitely the mandate of the Chabad-Lubovitch movement. Bottom line—you never know where you might find Jews!

Frankfurt: En route

When traveling to almost any location in Europe from Ottawa, we flew to Frankfurt Airport. Usually our flights did not connect, and we had to overnight on our way back. One time, we went into the city of Frankfurt and tried to go to the Jewish museum. Of course, it was closed, our usual timing problem, but we could see the memorial that was on the wall right behind the museum. This cement wall had small boxes mounted on it. Each box had a ledge where a stone could be placed. Fourteen thousand citizens of Frankfurt were deported and died during World War II. The fourteen thousand names were arranged in alphabetical order in perfectly straight lines. It was a most impressive and moving memorial.

We were surprised to find that Anne Frank had a box on that wall. She was born in Frankfurt but was hidden in Amsterdam. She was discovered there and transported to Bergen-Belsen, where she died. I have visited the Anne Frank House three times, once in 1958 with my parents, the second time with Stanley in 1965, and then in 2008 with my two graduate students. *The Diary of Anne Frank* has become world famous, translated into sixty-seven languages with over thirty million copies sold. The increase in popularity of both the book and the play and, therefore, the house changed my perception of the tragedy. In 2008, there was a line several blocks long waiting to get in, with food and souvenir venders lining the street. We decided not to wait. Frankly speaking, I found the scene disturbing and detracting from the deeper meaning. Perhaps I am wrong.

I Googled Anne Frank House and found this online about Garance Reus-Deelder, managing director of the Anne Frank House:

It's well known that there are often long queues outside the Anne Frank House, and it's remarkable to see how visitors wait patiently in line to see and experience Anne Frank's hiding place. In recent years, we have seen the interest in our museum increase considerably, and so the waiting time has grown too. By only opening the museum to visitors with a pre-booked ticket for a particular timeslot for part of the day, we can offer more visitors the opportunity to visit the museum without having to wait in that well-known queue. But later in the day we will still offer the opportunity to visit the museum to people who don't want to commit themselves to a particular timeslot or order a ticket in advance.

There is probably no perfect way to memorialize the Jews who died in the Holocaust. There have been many atrocities carried out between humans from the beginning of time, but at the risk of being called chauvinistic, I cannot help but feel that the systematic attempt to annihilate the Jews of Europe when Hitler was in power is unique.

Although unique to us, the next chapter describing our volunteer surgical missions provides an insight into NGOs (nongovernmental organizations) and volunteering in developing countries. Although for the most part "doing good," there are many conflicting aspects.

Chapter 16

SURGICAL MISSIONS: OUR NICARAGUAN EXPERIENCE

There is a saying that claims that everything happens for a reason. On our last night in Nicaragua as tourists in 2007, my husband and I happened to speak to someone in the lobby of our hotel. The consequences of that conversation proved that saying to be true. This first trip, as tourists, would be the first of twenty trips to Nicaragua. We started to talk to the gentleman about the slow computers and what he was doing in Nicaragua. He was not a tourist. He was a volunteer with an NGO that was helping build houses in small villages around the country. He was connected to several NGOs. So when Stanley said that he had always wanted to volunteer to operate in developing countries, he suggested that we contact a friend of his. The friend led a team of physicians, nurses, and helpers who traveled to Nicaragua to carry out surgery and visit health clinics. Stanley and I were welcomed into that team and joined them for a mission in February 2008. Our time with this group was a life-altering experience.

The origin of many humanitarian and medical missions to Nicaragua was Hurricane Mitch (October 1998)[79] still ranked as the worst hurricane in the western hemisphere since 1780 in terms of deaths and damage. Even though there have been hurricanes with stronger winds and lower pressure, the damage caused by Mitch set both Honduras and Nicaragua back fifty years. So it may be possible to say that both countries are still feeling the effects.

Our trips to Nicaragua had three distinct arms. One was the surgical/medical mission. The second, although not the initial objective, was equally important to us, the humanitarian arm. Third, and probably the one with some of the best stories is the part of our trips that was pure tourism. Entonces (one of my favorite Spanish words, meaning and so or then) I will tell our Nicaraguan story in three parts—first the surgical, second the humanitarian, and third our adventures as tourists.

After deciding to join the medical team, Stanley first wanted to check out the facility, and we planned a trip in October 2007. It is not easy to get from Ottawa to Nicaragua. We have traveled many different ways, but it always takes three flights. On this occasion (October to November 2007) we stayed overnight in New York, visiting our family. Then we flew to Miami and from Miami to Managua, a mere one and half hours. We had four hockey bags and a letter from the local sponsoring NGO. When we traveled with the medical team, we always had a host

---

[79] History of Hurricane Mitch, http://www.history.com/topics/hurricane-mitch.

organization that provided accommodation, interpreters, and other support staff for us. The local NGOs in Nicaragua were involved in a huge variety of activities, which included construction, health services, and educational services. Many involved religious activities, converting Nicaraguans from Catholicism to a variety of Protestant evangelical faiths.

During this first exploratory trip, we made it through customs with our four hockey bags with no trouble at all. This was almost never the case subsequently, and we never knew what red tape we would meet when we arrived, in spite of filling out all kinds of forms, inventories, and résumés of the people participating. But more on that later. On each trip, we had to provide Stanley's diploma from medical school, as well as my university diplomas, and there was always one or another document missing or one that didn't look quite right.

We were picked up by a taxi driver arranged by our sponsoring NGO, and after a most crazy drive in the dark on narrow, windy roads, we arrived at a large house, rented by our sponsoring NGO for their permanent and semipermanent staff. After that rather hair-raising drive (and, later on, a few others) we usually rented a car. I trusted Stanley and the cars we rented more than drivers and vehicles we didn't know. But more importantly, we stayed off the roads after dark, or at least we did our best to. We settled in, and after a cold shower, we tried to sleep. Aside from the rudimentary shared accommodation, the most difficult part of these missions was the temperature of the water supply in most small towns in Nicaragua. It was very cold. No hot showers and certainly not my favorite form of washing, a bath!

After many trips to Nicaragua, aside from the many wonderful friends we have made, there are three things that stand out in my mind that one cannot get anywhere else. One is the exquisite pottery. We bought some on every trip. Another of the highlights of each of our trips became the ice cream, by the company called Eskimo. It seems ironic that this very warm country, almost always over thirty degree Celsius, in my opinion, has the best ice cream in the world. Our favorite flavor is *ron con pasas* (rum and raisin) which probably is due to the fact that rum manufacturing is a huge industry in Nicaragua, with sugar cane grown all over the country. Flor de Cana is the rum company and clearly has a huge economic impact on Nicaragua. Not being a fan of rum, I discovered Tona, the local beer, which also is excellent. As for the food, rice and beans is still a staple, although there are now many pretty good restaurants in Managua, the capital, and in San Juan del Sur, the most popular tourist location on the Pacific coast, which borders on Costa Rica.

Humanitarian arm

To continue describing our first trip to Nicaragua, the morning after our arrival, after a buffet breakfast, we met two young people from the States who were working for the NGO. Both were there on a temporary basis, having just graduated from university. There are many NGOs with an American connection that have young volunteers who come to Nicaragua to carry out a variety of activities, such as building homes, as well as education in many areas—for example, basic literacy and health.

On this occasion, we were introduced to a family that we have supported from 2007 until now (2017). We were taken to a villa, a small housing development by one of the young volunteers, Erin. There are many villas in rural areas that are not too far from average-size cities. The families living there were given the opportunity to move from the dump to a small cinder block house with three rooms. The houses were deeded to the women of the household and, hopefully, to a stable family who paid off the cost of the mortgage in very small monthly amounts.

As we walked down the dirt road in the villa with Erin, many kids ran up and hugged her. One, a young girl, ten years old, named Mariana clearly was Erin's favorite. It was clear that she was very bright. But she wasn't going to school full-time, even though the school was in the villa and was free. No uniforms were required here. We asked why she wasn't attending full-time, and it was explained that her mother had many children to feed and needed the older ones to work, which usually involved picking coffee. They were sent away for weeks at a time to work in the coffee plantations and so got very behind in their school work.

Stanley asked how much Mariana made. The amount was approximately a few dollars a day, and so began our support of Mariana and her family. Our plan was to give the mother the money that she would have received if Mariana was working. We offered the same opportunity for the other children, three boys and two girls. Their father worked at a variety of jobs, depending on where there was a need. This could be in the city close to the villa or more than a day's drive to farms or companies where help was needed. Often, he worked in the coffee plantations when it was the picking season. From time to time, he took Mariana and her brother with him and out of school. Early on, it was clear that the older boys had no interest in school. They were both so far behind their age group that it was embarrassing for them to attend their classes. However, we persevered with the girls, especially Mariana, as she was the first one in the family to be promoted from sixth grade to high school.

It was important to us that—although many NGOs carried out proselytizing and conversion that went hand and hand with health care and construction of homes—the ones we affiliated with applied no conditions to the surgical care that we provided. No conditions for their surgery were required and our services were entirely free. It was only because of this that we felt comfortable being part of this mission, as we were the only Jews. Our local NGO connection organized our accommodations and transportation and supplied interpreters. In addition, the organization found the patients and medical clinics that needed the team's work.

It was on the first surgical mission in February 2008 that we met Manuela, who worked for the NGO we were affiliated with. Her job was to help organize the team's schedule and make sure we had everything we needed. We have maintained the friendship since then, and each time we came to Nicaragua, Manuela was there to help, as conditions changed continuously. She was the constant. It was only because of her that we were able to continue to support Mariana and her family.

After this first surgical mission in February 2008, we were so taken with Nicaragua and what our affiliated NGOs were doing that we planned another trip in November 2008 on our own. Manuela and a few other members of the NGO met us at the airport. We spent a couple of days during which they showed us around other homes that they had built in other areas close by. We rented a car this time, and so began our many encounters with the Nicaraguan police, which was detailed earlier (see chapter 12, "Police Encounters"). If it was clear that the car you are driving was rented because there was a logo of the rental agency on it, you became a target. It took a while for us to figure this out and we requested the rental agency to scrape the logo off.

Manuela took us to the villa, a place we always visited whenever we were in Nicaragua. Mariana was thrilled to see us and showed us her schoolwork. Both of her parents were working when we visited this time. Her mother, Lucia, was in town doing laundry, and her father was working at a factory. It seemed that the family was on track and doing well. But an up-and-down pattern has continued over the years that we have known the family—a pattern based on work and health issues, which constantly changed. If both parents had work locally, the children could stay in school. On this trip, no one was pulled out to go pick coffee. Stanley bought stuff for everyone at the local store and gave Mariana a dress that Manuela had bought for her. We took the NGO staff out for dinner and bought ice cream for everyone at Eskimo in El Parque. The ice cream purchase on our last day became a ritual no matter what town we were in or what NGO we were working with.

There were mayoralty elections in November 2008, and we were warned that there could be demonstrations. We did meet a big parade on our way back to Managua from the villa. Although this delayed us a fair bit, we made it back to Managua before dark. At this time, we still thought we could find our way around Managua. We set out to find Price Smart, the equivalent of Costco we were told. We thought that we could purchase our humanitarian supplies in Nicaragua, rather than bring them from Canada. We had heard that there had been riots the night before and that a big parade had been planned for the afternoon.

Surprisingly, we found Price Smart without a problem. Stuff was much too expensive, and so we started on our way back. Somehow, we ended up at the central market, a place we found out later was one of the more dangerous spots in Managua. We had just asked at a gasoline station how to get back to Camino Real, the much better hotel we had found for our surgical team, when the gasoline attendant ran up to us and said, "Policia." Stan saw a truck full of armed men and immediately went in the opposite direction. I had said that he was going in the opposite direction of the way back to the hotel, but it was probably a good idea, since the man at the gas station seemed very nervous. We eventually found our way back and decided not to venture off the main road back from the villa to Camino Real and not to wander around Managua, day or night. This wasn't always possible, as will become apparent as future trip stories unfold.

We did do a few more "risky" things, and I guess we have been lucky. On this same trip, we walked from the Camino Real Hotel to a restaurant about one and a half kilometers away. Someone at the reception desk said it was an easy walk and safe. It was a very uneven sidewalk, very dirty with rundown buildings on either side. When we mentioned to someone at the NGO that we had walked there, he went crazy and said we were lucky to be alive. This road, called the Carretera Norte, had become known for carjackings and muggings and was considered unsafe, although the assessment of the danger there was mixed.

It is important to have a word about the danger in Nicaragua. People's reactions when, in the past, we said that we were going to Nicaragua was that we were headed into a country where the violence at the time of the Iran-Contra affair[80] still existed. Although that general opinion has shifted somewhat, people always ask, "Is it safe?"

On our last trip to Nicaragua we met Manuela's colleagues from her new job. One young man gave me a statistic that I will not forget. Before accepting the position, his father undertook a security assessment. The results were remarkable. The safest country in the western hemisphere is no surprise. It is Canada. However, the second safest is Nicaragua, amazing! It is hard to know exactly what data were compared. But certainly, you can go to Nicaragua and, with reasonable precautions that you would take anywhere, be safe.

Our next surgical mission was in February 2009. We went with a very large group, with a couple of surgeons bringing their families along. We all went to the villa and had a great visit with Mariana and her family and friends. She was very enthusiastic about school and was so proud to show us her schoolwork again. We also visited her in her classroom. The NGO had built the school and a medical

---

[80] http://www.u-s-history.com/pages/h1889.html.

clinic, but the school was run by the Ministry of Education and the medical clinic by the Ministry of Health. The philosophy of this NGO's humanitarian activities was to provide sustainability, with the government taking over the operations of what the NGO had introduced and constructed, but it definitely was an uphill battle.

We went back to Nicaragua in October and November 2009. The October trip was with a small medical team, working now with another NGO in another location where a new medical clinic had just opened. This facility was superior to our previous location, and from that time on, that was where we went.

In November, we attended and were honored during the sixth-grade promotion ceremony in the villa. Mariana, who was in fifth grade, was chosen to present the flag. She had been singled out as one of the best students and was given this honor. The promotion ceremony was ready to start, and the sound system speakers hadn't arrived. Manuela was in charge of the sound system, and we were part of the ceremony. We waited and waited and finally the equipment arrived but did not work properly. With much effort, Manuela, hours later, got the ceremony underway.

The big problem was that we had to drive back to Managua from the villa (almost a three-hour drive) that day because we were leaving very early the next morning to return to Ottawa. Eventually, we were able to leave, but by the time we arrived in Managua. it was dark, against all our travel driving principles. That wouldn't have been a terrible problem, but our simple route along the Carretera Norte that led to the Camino Real was blocked. Around the end of November, a huge display of Christmas dioramas lined one of the main streets that intersected with the Carretera Norte, and it was impossible to cross. We took the designated detour and had no idea where we were. We decided to hire a taxi and follow the driver around the blocked road. We quickly lost the taxi and ended up in a parking lot. We tried again, and this time we were guided to a gasoline station on the Carretera Norte, where we knew where we were. The taxi driver wanted twenty-five dollars. This was ridiculous, since normally a taxi ride is twenty cords a person, which is a dollar. Anyway, we gave him ten dollars after an argument and went on our way. We arrived at the Camino Real and fortunately no harm done! But after this incident and to this day (February 2016), we left wherever we were in more than enough time to arrive at Camino Real before dark. Although we have rented cars in many different countries, it has become one of the many Labow travel rules. No driving in the dark in foreign countries!

We tried to model our support of Mariana's family on the NGO's scholarship program. Once a month, the students would come for their money, but they had to show that they had done ten hours of voluntary social service and some paid work to supplement their tuition. With much effort, it seemed to be working for most of the students most of the time. Still ignorant and inexperienced, we thought that we had an agreement that if we provided economic assistance to our family, the kids would stay in school. Our trips were in February and November for the most part. The February trip usually coincided with the beginning of the school year. November was the end of the school year, with promotion at the very end of November or beginning of December. The kids went to school during the rainy season and had vacation in December and January when the dry season started.

After out February 2010 surgical mission, we planned our visit in March with our granddaughter, Hannah. Hannah was eleven years old at the time, living in New York City, but despite her life of privilege, she was an outstanding traveler. The only issue may have been Nicaraguan food. When we ate at Manuela's family's home, Hannah had mac and cheese. The motivation for this trip was to show Hannah the reality of poverty. We stayed in the very basic accommodations provided by the NGO, slept on bunk beds, and traveled to the villa. We took Mariana and her friends swimming at a hotel, as well as the beach.

But before heading out to the beach, we visited the local dump and arrived just at the time a truck was unloading its garbage. The kids still living in the dump crowded around, ready to scavenge whatever they could. Hannah's comment when asked what she thought was that it was "overwhelming."

We also visited a *finca* (farm) a very interesting concept in caring for orphans. This particular finca was also started after Hurricane Mitch to house the orphans. The orphans were placed with individual families who also lived on the farm. That way, the orphans were more easily integrated into a family setting. There were many common services, such as a school and medical clinics, on the farm as well.

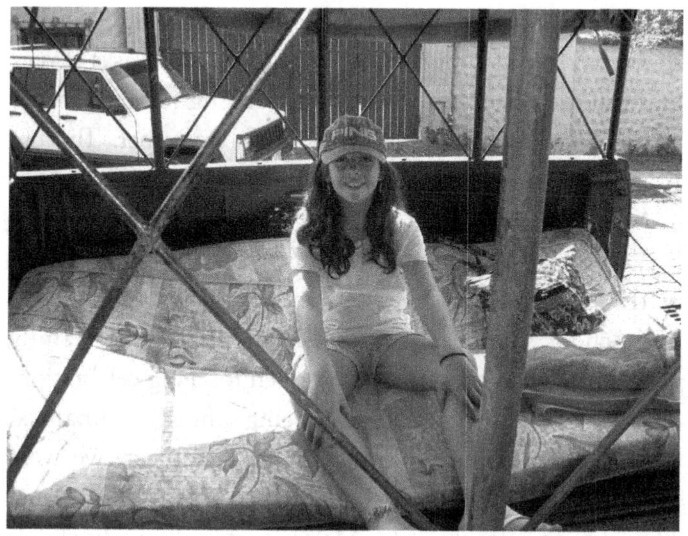

Hannah on the back of the truck in Nicaragua, March 2010

We continued on in the back of a truck (I think one of the highlights for Hannah since she knew that her mother would probably not approve). It was so remarkable watching Hannah and Mariana and her friends swimming at the beach and having a great time in spite of the language difference, but especially the extreme differences in the way Hannah and Mariana were living. We will never forget her Bat Mitzvah speech, when she commented on how this trip with us had affected her and made her so appreciative of the very privileged life she leads.

The leader of our team couldn't organize a team again in 2010, so we went alone in September. It turned out to be a terrible time for Nicaragua, with the rainy season causing dangerous flooding. However, we still visited Mariana again in September 2010 and gave her a photo book that we made from our visit in March with Hannah. She showed us her schoolwork, and it looked very good. Mariana was still very enthusiastic about school and was looking forward to her sixth grade promotion at the end of November. The big promotion ceremony took place in the villa on December 1. Manuela took photos for us.

After our surgical mission in February 2011, we arrived at the villa and took everyone shopping for bathing suits and school supplies. We took Mariana and her family swimming at the beach and for lunch for a big celebration. Our "program" for education being linked to financial help seemed to be working. But in retrospect, we were very ignorant. Situations change on a dime in Nicaragua. However, in October 2012, Mariana was still in school. We visited the high school near the villa and watched a lesson about reuse and recycle. The school was in great need of many supplies. There was no discipline in the classroom. It was understandable that this environment was not conducive to wanting to study.

Until February 2014, Mariana was going to school. After that, in spite of our efforts and that of her mother, Mariana kept skipping classes, even after her mother made her change schools. It seems that school was no longer something she wanted to do. She had found the boy she wanted to marry and was happy living with him and cleaning and cooking for him and his father and brother.

We finally came to a decision. It took us a long time to realize this, but conditional giving of money does not work. We found out that even our NGO, a while ago, had given up its scholarship program. If an organization like our NGO, with people on the ground, had given up conditional giving, how could we hope to continue? It is interesting what you learn about NGOs and assistance and money. It is anything but simple, and trying to impute North American first-world values on third-world, impoverished people may not be possible in a way you would want to do it. After almost ten years, this was a lesson learned.

Surgical arm

Our first surgical mission took place in February 2008. We decided that we should meet our group in Houston and not arrive separately in Managua. So after spending the night with cousins, we went to the airport and met our surgical team. The flight from Houston was two hours and fifty minutes, and when we arrived, there was no problem with customs. All eighty bags of stuff got through without a problem and were loaded onto a truck for delivery to the clinic where our NGO had organized for us to operate.

We were part of a huge team, forty-four members that included two general surgeons, two family doctors, one gynecologist, fourteen nurses, and some spouses and children. There were also local physicians and nurses who were assisting. Their role was never really clear, and although it became apparent that simply arriving and operating did some good, a much better role would be to teach. The missions evolved to that, or at least tried to, as time went on.

It was understandable that organizing such a large, diverse team would not be easy. Some people knew each other, but many did not. There was one head of the team, but there were other "heads" of each area of responsibility, and eventually this became a logistical problem. There were heads of humanitarian activities, nurses, and food and accommodation where we stayed and an organizer of some trips. There were two NGOs involved as well. One was where we stayed; one was the liaison with the clinic where we operated, who also organized the interpreters and the clinics in the countryside we would go to. In retrospect, there were too many heads and too many people without a clear role. Certainly, roles overlapped.

However, the first task at hand was to unpack the eighty hockey bags that accompanied the forty-four team members. The amount of supplies was grossly over what was really needed, but eventually they found a home in the medical clinic where we ended our surgical missions.

The patients for the OR arrived the next day and were triaged. There were far too many at first, and it was very difficult to organize the list. It was disturbing to deal with the huge mob of people who were given a color-coded ticket that determined which procedure they needed or whether they were going to be refused surgery. The patients referred to us supposedly had been previously organized, but that didn't appear to always be the case.

Stanley's room was run as an outpatient clinic, and his patients, for the most part, were operated on there. There were many children with cleft palates, but the clinic where Stan was operating was not a facility that could handle those. And then we found out that Operation Smile[81] was coming to Nicaragua and was going to operate in the main hospital in the city nearby. This organization had done over a hundred thousand cleft palate operations worldwide and had organized surgical teams that were experts, including

[81] Operation Smile: http://www.operationsmile.org/.

Americans as well as local physicians. It was always difficult to refuse to operate on a patient, but it was especially not in anybody's best interest to take on a case that might go wrong.

We also went out to medical clinics in the countryside. It was here that we gave out medication, mostly for parasites, pain, and colds and coughs. This occurred every day for almost two weeks. One exceptionally large clinic was one we held in the market. For the most part, there was nothing wrong with the women who attended, and they just wanted some attention for all the hard work they performed daily to feed their families. Other projects included teaching the women about hand washing and birth control. We strung beads of different colors that would mimic the menstrual cycle and handed them out at the various clinics. I am not sure this had much impact. In 2015, the births per a thousand women age fifteen to nineteen was 89.6 percent. Abortion is still illegal, even to save a mother's life. But it seems that in the main hospital in Managua medication to cause miscarriage is now (2017) quietly being given to save a mother's life and also for Zika virus infection.[82] In addition, education is not valued as much as it should be. Only 67 percent of children in Nicaragua finish sixth grade,[83] the evidence of which we experienced firsthand as we tried to keep Mariana in school after sixth grade. It took us a while to understand that it is very hard to change an ingrained culture. Hopefully changes will come eventually.

---

[82] Abortion illegal: https://www.pri.org/stories/2016-08-16/women-nicaragua-fight-right-get-abortions-could-save-their-lives.

[83] Education level achieved, http://www.epdc.org/sites/default/files/documents/EPDC%20NEP_Nicaragua.pdf.

We had some time off. One was a day trip to Leon, the previous capital of Nicaragua and the location of the university. The beach there was close by with a variety of restaurants to choose from. On our weekend off, we chose to go to Redwood Beach Resort. It was on a remote beach off a terrible road that had been under repair for years. We took two of the nurses with us. Stacey and Mike from New York and Chicago had just bought this resort and were fixing it up. It was in a magnificent location on a twenty-four-kilometer, pristine beach near the town of Mechapa, also located near the Padre Ramos estuary in the northwest Pacific coast of Nicaragua. On our way back, we stopped in at Monty's surf club. Monty is from British Columbia, and the surf in Jiquilillo is amazing I'm told.

There was another very interesting issue that arose during our mission, which was that of obtaining consent. I had recently attended a bioethics workshop about just that. One of the guest speakers was Dr. Lois K Cohen.[84] The title of her presentation was "Protecting High Standards of Ethics in International Collaboration. She was the Paul K. Rogers Ambassador for Global Health Research and had founded and directed the National Institute of Dental and Cranial Research (NIDCR) Office of International Health at NIH. She spoke about the difficulty of obtaining a meaningful consent from patients who were not English speakers or, even more importantly, were functionally and/or completely illiterate. It was hard to explain exactly what was going to be performed. She described a study in which a show of hands was taken as consent from women whose

[84] Lois K. Cohen and Global Health, https://www.usciences.edu/events/cohen-lecture-series/about-program.html.

children were going to be part of a dental research study. This was certainly relevant for many of the patients we were treating, considering the literacy rate in Nicaragua. One of our anesthetists became very upset about the fact that we had taken photographs and had not specifically asked permission. The head of our mission called a team meeting and assured the team that we were not doing anything wrong, since we were not profiting or publicizing these photos (not exactly true), but in the future, would include a question about photographs in obtaining the consent.

Stan did a variety of cases in that first mission. They included several general anesthetic cases (dermoid cyst excision, burn scar contractures, and adult hare lip revision). But most required local anesthesia (multiple lesions in all locations, a tumor on an eyelid, and carpal tunnel decompression). The total number of patients was over a hundred. This was true for the missions when we operated for two weeks, but when we were on our own, we only stayed for a week. That was exhausting enough, since we rarely had any help. Our patient totals were lower.

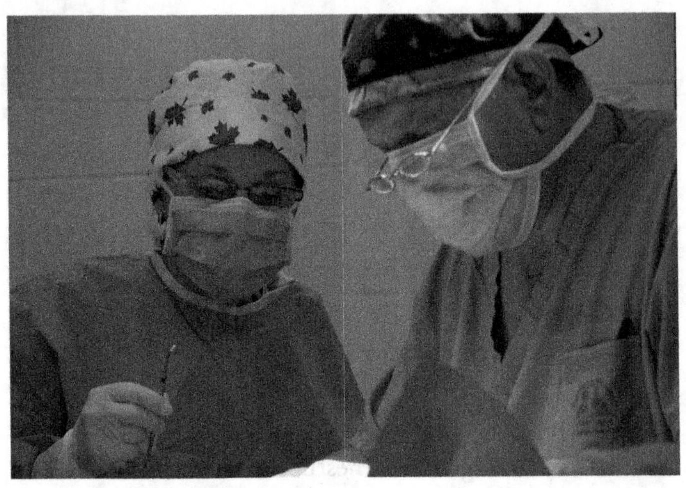

Stan and his scrub nurse, Nicaragua 2008

At the end of this first mission, we had already made great friends with other participants. We went to the Intercontinental Hotel to show them that there was some luxury in Managua and then to a very good restaurant called La Stradivarius. Stanley had his usual fight with a taxi driver. The driver wanted to charge us sixteen dollars for a very short drive. As I had previously said, usually a ride is about two dollars a person at the most. We went into the restaurant, and the driver followed. Stan gave him four dollars. Our friends still comment on their initial experience with Stan.

When we visited in November of 2008 (see humanitarian arm above) we found a much better hotel in Managua just a little bit farther from the airport, called Camino Real, and well worth the one-kilometer drive. Stanley met with the sales manager and negotiated a deal for seventy dollars plus tax, including a fabulous buffet breakfast. Eight years later, it still ranks as one of the best buffet breakfasts in Latin America in our opinion.

The only problem with finding this hotel is it came with a curse. I was in charge of organizing all the reservations for the next surgical mission, which was in February 2009. This included all the reservations at Camino Real both before and after the mission and the shared accommodation in the town where we operated. In February 2009, the mission was even larger and even more diverse. Problems seemed to arise constantly.

Here is the list so you can see what I mean:

4 surgeons (2 general, 1 gynecology, 1 plastic)
3 anesthetists
2 general practitioners
5 OR nurses
4 recovery room nurses
8 pre- and post-OR nurses
1 small procedure room nurse
3 unit clerks
2 central supply personnel
1 maintenance worker
8 "support staff" (including wives and children)

First, I communicated with the travel agent to arrange the flights, and that was fine. She lived and worked in BC, where most of the team was coming from. Then communicating with our NGO for the accommodation was not so simple.

There was confusion as to whom I should communicate with, and this led to problems with room assignments. And so the complaints started ("I want to room with her"; "I don't want to room with her"). I was also involved with planning some activities during the mission. The closing dinner and the day in Leon went well, but again, I received complaints from people for the weekend away trip. Granada, the top tourist destination in Nicaragua, was hosting the annual poets' convention, and accommodation that weekend was difficult to find. Manuela worked tirelessly to find space for those who wanted to go there, and eventually she could split up the group and get available hotels. Instead of thanks, I got complaints that the hotel was noisy because there was a wild party going on. It was interesting that these came from first-time travelers to Nicaragua and to a mission, and they never returned again. The mother of one family in particular also complained that she and her daughters had nothing to do. The member of the surgical team, her husband, was sightseeing when he was supposed to be assisting surgery. It was clear that they really didn't understand that this was not a vacation but a chance to initiate and participate in the needs of the mission and that of the community.

I prepared a list of recommendations after the last mission, which were followed for the most part but not because of what I had written. It was mostly because a new medical clinic had opened in another location, not too far from Managua, and the surgical missions switched there. We also switched NGOs on the ground. Another NGO took over all the arrangements. And although the organization was located in a very out of the way place, a small group went to check it out at the end of the February 2009 mission and were amazed at the facility. In October 2009, a small mission was organized to check out this new medical clinic, and it was a huge success. The medical director was thrilled to have us and did everything she could to help.

So, in February 2010, the mission went there and was more focused, with no children along and certainly much smaller. The dynamics were very different in this location. The medical director there encouraged teaching, and the goal became to teach as well as perform surgery. We interacted with the entire staff in the clinic. We ate in the staff dining room with everyone else, although we got special meals and were served from a separate window. It was interesting that at one time we were there with another group from the United States who had their own food. They didn't eat there. They only worked with their staff, came in, did their surgery, and left. Their explanation was that they did so to keep the team healthy.

Our team leader changed the team's focus, trying hard to ensure its goals became sustainability. It was clear that two missions a year would go a long way in achieving it. The surgeons that came along limited their surgery and tried very hard to teach specific procedures to the staff at the clinic. Our team provided the equipment, and it was left there for them to use. One of the staff doctors helped Stanley, who taught him basic suturing. He often helped with patients who arrived in the emergency room and were going to be operated on in the main OR and also helped giving the local anesthetic to patients in advance of Stanley operating.

Stan also had a couple of fourth-year medical students, who were required to do a year in a rural clinic. They were not too badly trained but certainly could improve their technique. One in particular helped us a great deal, since she spoke English. Entonces, never assume things remain the same for long. Each time we returned to Nicaragua, there was a different story about almost everything.

However, in spring 2010, the leader of our team decided that he couldn't plan another mission in that year. We happened to be there in March at the time with our granddaughter and made plans to come on our own in September. As usual, getting permission to come became a major deal. Once more we had to provide all the documents (medical school diploma, plastic surgery fellowship, license, CV, American college membership, Royal college membership, and for me my PhD diploma and my CV). Then we needed an invitation letter from the clinic director and the local head of MINSA, the Ministry of Health. Another letter needed to state that we were donating the supplies we brought.

We rented a car as usual and drove up to where we were going to stay this time, what we thought would be closer to the clinic. However, the road was under construction, and it was the rainy season. It took us around an hour to negotiate the terrible roads every time we drove from where we stayed to the clinic. There was a section of road just before the clinic where our car was almost halfway under water, but somehow we made it every time.

It was a terrible time in Nicaragua but especially around where our NGO headquarters was. That year, 2010, had an unusually bad rainy season, with devastating effects throughout the country. Starting with Tropical Storm Agatha in early June, the country suffered several months of severe floods and landslides. There were five members of the Nicaraguan Red Cross who lost their lives during a field mission on our last day. People were lacking food since the fields were flooded and the crops ruined. We bought beans and rice in town near the clinic, and our NGO members supplied the people stranded because of the flooding. For future missions, we did find accommodation closer to the clinic and organized it for the next (and as it turned out final mission) with our big team.

The next mission and what turned out to be the last for the team took place in February 2011. This was one of the worst experiences at the airport. Our bags were impounded by customs. It was some kind of fight between customs and the Ministry of Health because customs wanted to collect duty on the supplies, saying that they were being sold. It wasn't just our mission. We saw one group after another having their bags taken. Some people had their clothes in with their supplies. At least ours were in our carry-on bags, and they were not taken.

We were only around twenty again in this mission. I had organized the rooms at a small hotel, which I'd found during our last mission alone. Rooms were pretty bad, but the reason for not going there originally was that supposedly there were problems with the water supply. This turned out not to be the case, and except for very short periods of time, we always had enough running water. Of course, it was freezing cold. And where we were, the temperature early in the morning was not hot. Although there was no dining room at the hotel, there was a large terrace, where the owner had terrific breakfasts catered. We had negotiated a deal last fall with him. Again, I was in charge of managing the funds for all meals and the hotel as well. Somehow, like last time, the totals never quite added up. It was complicated as you can imagine, with meals for twenty people.

Aside from planning and organizing the funds for all the accommodation, my job was to help in the office where we screened the patients for basic medical information. It was important to document any allergies, as well as to give all the women pregnancy tests prior to the surgery so that no one was operated on who might be pregnant. As we participated in several missions, it was apparent that although everyone's motivation was to help the disadvantaged women of Nicaragua, personalities and issues come along also. We were learning a great deal about being volunteers within a large group and the interactions with other NGOs and surgical teams. Operation Smile was in Managua this time, and meetings with all of them and our team complicated our schedule. However, in spite of logistical problems, the bottom line, when the final numbers were tallied, confirmed Stanley had performed 220 procedures in the two weeks, and everyone had been operated on successfully and gone home well and happy.

From November 2011 on, Stan and Roz were their own surgical mission. Our local NGO leader had left Nicaragua, and our team leader decided that he couldn't bring another mission there without the local NGO. We organized the mission with the medical director of the clinic, who greeted us at the airport with the keys to our clinic room, and immediately leveled with her that there wouldn't be a February mission. Everyone kept asking, and certainly all were very disappointed.

Our travel routine for the missions we did on our own was as follows: We flew down to Nicaragua on a Thursday. We arrived at night, and the medical director and Manuela met us at the airport with the keys to our clinic room. We rented a car Friday morning and drove up to the villa to see Mariana and her family. We brought them clothes from Ottawa, shopped for new clothes and whatever else they needed, and then went out for lunch. We stayed overnight and then on Saturday took the family out for lunch and swimming and drove back to Managua with more than enough time before sundown. We stayed overnight in Managua; usually met with Manuela, who now lived there and not in the town near the villa; and then, on Sunday, drove up to the new medical clinic where we operated. We set up our clinic for work on Monday. We operated Monday through Friday morning. Then we packed up and drove back to Managua, staying overnight to leave early Saturday morning to return home. We didn't break with this routine, as it seemed to work very well for every mission from November 2011 until February 2015, a total of seven missions. From our first mission at this new medical clinic, we were given a room where we could store most of what we needed for our next mission. Everything was always there when we returned.

Before our arrival, the medical director always advertised on TV that we were coming. During the mission in February 2012, we were celebrities. We were interviewed for TV twice and then also by someone doing a psychology project. Our February 2013 mission was the best, in that we saw the most patients, 180. This was almost as many as the number we had done in the two weeks with the previous larger missions.

However, in November of that year, the surgery on which we had trained the surgeons previously was not being performed. There was a large turnover of doctors who'd worked at the clinic and many who'd been previously trained were no longer there. But more important, the equipment that we had donated for them to use was not working. This was something else that became apparent to us over the years. It is possible to supply high-tech equipment and train the professionals how to use it. But then, when it breaks down or parts need to be replaced, the equipment can no longer be used because the technicians required to fix it aren't there. Nor are the parts available, not to mentions the funds to purchase them.

One other problem at the clinics in both of the places we operated in was the power outages. Some of these were deliberate by the government, since it was necessary for repairs; some just happened. There were generators available at the clinic, and usually we could at least continue with the bifrecator, which was the instrument Stan used the most to cauterize the wounds after he removed the lesions. It was always a fear that the bifrecator wouldn't work because that would end the surgery. We brought down a backup that we returned with every time. We left one there, and that was never taken. For the whole time that our friend was the medical director, our supplies were safe. Nothing important was ever missing. On this trip, Stanley took all the stuff remaining in our storage room that he did not want and took it out of the room and brought it to the supply room of the hospital. We just left what we needed for our next mission.

Things seemed based on our last visit to be going fine but one never knew for sure that things were going fine in Nicaragua. On all our visits, even though often they were only a few months apart, we could not anticipate what situations would exist upon our arrival. In September, before the November 2014 mission, we got an e-mail from our medical director friend. She had been relieved of her position at the clinic. We never really knew why. The new medical director did get us a license for November, but that turned out to be our last surgical mission.

On our farewell morning in November 2014, we went to say good-bye to the new medical director. He hadn't visited our clinic the whole week. However, when we were asked to supply funds for the clinic soccer team, we agreed, and at this meeting, the captain of the soccer team presented us with shirts. Everybody on the team wore shirts that said Dr. Labow, along with his number.

That didn't seem to matter when it came to getting permission for our next mission, which was supposed to be in February 2015. Our invitation and license never came. We had no idea why we were refused, but we packed up all our instruments in February and went home. Although we had very mixed feelings about not being invited back, it was a great excuse. It wasn't us who said we were no longer coming or no longer able to come. It was the new medical director who had refused us. We promised everyone we would come and visit our friends in February 2016, which we did. We had Sunday lunch together, and everyone cried, including us.

Tourism arm

On our first trip to Nicaragua, we were only tourists. We had combined Panama and Nicaragua, and I described how we got there in chapter 2 "Getting There." It was one of our craziest combinations of weather and road problems. We rented a car in Managua and took a very roundabout way to get to San Juan de Sur. It is hard to describe just how horrible the roads were at that time (2007). We got lost many times and had to ask many times. In the town of Tipitapa, we ended up going the wrong way on a one-way street. We finally found Masaya and then Nanaime, where the Pan-American Highway began. The road until the Pan-American was a series of huge potholes. There were kids along the road filling the holes with sand. Along came an ice cream vending bicycle, and we bought everyone ice cream. The signs often existed after the intersection, so you only could see them after and so you had to turn back because you had gone too far. Often a sign was hidden by a tree or tall grass. The road to San Juan was even worse than the one to Nanaime. The eighteen kilometers took over an hour. It took us four hours from Managua to get to the beautiful resort of Morgan's Rock in an out of the way place on a dirt road. All of that is gone now. In February 2016, every road was beautifully paved, and it only took two and a half hours from Managua. Nicaragua had become a tourist destination.

Morgan's Rock is a beautiful ecotourism resort. It is owned by a French family who grows their own food. When we were there in 2007, all meals were included, as were all activities, hiking, and horseback riding. And the resort was situated on a pristine beach with a beautiful pool. We walked on trails in the hacienda and then drove for miles on the property where, from a hill, it was possible to see Lake Nicaragua and the Pacific Ocean. It was easy from that point to understand how the Panama Canal was originally going to go that route. From the Atlantic Coast, it is a short distance to Lake Nicaragua, which again with a very small land portion could get you to the Pacific.[85] The United States wanted Nicaragua as the site, but the French had started to build the canal through Panama. By lobbying the Americans with a stamp showing an erupting volcano, the company building in Nicaragua took over construction through Panama. For the past few years, new plans for this canal began. A Chinese consortium from Hong Kong had plans to build another canal through Nicaragua. However, with the downturn in the Chinese economy, things were on hold again and the whole deal is still shrouded in mystery.[86]

One day we went with a guide to the local school, which Morgan's Rock was helping. We had brought lots of school supplies with us and distributed them to the school. The kids were in uniforms, and each did have a desk. Grades one through six were together, with two teachers. There was a small preschool there as well. While we were there, a woman came with a meal for each child. The teachers and kids walked up to five kilometers to get to the school.

The Yaris we had was driving terribly, and Alamo sent up a new car. When we checked out of Morgan's Rock, we followed the old car into town and had to fill up. They wanted fifty dollars. So we went to the nearest gas station and filled up for eleven dollars. We set out for Granada, the tourist destination city in Nicaragua. And then, for the first

---

[85] Nicaragua and the Panama Canal, https://en.wikipedia.org/wiki/History_of_the_Panama_Canal.

[86] The plans for another canal, https://www.nytimes.com/2016/04/04/world/americas/nicaragua-canal-chinese-tycoon.html?_r=0.

time of many, we were stopped by the police. This happened over and over, almost every trip. More about that in chapter 12, "Police Encounters." Granada is a beautifully restored colonial city. We have returned here several times. The last time, in 2015, we found it too congested and touristy and said we would leave it off our list for subsequent trips. The first time we were there, we took a boat ride on Lake Granada and, when you were far enough away from the city shore, which was terribly polluted, it was beautiful. The walk down from the city square was full of garbage, and the park along the water was very rundown. However, a new ecolodge, which was quite luxurious, has been opened on one of the islands, and there were many small islands where there were private luxurious homes. In contrast, the city square was filled with kids who went around eating the leftovers from peoples' lunches. There were beggars, but mostly there were people selling all sorts of food and trinkets or polishing shoes.

The other huge tourist attractions in Nicaragua are the volcanoes. Mombacho is the one near Granada, and we took a tour up the volcano in a huge truck. We stopped at one of the coffee plantations on the volcano. Coffee and sugar cane are the two big crops in Nicaragua. The volcano is still active now, and that day it was possible to walk around the opening and feel the heat. The views from up there were amazing, but the battery had died in the camera! On our way back to Granada, we stopped in Catarina, a beautiful town near Lago Apollo. That is a crater lake surrounded by restaurants; parks; and, at the bottom, hotels.

Our next stop on this first trip was Leon, the former capital and one of the main campuses of the university in the country. The cathedral there is quite amazing but very rundown. We did climb up to the roof and got a few good photos, although the view was not anything too special. We returned to Leon several times when we were working in the villa. It is fairly close by and the closest to the ocean. Puneloya is the town with the closest beach, with excellent seafood restaurants, which we took advantage of several times.

After Leon we checked into the Intercontinental Hotel in Managua. It is in a shopping center (Metro Centro) and close to a number of good restaurants. We may have been more lucky than careful, but we walked around that area quite freely and never felt any danger. We did head down to a very interesting archeological site called Huellas de Acahualinca.[87] Footprints that had been preserved in the sand mixture that came from the volcanoes were discovered by construction workers in 1874 by accident. Carbon dating put them at about 6000 BC, extremely old by Latin American standards. Mayan civilization was around 3000 BC. The staff at the hotel told us not to go there or to at least take a taxi. We drove there, found it all fenced in, and parked right in front, where someone from the museum watched our car. There were lots of people just hanging around—beggars and handicapped people in wheelchairs going in and out of the traffic—and it did look like a very poor area. But once again, nothing happened to us, and we returned to our hotel, safe and sound. We returned our car to the airport and checked into the Best Western. That was

---

[87] https://en.wikipedia.org/wiki/Ancient_footprints_of_Acahualinca

when we met our contact to the NGO who brought us to Nicaragua subsequently.

On our next trip, in fall 2007, we went down to San Juan del Sur again for a few days of tourism. This time we stayed at Pelican Eyes. The accommodation was made up of large villas with kitchen facilities, a living room, and two bedrooms. The location had a beautiful view of the ocean, but being perched on top of a very high hill, the access was a bit difficult. We decided to drive to Morgan's Rock and try to visit the school that we supported. This was the end of the rainy season, and the road to Morgan's Rock was not the best even when everything was dry. Somehow, we managed to get up there. What we found was amazing. The resort was transformed into the location for a photo shoot for the swimsuit issue of *Sports Illustrated*. We told them what we were doing in Nicaragua, and many members of the crew as well as the model herself wanted to come with us to the school. The Morgan's Rock truck led us out of the worst of the road, and we went back to San Juan.

The next day, we decided to drive to Catarina. We'd loved that location so much on our first trip. Catarina is known for its flower markets and also for its pottery vendors. If I had to choose one thing that is available in Nicaragua that I love (and that almost everyone who's received it as a gift from me loves) it's the pottery. On every trip, we always bought pottery, which I found to be unique and beautiful. We parked our car and started to walk along the fence bordering the lookout over the Laguna. We came up to a tent advertising a sort of motorized bike that could drive us down to the Laguna shore. We hired two young boys who drove us down a harrowing, steep, windy path, fully paved with interlocking brick. Thirty-five minutes later we arrived at the bottom.

We reached the shore, which even had a sandy beach with many hotels all around. After taking a photo, we climbed back into the little motorbike taxi, and after going about a kilometer up the steep hill, it sputtered and died. There was no cell phone service there. Even so, the kids had run out of minutes. I don't know how they got back up, but we started to walk and were at a crossroads when a bus drove up. It said Masaya. We got on and, for fifty cents, arrived at the Masaya bus terminal. Small problem! Our car was in Catarina. However, for seven dollars, we got a taxi to Catarina and our car. The whole excursion took two and a half hours. After all this, somehow we made it back to San Juan just before dark. There was always an adventure in Nicaragua!

The next day, Gladys from Morgan's Rock came to get us. We were going to meet the group from *Sports Illustrated* at the school. We met up with the two other vehicles and set out for the school, where our money had built a well. We arrived at a school, and after a few minutes, we realized that was not the one where we had been the previous March. It was in terrible condition, but we all went in and took photos. The children were not well dressed. Some were not in uniforms. We explained to Gladys which school we wanted to go to, and she figured it out. It was nearby. We reached a fork in the road, which appeared to be a river, and turned to drive along it.

We climbed up to the school, and we recognized the teachers. Certainly, this school was much better equipped. After giving the teachers some money, we climbed back into the truck. The truck got stuck after turning around and hit a rut in the water. The truck leaned over, and it started to fill with water. We figured we'd better get out. Eventually, Gladys got a cell phone to work and managed to reach Morgan's Rock. One of the other trucks on route got to us an hour later. And with a rope attached to the other truck and all the kids pulling also, the truck got out just as the rope snapped. We drove back to San Juan and relaxed for the rest of the afternoon. The next day, we drove back to Managua and, the following day, flew back to Ottawa, via Miami and New York that time.

After packing up our equipment when we realized it was our last trip where we would be doing surgery, we went to Granada and stayed in Plaza Colon again. The hotel was just as nice as it had been before, but the city was just too crowded. Driving in it was crazy, until we could find the hotel parking lot. We then went to Tola, near Rivas, at a resort called Aqua Wellness. We stayed in a beautiful wood cabin facing the beach. The ocean was warm and lovely, and the shoreline beautiful. The cabins of the resort were placed all the way up the side of the hill. Breakfast was included, and you could eat at the open dining hall right on the beach. There was nothing else around there, and it was a great place to relax. We found out that we were just around the corner from Mukul, the resort now owned by Flor de Cana, the rum company. It used to be the private preserve of Samosa, the dictator that was overthrown during the first revolution in 1979. Mukul can be accessed by a new airport that serves Rivas and Tola, where many condos and resorts are under construction. So it is possible to fly to Managua and transfer to a plane that will take you right near Mukul for a mere

$1,000 a day! Nicaragua has come a long way; it was a hot destination for New Yorkers and superstars like Morgan Freeman and Michael Douglas.

On our last trip in February 2016, we just visited our friends and the family in the villa. We also went back to San Juan del Sur and stayed at Pelican Eyes again. Sadly, the hotel was not in good shape. It seems that the manager ran off with the money several years ago. Interestingly, he was just being brought to trial in Texas for tax evasion. We met people who lost their entire down payment on a condo that was going to be built. So, they go there every winter for 6 weeks at a very reduced rate in order to partially make up for it.

Through e-mails we stay in touch with all our friends, and with Manuela's help we continue to support our family in the villa. But the very long chapter of our other life for ten years is over. It has changed us forever.

Surgical mission to Paraguay

We were all set to join yet another mission with our friends from the Nicaraguan team on their first mission to Paraguay. But in May 2013, there was a terrible dengue epidemic, and the hospital where our friend was supposed to go canceled the mission. We decided to go anyway but left all our surgical stuff in Ottawa. We had become very friendly with the Paraguayan ambassador to Canada. The ambassador was wonderful and helpful, very different from the Nicaraguan situation. Our documents were easily worked out, and licenses were given with no problem. We were greeted at the airport by two people from the Ministry of Health and a doctor friend of the surgeons who were supposed to come. We checked into the Ibis but found a wonderful Sheraton right next door. It was very busy with a delegation from the EU that was monitoring the elections in Paraguay, but Stanley managed to negotiate a great rate, which included a fabulous breakfast.

The next morning, we were picked up by someone who spoke perfect English, and we went to visit the national hospital in Itagua. Itagua is a small town about an hour from Asuncion. Not much is there to see or do; nor are there too many restaurants to eat at. But there was a huge national hospital that had many medical and surgical specialties. We met with the chief of gynecology. She immediately gave us dates that were good for her for our group to come. She said that she would organize a course for her staff and the gynecology residents. She wanted them to learn laparoscopic procedures. General surgery was being performed that way at the hospital but not yet gynecology.

In spite of the dengue epidemic, no cases had been canceled at that hospital. She had a resident who spoke English, and when we asked about a hotel, he suggested the Olimpo. What a find! This hotel was very new and very nice and very inexpensive.

We drove back to Asuncion, and the next day we were picked up by the two people from the Ministry of Health who were at the airport when we arrived. We drove almost three hours to Villarica and visited the hospital where we were supposed to go. This town is even smaller than Itagua, and the hospital there was not suitable for a surgical mission for many reasons. We went back to Asuncion and, the next day, stayed in Asuncion organizing the rest of our trip, which was touring that part of Paraguay and going into local health clinics.

We rented a car from Avis at the Sheraton and set out for Itagua. We stayed at the Olimpo in a beautiful suite. The hotel served breakfast, and we found out it also served dinner. The management went out of its way to accommodate us. There was a pool, and although it should have been spring and warm enough to swim, it was really cold and rainy. That certainly helped the dengue epidemic, but we still sprayed with lots of DEET every day.

Another great thing about the Olimpo was that a great ice cream place was just around the corner. We had some every night. The hotel had lots of guests, the strangest being twelve Korean businessmen who were training workers at a Hyundai factory. They had their own special food, gobbled it up, and went upstairs to their rooms.

We drove around for the next five days with the Olimpo Hotel as our base. Every small town around Itagua had a story. The town of Piribebuy was the most interesting, both for what we saw there and later on when, by accident, we met a descendent of a survivor. More about that later. There was a battle there fought on August 12, 1869, part of the Triple Alliance War.[88] Piribebuy was then serving as the temporary capital of the Paraguyan government. The story told there was that the Paraguayan defenders were poorly armed and included children led by their teachers into battle. They were certainly no match for the allied forces, who had overwhelming numerical advantage and included

[88] The Triple Alliance War in Paraguay, http://www.economist.com/news/christmas/21568594-how-terrible-little-known-conflict-continues-shape-and-blight-nation.

Brazil, Argentina, and Uruguay. The children, along with the women who tried to defend the town, were captured and executed.

We also visited several *centros du salud*, health centers, as we drove around the countryside, visiting the small towns. We found very difficult situations everywhere. Some had a nurse but not a doctor. Some had a surgeon but no anesthetist, so surgery couldn't be performed. Some places were completely empty.

We returned to Asuncion and walked in the area around the Sheraton, went downtown, and saw the old Asuncion, which was where we stayed when we were in Paraguay in 1987.

One of the most remarkable occurrences happened when we were crossing the Mariscal Lopez, one of the busiest streets in Asuncion. Stanley and I were talking, and a woman who was also crossing the street heard us and started speaking English to us. She was with her friend, and they were meeting other friends at a coffee shop in a shopping center nearby. She asked us to join them. She was visiting her mother who was still living in Asuncion, but she lived in London. She was certainly a very wealthy woman whose estate in Highgate could accommodate her sons and their families who were building homes on the grounds. As we spoke further, she told us about her family. Her grandfather had entered the battle of Piribebuy with his mother. His mother was slaughtered as she described it, "stabbed with a lance by a Brazilian solder," but he managed to escape. He was only eight years old at the time. This was a truly extraordinary story that was especially meaningful to us, having just been in Piribebuy and learning about the Triple Alliance War.

When people always said how wonderful we were to volunteer and donate both our services and equipment so many times, we always say that those trips were more beneficial for us than they were for the people we treated and helped. More than anything, it was an educational experience. As a result, we contemplate the way foreign aid is given and the benefits that result. It is hard not to be patronizing while assuming that what we have to offer is superior to what the people have and want. Providing medical care and aid without sustainability may actually be doing more harm than good. We are certainly very happy to have participated in our surgical missions and humanitarian aid, but I think more and more about how much good did we really do. Have we changed their lives as much as they changed ours?

Is there one word that describes travel? Stanley said, "Education."

Conclusion

This chapter is the most difficult to write. There is no final word on travel. And what pleases some is an anathema to others. But over the years I have bought and received as gifts many diaries to record my trips. Many have outstanding quotes, which describe my feelings about travel and highlight some of the differences between different philosophies of traveling or touring—in other words, the differences between a tourist and a traveler. Using those quotes may be the best way to summarize this book about my travel stories.

Traveling in the company of those we love is home in motion.
—Leigh Hunt

This book is about traveling with Stanley, my husband for, as of June 11, 2017, fifty-six years. Although we differ on many subjects, we often say when we are somewhere away from home that this is the area where we are truly compatible, traveling.

The traveler sees what he sees. The tourist sees what he has come to see.

—Gilbert K. Chesterton

That quote definitely summarizes our feelings. We have been on trips with friends and with our kids as well, where they felt it was necessary to check off items seen that were listed in a travel guidebook. We have never felt that way. Some of the best experiences we have had have been getting lost trying to find something and finding something else. One time, by chance, we met another couple who deliberately avoided going to see a well-known site in a specific location—in that case, Knossos in Crete. Another time I remember driving through Cyprus, and the Blue Grotto was listed as something to see. When we arrived there, dozens of buses lined the road. Stanley just kept driving. If there were that many buses, he wouldn't stop. He would always say, "Too touristy" or "Too many people."

Travel teaches toleration.

—Benjamin Disraeli

No matter how much a trip is planned, it is never possible to anticipate everything that could happen. Sometimes the best-laid plans cannot be realized. Weather cannot be controlled, an obvious statement, and certainly weather can affect your activities and, even more importantly, flights to where you have to go. It's important to always keep calm and flexible. Who can always do that?

Travel is fatal to prejudice, bigotry and narrow-mindedness.
—Mark Twain.

It is possible to arrive somewhere with preconceived ideas about the place you are visiting, but it is inevitable that if you have to negotiate anything on your own it is necessary to behave in a respectful way. Acting in a superior and judgmental manner will usually get you nowhere fast. It is important to act in a culturally sensitive way in order to get results. Hence, the subtitle of this book, *Don't Step on the Garlic.*

The use of traveling is to regulate imagination by reality and instead of thinking how things may be, to see them as they are.
—Samuel Johnson in *Anecdotes of Samuel Johnson* (1780)

This is an excellent piece of advice. I remember one camping trip we took years ago where we were with a group of young people. One of the young women halfway through the trip was in tears of frustration over how this trip was going. The weather had been bad, very windy and rainy. There were loads of insects that were so small they couldn't be kept out of the tents. Through her tears, she said that this was her dream trip. She had saved money to come sea kayaking and snorkeling and the conditions were not what she had expected or hoped for. It is not a good idea to expect and hope for what cannot be guaranteed, even by the best tour company.

Traveling is one way of lengthening
life, at least in appearance.
—Benjamin Franklin in a letter to Mary Stevenson

And of course, sometimes things go terribly wrong. Will we ever get over this terrible time? This is the moment when we're camping and a thunderstorm causes our tent to collapse, and we are cold and wet. We usually say, "Are we having fun yet?"

Air Canada's magazine *En Route* has won many awards. I always pick it up and read some of the articles when I'm on an Air Canada flight. My favorite article when I was traveling to Bermuda in November 2016 was the Letter of the Month from Shannon Hargreaves, Winnipeg. She wrote while on a flight from Ottawa to Winnipeg that she had read the Leaders of the Pack piece entitled "An Exchange Student opens Her Bag," by Elizabeth Pare, published in the September issue *En Route*. I had the pleasure of reading this letter, which expressed our philosophy of travel exactly.

Expectations can ruin a trip. Just let things happen,
be present and make the most of the experience[89]

And another article in the same issue was entitled "The Frequent Flyer" by Robin Sharma, founder of Sharma Leadership International Inc.

[89] En Route September 2016; Elizabeth Pare

Get lost in the cities you travel to. The brain craves novelty; we fire new neural pathways when we're experiencing new things. There's great humanistic value in becoming an adventurer again.[90]

We still follow one of our travel rules of arriving in a new place or a place where we haven't been for many years and searching for a place to stay. We always have a room on the day we land, but after that, part of the adventure is finding a place we like and negotiating a deal. Lately, the hotel discount websites can be very misleading and intimidating: "One room left," "Two rooms left," and even "Fully booked." We have found that not to be true. Maybe it is true on that website at that time, but we have found that there is always a room, again if you don't have expectations.

And last but not least, this quote from Nehru:

We live in a wonderful world that is full of beauty, charm and adventure. There is no end to the adventures that we can have if only we seek them with our eyes open.

—Jawaharlal Nehru

Still, after years of traveling in many countries and in many different ways, travel is our favorite form of enjoyment.

---

[90] En Route November 2016, Robin Sharma

Appendix

All websites in the footnotes were accessed in 2017.

Printed in the United States
By Bookmasters